Workers Can W

'Just at the time when workers are mobilising to tackle the economic and climate crises we all face, this invaluable handbook comes along to provide an essential guide to winning.'

—John McDonnell MP

'A must read for every trade union activist.'

—Lyn-Marie O'Hara, Glasgow equal pay striker

'Workers have needed a practical, positive, accessible guide to organising in Britain for a long time and Ian, using his vast experience in the area has created just that. It will be a valuable resource for union representatives and organisers wanting to grow their branch and union!'

—Sarah Woolley, General Secretary, Bakers, Food and Allied Workers Union

'In the age of climate breakdown, militant worker organising is as urgent as ever. Workers and environmentalists share a common enemy in the capitalist class and Allinson gives us all a powerful guide of how to effectively organise for social change from our workplaces. If you're wondering what you can do in the fight for climate justice then read *Workers Can Win*, join your union, and get organising.'

—Chris Saltmarsh, co-founder of Labour for a Green New Deal and author of *Burnt: Fighting for Climate Justice*

'Drawing on years of experience, Unite activist Ian Allinson has written an organising handbook that will be invaluable for rank-and-file organisers and trade union professionals alike. Allinson offers timely, concrete analysis and advice that will be an aid to activists across the trade union movement in today's difficult work environment.'

—Kim Moody, author and founder of *Labor Notes*

'Workplaces are key sites of struggle against the hostile environment for migrants, and so to tackle these injustices against migrants we need strong unions. *Workers Can Win* is a readable, practical guide for organising at work and building the power we need to fight back against oppression.'

—Ida Jarsve, co-founder, Lesbians and Gays Support the Migrants

'This book is just brilliant. It is not only packed full of invaluable advice and practical tips for anybody organising in the workplace, but it is also hopeful. Crucially, it offers an accessible political analysis of why it is so important for working-class people to build power in the workplace and beyond, demystifying the process as it goes.'

—Laura Pidcock, National Secretary of The People's Assembly

'A vital resource for anyone serious about taking part in trade union work at any level, and also extremely useful for anyone working for positive change in their community.'

—Brendan Montague, editor, *The Ecologist*

Wildcat: Workers' Movements and Global Capitalism

Series Editors:
Immanuel Ness (City University of New York)
Peter Cole (Western Illinois University)
Raquel Varela (Instituto de História Contemporânea [IHC] of Universidade Nova de Lisboa, Lisbon New University)
Tim Pringle (SOAS, University of London)

Also available:

The Cost of Free Shipping:
Amazon in the Global Economy
Edited by Jake Alimahomed-Wilson and Ellen Reese

Choke Points:
Logistics Workers Disrupting the Global Supply Chain
Edited by Jake Alimahomed-Wilson and Immanuel Ness

Power Despite Precarity:
Strategies for the Contingent Faculty Movement in Higher Education
Joe Berry and Helena Worthen

Dying for an iPhone:
Apple, Foxconn and the Lives of China's Workers
Jenny Chan, Mark Selden and Pun Ngai

Just Work?:
Migrant Workers' Struggles Today
Edited by Aziz Choudry and Mondli Hlatshwayo

Wobblies of the World:
A Global History of the IWW
Edited by Peter Cole, David Struthers and Kenyon Zimmer

Arise:
Power, Strategy and Union Resurgence
Jane Holgate

El Golpe:
US Labor, the CIA, and the Coup at Ford in Mexico
Rob McKenzie with Patrick Dunne

Augmented Exploitation:
Artificial Intelligence, Automation and Work
Edited by Phoebe V. Moore and Jamie Woodcock

Organizing Insurgency:
Workers' Movements in the Global South
Immanuel Ness

Southern Insurgency:
The Coming of the Global Working Class
Immanuel Ness

Amakomiti:
Grassroots Democracy in South African Shack Settlements
Trevor Ngwane

Workers' Inquiry and Global Class Struggle:
Strategies, Tactics, Objectives
Edited by Robert Ovetz

The Spirit of Marikana:
The Rise of Insurgent Trade Unionism in South Africa
Luke Sinwell with Siphiwe Mbatha

Solidarity:
Latin America and the US Left in the Era of Human Rights
Steve Striffler

Working the Phones:
Control and Resistance in Call Centres
Jamie Woodcock

Workers Can Win

A Guide to Organising at Work

Ian Allinson

With illustrations
by Colin Revolting

PLUTO PRESS

First published 2022 by Pluto Press
New Wing, Somerset House, Strand, London WC2R 1LA
and Pluto Press Inc.
1930 Village Center Circle, Ste. 3-384, Las Vegas, NV 89134

www.plutobooks.com

Copyright © Ian Allinson 2022

The right of Ian Allinson to be identified as the author of this work has been asserted in accordance with the Copyright, Designs and Patents Act 1988.

British Library Cataloguing in Publication Data
A catalogue record for this book is available from the British Library

ISBN 978 0 7453 4782 0 Hardback
ISBN 978 0 7453 4781 3 Paperback
ISBN 978 0 7453 4784 4 PDF
ISBN 978 0 7453 4783 7 EPUB

This book is printed on paper suitable for recycling and made from fully managed and sustained forest sources. Logging, pulping and manufacturing processes are expected to conform to the environmental standards of the country of origin.

Typeset by Stanford DTP Services, Northampton, England

Simultaneously printed in the United Kingdom and United States of America

Contents

Table and figures

TABLE

FIGURES

Series preface

Workers' movements are a common and recurring feature in contemporary capitalism. The same militancy that inspired the mass labour movements of the twentieth century continues to define worker struggles that proliferate throughout the world today.

For more than a century, labour unions have mobilised to represent the political-economic interests of workers by uncovering the abuses of capitalism, establishing wage standards, improving oppressive working conditions, and bargaining with employers and the state. Since the 1970s, organised labour has declined in size and influence as the global power and influence of capital has expanded dramatically. The world over, existing unions are in a condition of fracture and turbulence in response to neoliberalism, financialisation, and the reappearance of rapacious forms of imperialism. New and modernised unions are adapting to conditions and creating class-conscious workers' movement rooted in militancy and solidarity. Ironically, while the power of organised labour contracts, working-class militancy and resistance persists and is growing in the Global South.

Wildcat publishes ambitious and innovative works on the history and political economy of workers' movements and is a forum for debate on pivotal movements and labour struggles. The series applies a broad definition of the labour movement to include workers in and out of unions, and seeks works that examine proletarianisation and class formation; mass production; gender, affective and reproductive labour; imperialism and workers; syndicalism and independent unions, and labour and Leftist social and political movements.

Acknowledgements

This book would have been impossible without my former workmates and countless other activists, organisers and writers I have learned from or whose stories I have used. The late Colin Barker encouraged me to write, and my confidence to do so owes a lot to my tutors at Keele University, and to Unite and the TUC, whose education bursaries contributed towards my study costs.

My wife Isabel gave me huge encouragement and support as well as comments on the draft. Nick Cimini was a constant help and support throughout the process. The socialist group rs21 not only encouraged me but allowed me to use some of my time working for the organisation for writing the book. I am grateful to all those who gave comments and suggestions including Adam Herriott, Brendan Montague, Danny Budzak, Dave Allinson, Dave Lyddon, David Renton, Gareth Dale, Hazel Croft, Hilda Palmer, Kate Bradley, Katy Fox-Hodess, Kim Moody, Lynne Hodge, Matt Whaley, Sadie Fulton, Stephen Mustchin, Stu Melvin, Raymond Morell, Sue Bond, Vik Chechi-Ribeiro and Willie Howard, and to Nick Evans for helping me edit the draft. Thanks to Adam Bell, David Shulman and the team at Pluto for turning my manuscript into a book. This book is the product of a collective effort, but some who contributed will undoubtedly disagree with aspects of it, and responsibility for any errors lies with me.

Glossary

1199	A union organisation of health workers in the USA, currently part of the Service Employees International Union (SEIU).
AA	Automobile Association.
AAR	Acknowledge, Answer, Redirect.
Acas	Advisory, Conciliation and Arbitration Service.
accompany	Attend an individual grievance or disciplinary meeting with a worker. See Chapter 4.
ACOP	Approved Code of Practice.
ACORN	A community union.
activist	Someone with lots of energy and commitment to taking action for a cause.
ADCU	App Drivers and Couriers Union.
advocacy	A model of trade unionism where the union advocates as a third party on behalf of workers, individually or collectively. See Chapter 4.
agitation	The process of helping a worker to get angry about their issue.
ASOS	Action Short Of a Strike. See Chapter 9.
attitudinal structuring	Shaping the ideological terrain on which battles are fought. See Chapter 8.
BA	British Airways.
BAILII	British And Irish Legal Information Institute.
ballot, aggregated	A single ballot covering multiple workplaces or associated employers producing a single ballot result. See Chapter 9.
ballot, disaggregated	A ballot with separate results for each workplace or employer. See Chapter 9.
ballot threshold	A level of turnout in an industrial action ballot required to enable lawful industrial action following a 'yes' vote.
bargaining unit	A defined group of workers that the employer(s) recognises the union(s) as representing and for which agreements may be reached.
battle for interpretation	The battle after an action or conflict to popularise an interpretation of what happened that equips workers for future action rather than demobilising them.

BESNA	Building Engineering Services National Agreement.
big bargaining	Negotiations with lots of workers in the room. See Chapter 10.
BMA	British Medical Association.
BNP	British National Party.
bogus self-employment	Workers being treated as self-employed when they are not really.
branch	A grouping of union members, usually by geography, employer and/or industry. See Chapter 11.
Brexit	The UK leaving the European Union (EU).
Britain	England, Scotland and Wales.
broad left	A faction within a union that seeks to win votes for more democratic rules and left-wing policies, and to elect supporters to union positions. See Chapter 11.
bureaucracy	The institutional apparatus of a union, including its paid staff. See Chapter 11.
CAC	Central Arbitration Committee.
CAIWU	Cleaners and Allied Independent Workers Union.
capability	An employee's ability to do their job. This might relate to health or skills and is often used in relation to disciplinary procedures.
capitalism	The current economic system, based on workers selling their labour power and employers competing with each other to grow.
casework	Supporting workers with grievances and disciplinaries, usually through formal procedures. See Chapter 4.
CEO	Chief Executive Officer.
charting	Listing all workers and grouping those who interact most, to record information about them. See Chapter 6.
charting, social	Drawing out social relationships between workers. See Chapter 6.
collective bargaining	The process through which workers collectively reach agreements with employers through one or more unions.
combine committee	A committee of representatives from different workplaces (and sometimes different unions) in one employer, group of employers or industry.
communication tree	A tool for passing information through a large group by one-to-one communication. See Chapter 6.
companion	Someone who accompanies a worker at an individual grievance or disciplinary meeting. See Chapter 4.
concession cost	The financial and non-financial cost to a decision-maker of giving workers what they want. See Chapter 8.

conduct	Employee behaviour. Often used in relation to disciplinary procedures.
contract, fixed-term	An employment contract that ends automatically, without the employer giving notice. This could be on a particular date, on the completion of a task, or based on a particular event.
consultation	A process where the employer shares information and proposals, workers or their representatives consider them and have the opportunity to respond, and management considers any response before taking a final decision.
consultation with a view to reaching agreement	A version of consultation with an onus on the employer to seek agreement from workers or their representatives. There is no obligation on workers or their representatives to agree anything.
CORE	Caucus Of Rank-and-file Educators.
COSHH	Control Of Substances Hazardous to Health.
craft union	A union organising workers in a particular occupation, rather than diverse workers in certain employers or industries.
CWC	Clyde Workers' Committee.
CWU	Communication Workers' Union.
D&I	Diversity and Inclusion.
delegation work	Groups of strikers touring other workplaces, union branches and towns to raise support.
demonstration strike	A strike intended to express discontent rather than force the employer to concede.
detriment	Disadvantage, e.g. financial loss, distress.
direct action	Action which uses our own power rather than appealing to those in power. See Chapter 9.
discontinuous action	Action that is not continuous, such as when workers return to work between strike days.
discrimination, direct	Treating someone less favourably because of a protected characteristic. See Chapter 7.
discrimination, indirect	A provision, criterion or practice that puts people with a protected characteristic at a substantial disadvantage. See Chapter 7.
disruption cost	The financial and non-financial costs that workers can inflict on a decision-maker in pursuit of their goals. See Chapter 8.
distributive bargaining	Bargaining that focuses on maximising your share at the expense of your opponents. See Chapter 10.
DOCAS (also known as check off)	Deduction Of Contributions At Source.

DSE	Display Screen Equipment.
dual card	Dual carding means being a member of two unions at the same time.
EEA	European Economic Area.
EETPU	Electrical, Electronic, Telecommunications and Plumbing Union.
EHRC	Equality and Human Rights Commission.
EIA	Equality Impact Assessment.
employee	A worker with a contract of employment (whether written or not). See Chapter 7.
employer association	A group of employers who may share advice and resources, bargain collectively with unions in a particular industry, and help association members to break strikes.
EPIU	Electrical and Plumbing Industries Union.
ERA 1996	Employment Rights Act 1996.
ERA 1999	Employment Relations Act 1999.
escalation	Increasing the impact of action over time.
ET	Employment Tribunal.
EU	European Union.
EWC	European Works Council. See Chapter 7.
exploitation	I use 'exploitation' in the economic sense, not the moral sense. Wealth is created as employers exploit workers and take from the environment.
facility time	Work time when a worker is allowed to carry out union duties or activities. See Chapter 7.
fire and rehire	A process where employers dismiss employees and offer them re-engagement on worse terms, or threaten to do so.
flexitime	Systems where workers work a defined number of hours over a period but choose starting and finishing times each day, within defined limits.
framing	Describing an issue in a way which helps your side. See Chapter 5.
franchise	A business whose owners and managers use a brand, other rules and sometimes supplies from a larger company in exchange for fees.
FTO	Full-time officer (see 'paid officer').
GDPR	General Data Protection Regulation.
GFTU	General Federation of Trade Unions.
gig economy	Where workers are temporarily engaged for particular tasks, often as 'self-employed' contractors.
Global Address List	List of all users on an email system.

harassment	Conduct with the purpose or effect of violating someone's dignity or creating an intimidating, hostile, degrading, humiliating or offensive environment. See Chapter 7.
HMRC	Her Majesty's Revenue and Customs.
HR	Human Resources.
HSE	Health and Safety Executive.
ICE	Information and Consultation of Employees.
ICO	Information Commissioner's Office.
ID	Identification.
ideology	A set of ideas that justifies social arrangements and inequalities.
illegal	Banned by law.
indefinite action	Action with no specified end-date.
industrial action	Strikes and Action Short Of a Strike (ASOS).
influential worker (also organic worker leader, natural leader, opinion leader)	The worker who has most influence with their workmates. See Chapter 6.
injunction	A court order to do or not do specific things. Failure to comply is contempt of court.
inoculation	Helping workers explore their fears about how management might react, so that the bosses' poison has less effect.
integrative bargaining	Bargaining that focuses on maximising shared interests. See Chapter 10.
interim relief	A legal claim following dismissal on certain automatically unfair grounds including lawful union activities. See Chapter 4.
IT	Information Technology.
IWGB	Independent Workers' Union of Great Britain.
IWW	Industrial Workers of the World.
Joint Shop Stewards Committee (JSSC)	A committee involving reps from all unions in a workplace.
Just-in-Time	A system where goods are received as close as possible before they are needed, minimising stocks.
labour power	A worker's capacity to work. Workers sell this to their employer. See Chapter 2.
lawful	Permitted by law.
lay	Not employed by a union, e.g. lay member, lay rep.
leader	Someone with followers.
Lean	A management approach based on eliminating any part of a process that does not contribute to the creation of value.

leader ID	The process of identifying influential workers.
level of bargaining	Whether bargaining takes place at a centralised (high) level, such as the employer or industry, or a decentralised (low) level, such as workgroup, team or department. See Chapter 10.
leverage	Applying greater pressure to a target by doing so indirectly. See Chapter 8.
levy	Where a group of union members make regular contributions to support other workers on strike.
Lib Dems	Liberal Democrats.
LRD	Labour Research Department.
managerial ideology	The ideas that justify managers' power. See Chapter 5.
managerial relations	Aspects of the employment relationship determined between a manager and a worker after they start work, e.g. management behaviour, work allocation.
mapping	Drawing the physical layout of a workplace or workplaces and marking it up with information. See Chapter 6.
market relations	Aspects of the employment relationship that can be specified in a job offer before work begins, e.g. pay, hours.
micro-unions	Very small unions, not affiliated to the TUC, often relatively new and specialising in organising precarious and migrant workers.
MMP	Mayr-Melnhof Packaging.
mobilising	Turning out people who already agree with the cause to take action.
motion	A formal proposal put to a meeting for attendees to vote on.
NACODS	National Association of Colliery Overmen, Deputies and Shotfirers.
NEON	New Economy Organisers' Network.
NEU	National Education Union.
NMW	National Minimum Wage.
NUM	National Union of Mineworkers.
OILC	Offshore Industry Liaison Committee.
ONS	Office for National Statistics.
open bargaining	Where any worker can attend and listen to negotiations. See Chapter 10.
oppression	Being subject to the exercise of power or unjust treatment. This is often thought of only in relation to those with 'protected characteristics' under the Equality Act but applies to all workers.

organiser	Someone who tries to systematically build workers' power. The term is also used as a job title in some organisations, often for jobs that bear little relation to this.
organising, self-selecting	Making a general appeal over an issue and organising the people who respond positively.
organising, structure-based	Organising a group of people defined by an existing structure such as a workplace or housing estate.
outsourcing	When an organisation pays another company to carry out work rather than employing people directly to do it.
PA	Public Address.
paid officer (see also 'FTO')	Officer employed by the union to bargain with employers. See Chapter 1.
partnership	An approach to trade unionism emphasising shared interests with employers and avoiding conflict.
PAYE	Pay As You Earn.
PCP	Provision, criterion or practice. See Chapter 7.
phone bank (and text bank)	A group of people make calls or send texts on behalf of a campaign.
picket	Pickets are people (usually strikers) who stand on a 'picket line'. Picketing means gathering on a picket line outside a workplace or other key location to prevent workers, vehicles or goods entering or leaving.
pluralistic ignorance	When a majority of people think something, but they assume that most other people don't agree.
politics	Who has what power, how they use it and what for. See Chapter 2.
power	The ability to achieve the outcomes you want, irrespective of opposition from your employer or others.
power, associational	Power derived from collective organisation. See Chapter 8.
power, ideological	The ideological resources available to legitimise causes and actions. See Chapter 8.
power, institutional	Power derived from legal enforcement, codes of conduct, and other standards. See Chapter 8.
power, market	Power workers derive from their position in the labour market, e.g. how hard it is to replace them, their capacity to survive without being paid. See Chapter 8.
power, moral	A type of associational power based on publicly tarnishing the reputation of an organisation behaving immorally. See Chapter 8.
power, structural	Power derived from workers' position in the production process or wider society. See Chapter 8.
PPE	Personal Protective Equipment.

precarious workers (also precarity)	Workers with little income security. Often seen as including those on temporary or zero-hours contracts, agency workers and bogus self-employment.
protected characteristic	The Equality Act 2010 defines nine protected characteristics: age, disability, gender reassignment, marriage and civil partnership, pregnancy and maternity, race, religion or belief, sex, and sexual orientation.
PSA	Power Structure Analysis.
PSED	Public Sector Equality Duty.
rank and file	Relating to union members (and sometimes lay reps and officers) rather than paid officers. See Chapter 11. A rank-and-file strategy is one that builds the capacity of workers to exercise power independently from the union bureaucracy.
RCN	Royal College of Nursing of the United Kingdom.
reasonable adjustment	A change to enable a disabled person to perform in their job. See Chapter 7.
recognition (also union recognition)	One or more employers recognise one or more unions as representing a group of workers. See Chapter 7.
red union	A union comprised of radical workers when the majority are in a less radical union.
rep (also shop steward, branch officer, branch official, Mother or Father of the Chapel, lay rep, senior rep or convenor)	A worker elected by their workmates to play a role in the union in relation to their own employer. See Chapter 1.
repression	Use of surveillance, imprisonment, fines, violence, etc., to subdue people.
repudiation	When a union encourages strikers to return to work to avoid legal liability for unlawful action.
RMT	National Union of Rail, Maritime and Transport Workers.
RoES	Representative of Employee Safety. See Chapter 7.
rs21	Revolutionary Socialism in the 21st Century.
safety rep	A rep dealing with health, safety and welfare issues. See Chapter 7.
scab	Someone who works though industrial action, undermining its effect – an activity known as 'scabbing'.
secondary action	Solidarity industrial action taken by workers over a dispute with another employer.
section meeting	A meeting of members in a particular team or department.

selective action	Industrial action taken by only some of the workers at any one time. See Chapter 9.
semantic drill	Practising saying or writing things to convey our meaning clearly, making workers' issues and activity central and avoiding portraying unions as third parties. See Chapter 5.
servicing (also 'business unionism')	Trade unionism based on unions as third parties providing (often individual) services to their members as customers. See Chapter 4.
SNB	Special Negotiating Body.
social reproduction	The process of producing and sustaining a compliant workforce through childcare, education, healthcare, etc.
SRSC	Safety Representatives and Safety Committees (Regulations).
staff turnover	The rate at which staff leave and are replaced.
statutory	Decided, controlled or required by law.
strike	A temporary stoppage of work by a group of workers to express a grievance or enforce a demand (Hyman, 1989).
strike, unofficial	A strike not formally authorised by a union.
strike fund	A fund to help sustain strike action.
strike pay	Money paid by a union to members when they are on strike.
structure test	An action organised through your organisational structure of influential workers where you record who takes part on your charts so that you can assess your strength and identify weak areas. See Chapter 6.
structure test, public	A structure test where a worker's participation is visible to other workers, the boss or their community.
Subject Access Request (or SAR)	A request for personal information held about you, using data protection legislation.
subscriptions (subs)	Members' regular financial contributions to their union.
TGWU	Transport and General Workers' Union.
third partying	Using language that depicts the union as a third party to the workers and the employer, rather than an organisation of the workers themselves.
trades council	Umbrella organisation made up of delegates from branches of TUC-affiliated unions in a particular geographical area.
TUC	Trades Union Congress.
TULR(C)A 1992	Trade Union and Labour Relations (Consolidation) Act 1992.
TUPE	Transfer of Undertakings (Protection of Employment).
UCS	Upper Clyde Shipbuilders.
UCU	University and College Union.
UK	United Kingdom. Britain and the north of Ireland.

UKIP	UK Independence Party.
umbrella company	A company that provides a PAYE system for another company and sometimes acts as an employer on their behalf.
union activities	Official union tasks carried out by members where the employer recognises the union, but which aren't union duties. See Chapter 7.
union duties	Certain tasks carried out by an employee who is a union official (e.g. a rep or branch officer) recognised by the employer. Apart from training, these typically relate to consultation and negotiation. See Chapter 7.
Union Learning Rep (ULR)	A rep dealing with staff training and education. See Chapter 7.
unlawful	Activity that no law permits.
UVW	United Voices of the World.
victimisation	Trade unionists use the word to mean being picked on for union membership or activity. In law, it means being picked on for exercising a statutory right.
wage labour	Labour carried out in exchange for wages.
wall-to-wall organising	Organising everyone in a workplace, irrespective of employer or occupation.
whistleblowing	Revealing a hidden truth about an organisation. See Chapter 7.
whole worker organising	An approach that recognises that workers have issues and connections far beyond their job and seeks to link them to the organising effort.
WHO	World Health Organisation.
worker	Someone who sells their labour power to live. It also has the legal meaning, explained in Chapter 7, of people (including employees) with a contract to personally do work that isn't on a client or customer basis. It does not include the genuinely self-employed.
workgroup	A group of workers who physically or virtually work directly together, whether organised as a team or not.
working class	People who must sell their labour power to live and those out of work, their dependents, and those too young, old, sick or busy with caring for other working-class people to do paid work. See Chapter 2.

1
Introduction

There are fundamentally two reasons to organise at work: to change things related to your job, and to change everything else. Organising is about building workers' capacity to take effective collective action and win change. It is the only realistic way for most of us to have any real influence over our work – a huge aspect of our lives. It's not just that work (or the lack of it) occupies much of our time and energy. The rest of our lives are shaped by its pay, hours, conditions, locations and stresses.

As individuals, we are relatively powerless, so power is often seen in a negative light – as something bad people have over us. But there are other types of power. As Martin Luther King Jr. put it:

> Power, properly understood, is the ability to achieve purpose. It is the strength required to bring about social, political or economic changes. In this sense power is not only desirable but necessary in order to implement the demands of love and justice.
>
> (King, 2010 [1968], p. 37)

Collective action at work is a major source of potential power to tackle wider issues, such as poverty, inequality, discrimination, housing, public services, war and the climate crisis. Action at work over such issues seems implausible to most workers in Britain at the moment, but historically and globally collective action at work has been a big part of almost every significant movement for social change. There is a yawning gap between workers' needs and the feelings of powerlessness that currently dominate the lives of working people. Bridging that gap requires organising, and while organising in other settings is important too, everyone concerned with social or environmental justice should see organising at work as a priority.

This book is aimed at workers who want to organise at work, and secondarily at individuals and organisations trying to help workers organise. There are many workers already organising who want to be more effective.

Many more recognise the need to organise at work and want to learn how to do it. This includes people inspired by Jeremy Corbyn's time as leader of the Labour Party, many involved in social movements, and those just fed up with bad treatment at work. I won't address the many important questions of strategy, such as where organisations should prioritise resources geographically or between industries and occupations. Whatever else we do, workers need to organise where we are. The book focuses on building organisation capable of winning change where you work. It won't tell you how to rebuild the whole working-class movement, but it does argue for building links and solidarity beyond your job.

Certain ideas are a prerequisite for effective organising: commitment to advancing workers' interests through their own collective activity, and a belief that workers generally make wise choices when confronted with important decisions and good information. This isn't about having a rose-tinted view of workers, but a belief in our potential – that the right situation can bring out the best in us. Though these ideas are paramount, the technique, skills and craft of organising are also essential. It's when the going is tough and workers' anger doesn't just carry us past difficulties that such skills are most important.

Organising isn't a matter of obediently following instructions – there is no 'one best way' to do it. Circumstances vary and there's also an element of luck. However, there are definitely some bad ways to organise. I explain some principles, ideas and techniques that generally work, and help you avoid some of the pitfalls as you learn and develop your skills. I have set up a website associated with this book (workers-can-win.info) and will post updates there. I'd love to hear about your experiences as you organise and your suggestions for additions or improvements to what I've written. While the book touches on many of the issues workers face, no book could cover them all. Instead, I will signpost where to find information and resources, and encourage you to build a network of people you can turn to for advice and support.

I was driven to write this book out of frustration. I spent years organising at work, picking up ideas wherever I could. I found many good books, but none that combined the nuts and bolts of organising with its political context or that were based on organising in Britain. While there is lots we can learn from organising in other countries (just as much of this book should be useful to those outside Britain), the legal, organisational, cultural, ideological and political framework makes a difference. The history of colonial occupation means that industrial relations in Ireland (north and south) shares many features with Britain, but also contributes to differences, including legislation, policing, politics, organisations, religious segregation and discrimination. The differences between the nations of Britain (England, Scotland and Wales) are much smaller by comparison. For this reason, the book does not cover either part of Ireland. I have sometimes, however, referred to the United Kingdom (UK) – Britain and the north of Ireland – where relevant to legislation or statistics.

Even within Britain, people in different industries and unions use different jargon for the same things or the same word for different things. I try to explain jargon when we first meet it, but you may find the glossary useful, particularly if you are dipping into the book rather than reading it cover to cover. A few points are worth explaining here. I will use the term 'rep' to signify a worker elected by their workmates to play a role in the union in relation to their own employer. You may also hear a rep referred to by names such as shop steward, branch officer, branch official, Mother or Father of the Chapel, lay rep, senior rep or convenor. The term 'lay member' is widely used to mean any member not employed by the union. There are also people who are employed by unions to deal with workers and employers. In this book, I refer to them as 'paid officers'. The most common term used in the movement is 'full-time officer' (FTO), but this isn't really appropriate given they may work part-time. You may also hear them referred to by terms such as officers, officials or organisers. Most unions appoint paid officers, but members elect them in a few. I'm not including in 'paid officers' the many others employed by unions who don't bargain with employers, for example, in organising, administration, research and other functions within the union apparatus. You'll need to learn the jargon for your bit of the movement, but when I say 'rep' I mean a worker and when I say 'paid officer' I mean someone employed by the union.

Many workers don't have a conventional workplace – you may travel, work at many locations or at home. I've sometimes used the word 'workplace' when it is legally relevant or as a shorthand when talking about a group of workers, whether or not they are physically together. Similarly, I've sometimes used the word 'employer' to denote the organisation you work for irrespective of whether you have employee status.

In making the case for organising at work, Chapter 2 talks about why work generates conflict and gives workers potential power. It discusses what is needed to turn that potential power into the ability to win change, to overcome the current weakness of the workers' movement. The final section addresses some of the real and perceived barriers to organising in the modern world of work.

The bulk of the book is structured to follow the journey of an activist from starting to organise in a new job in Chapter 3 to industrial and direct action in Chapter 9. Your own organising journey may mean you tackle issues in a different order or skip some altogether. The final chapters (Chapters 10–12) deal with challenges you may meet at any stage.

In Chapter 3, I cover some of the essentials if you are in a new job or starting to organise for the first time, including finding allies, staying safe, gathering information, choosing a union, getting trained, accessing

resources and building your network. Parts of this chapter will be of use to established activists too.

Chapter 4 discusses different models of how unions work, and how they often operate in ways that leave workers passive and disengaged rather than helping us build power. Union weakness and legislative changes have encouraged an emphasis on dealing with issues in an individual and legalistic way. You need to think hard about how you deal with 'casework' such as grievance and disciplinary procedures so that it supports rather than undermines your organising. Throughout the book, I explain relevant aspects of the legal framework in Britain, but of course this can't substitute for professional legal advice when appropriate. The chapter discusses workers' rights around some issues that often generate casework and that are common in unorganised workplaces – non-payment of wages and dismissal. It covers the pitfalls of casework and ends with some common 'non-work' casework issues.

Effective organising is around issues. In Chapter 5, I discuss how to choose issues to organise around and how to communicate about them. This includes the first of four 'techniques in detail' sections, about one-to-one organising conversations.

Chapter 6 introduces many more organising concepts and techniques, including identifying and winning over the most influential workers, being systematic about including everyone and knowing how supportive they are, and using trees and networks for communication. It also covers meetings, socialising and democracy, before introducing collective action.

We are told by governments, employers and the media that we have certain 'rights', but these are limited, infringed all the time and under attack. This was well illustrated when P&O boss Peter Hebblethwaite told MPs[1] that he knowingly broke the law by sacking 800 staff without consultation. He made clear that he would do it again because paying the compensation was cheaper than obeying the law. Laws and policies are useful, but reliance on them limits what we can aim for. In Chapter 7, I discuss how to organise using rights connected with contracts of employment, employer policies, health and safety, discrimination, redundancy, 'TUPE' transfers of workers between employers, whistleblowing, union recognition, facility time, and employee forums and works councils. While organising around 'rights' is no substitute for collective action, many activists will find themselves using rights before they are in a position to go on strike. This book is intended to be read through, but you may want to skip parts of this chapter and come back to them when you need them. However, I'd strongly encourage you to read the sections on contracts of employment and discrimination, which include fundamentals every workplace organiser needs to know.

Workers can win change when we know who has the power to concede what we want and when we can credibly threaten to take collective action that would cost these decision-makers more than the concession. Chapter 8 discusses the different types of potential power available to workers and those in authority, how to make a credible plan to win your campaign and how to plan particular actions.

Chapter 9 continues the focus on collective action by delving into industrial and direct action in detail. It covers the industrial action process, types of action, and the practicalities of going on strike, building solidarity, using the media and settling a dispute.

Management won't just sit idly by while you organise. Chapter 10 looks at management mischief. It starts by exploring the techniques management use to intensify work and keep control, as well as how to counter them. It then discusses how to respond to management attempts to derail, divide or attack union organisation.

Chapter 11 starts by looking at how to make use of the union structures and resources beyond your own work. Dealing with a union can be pretty perplexing. It's not just that unions are complicated organisations with lots of jargon, or that some individuals aren't always as helpful as you'd hope. A union is an institution in its own right, and parts of it pursue agendas that aren't always the same as those of its members. I advocate a 'rank-and-file' approach and offer tips on how workers can assert themselves, pressure paid officers to do the right thing, or take action independently.

The final chapter, Chapter 12, covers identifying and addressing common pitfalls in campaigns, including those caused by participants. It discusses creating a supportive organisational culture that avoids activist burnout. The book ends by returning to the limitations of unions and discusses the need for both rank-and-file and socialist organisation in overcoming them.

At the end of each chapter, I have included some key bullet points of what it has covered, and usually some questions you could discuss if you are reading the book with a group, maybe one from your workplace. I look forward to hearing how your organising is going, and your own ideas and tips that could be shared with other workers via the website (workers-can-win.info).

Organising and developing our skills are, after all, collective endeavours. I will also use the website to post new material as the world of work evolves, so please check it and subscribe to updates.

Key points

- Collective action at work is a major source of potential power to address issues at work and beyond.
- There's often a big gap between our needs as workers and our sense of our own power to address them.
- Effective organising requires a commitment to advancing workers' interests through their own collective activity, and a belief that workers generally make wise choices when confronted with important decisions and good information.
- I will use the term 'rep' to signify a worker elected by their workmates to play a role in the union in relation to their own employer.
- I refer to people employed by unions to deal with employers as 'paid officers'.
- Register for updates to the book via (workers-can-win.info) and send in your own experiences and ideas.

2
Why organise at work?

As well as those of us who want to change our working lives, organising at work should be a central concern for everyone interested in social justice or responding to the accelerating climate catastrophe. This isn't just because work is so central to most of our lives and so much injustice. Conflict is the inevitable consequence of how work is organised in a capitalist society. I'll explain how conflicts around work can build immense power in the collective hands of people with good reasons to use it to benefit the whole of humanity and our environment.

An argument about the potential of workers' power seems incongruous at a time when most workers aren't collectively organised, unions are shackled by repressive legislation, strikes are rare, and those that do occur are often defensive or only about the interests of small sections of the workforce. So why are struggles around work strategically important for supporters of social and environmental justice?

In this chapter, I will argue that there are structural reasons why conflict happens at work, that organising around it has particular potential which is currently unfulfilled, and that unions have an important role but also limitations. I will discuss the possibilities for systematic organising and spontaneous struggles.

WORK CAUSES CONFLICT AND SHAPES RESISTANCE

No matter how repressive the government or how downtrodden the workers, conflict is ever present in the employment relationship, even if it is often hidden. When a boss hires a worker, they buy her ability to work, what Karl Marx (2015 [1867]) called the worker's 'labour power', which is the source of profits. No employment contract can fully specify the quantity or quality of work she actually does. It might specify the time spent or certain metrics, but there's always room for workers to vary their effort. This is why bosses need to *manage* workers.

Bargaining (however informal) doesn't stop when the pay and hours have been agreed. Day in and day out, managers try to maximise the work extracted from the workers already on their books. Management concoct endless schemes to supervise, monitor, measure and assess us; force us to compete with each other; bombard us with propaganda to persuade us to prioritise their interests above our own; incentivise and threaten us. Meanwhile, workers have to find ways to cope with all this and to push back when we can. Our responses can be individual or collective, open or sneaky.

This isn't to say every manager is personally vindictive or unpleasant. The conflict that arises from managing our work isn't about managers' personalities or beliefs, though of course some are more obnoxious than others – it is structural. Employers – whether companies, states or 'not-for-profit' outfits – are locked in competition with each other, and that competition forces management to try to get as much as possible from their workers for as little

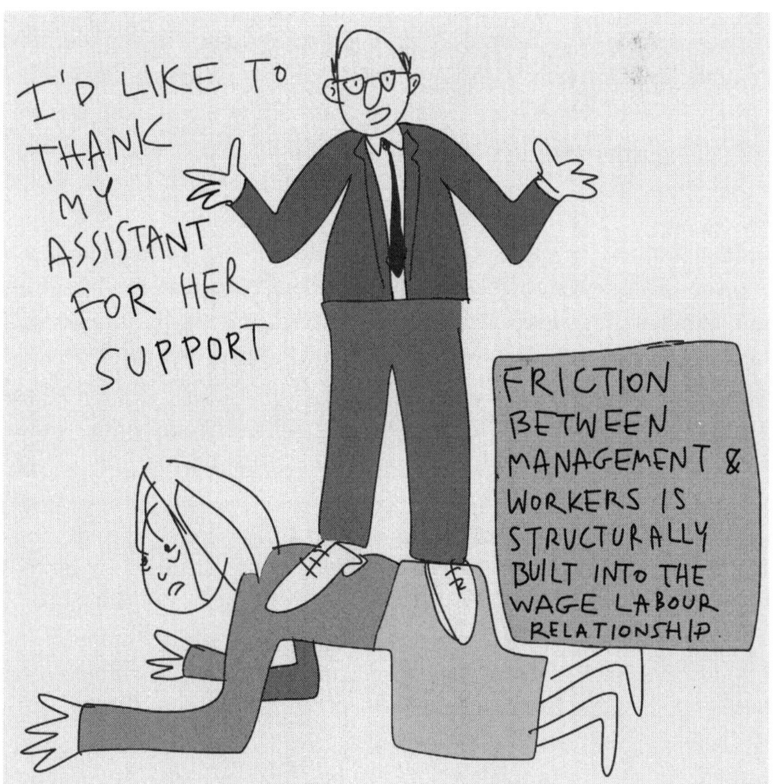

as possible. Their position can force them to act against workers' interests, so you can never trust them.

The level of conflict isn't always the same. It's obvious that managers in some industries and employers are more aggressive than others, and that employers go through periods of relative stability and times when they really turn the screw. But friction between management and workers is no accident or exception – it is structurally built into the wage-labour relationship.

COLLECTIVITY

In order to produce products, services and profits, bosses bring workers into relationships with each other. In most cases, this is pretty obvious. In 2020, 56 per cent of UK employees worked for an enterprise with 250 or more employees, and 84 per cent for one with ten or more (ONS, 2020): figures that haven't fallen much in recent years. In many cases, our jobs require workers to cooperate between different employers. Outsourcing and subcontracting often split workers between multiple employers, and many employers share large workplaces, such as shopping centres or airports. But workers aren't always under the same roof. Some workers have always worked at home, or in dispersed workplaces, and the Covid-19 pandemic saw a growth of home and remote working.

Even if remote or mobile, almost all workers have to communicate and cooperate in the course of their job – you are hard pressed to find a job advert that doesn't want a 'good team worker'. So, at the same time as employers try to divide, isolate and atomise us to control us better, they train us to cooperate and act collectively. We can't often act as small cogs in their machine without engaging with other cogs. Workers use these relationships in the routine tug of war with management over how much effort we put in. Every time we moan to each other about the latest ridiculous management request, we are testing the water, checking what other workers' norms for effort are. Few want to risk being far less productive than our colleagues, but neither do we want to be suckered into working twice as hard for the same money. These conversations, which take place in most jobs, whether unionised or not, are embryonic forms of collective organisation and collective regulation of the effort we put in to our work.

This collective character of workers' organising has important implications. Firstly, it begins to address the power imbalance between boss and

worker. Secondly, it creates a bias towards democracy rather than individualism – a point I will return to. Workers often organise things amongst themselves, covering for each other to get the job done if someone's circumstances get in the way.

The dominant ideology in our capitalist society claims that an individual worker signs her contract freely and on equal terms with her employer. This is utter nonsense, concealed by formal legal equality. The boss has all the economic power – they can afford to hire the worker; the law bans the worker from using the buildings, equipment and raw materials unless the boss wants her to, and she can't afford to buy them herself. The contract allows one party to tell the other what to do, but not the other way round. Nearly all employers are themselves collectives – whether of shareholders, managers, trustees or as the state. That usually makes it easier for an employer to replace one worker than it is for one worker to replace their employer. It is only when workers organise collectively that we begin to lessen this power imbalance.

Organising at work is more resilient than in most other settings. Even when governments impose curfews, bans on meetings or protests, restrictions on the media or internet shutdowns, they still need many of us to work and can't prevent us interacting on the job. Workers can build bonds of trust that enable us to take high-risk action together. We may think the anti-union laws in Britain are repressive (and they are!) but they pale in comparison with the kidnapping, torture and murders that workers face in many countries.[1] Workers keep organising even under such conditions.

Organising at work involves organising a group of people defined by a pre-existing structure, such as their workplace, employer, industry or occupation. Much campaigning in other settings involves a self-selecting group already sympathetic to your cause, such as those who respond to a leaflet or Facebook event. As Jane McAlevey (2016) argues, structure-based organising has far more potential to build power than organising a self-selecting group. You are aiming to involve a majority of a target group, which is inherently more powerful than a scattered minority. You will, of course, start with a minority who are willing to act and reach out to others. To grow, you are winning over and organising new people, not merely recycling existing supporters. For this reason, structure-based organising is usually harder, but it has more potential. Your organisation is built around existing relationships between workers, making stronger bonds of solidarity.

Organising around work enables collective action that can disrupt work, giving it great potential power. As the lyrics of 'Solidarity Forever' put it, 'without our brain and muscle not a single wheel can turn'. Few notice when

a company CEO goes on holiday or for a game of golf, but employers can barely cope if a couple of workers go off sick, never mind if their whole workforce strikes.

This was powerfully illustrated by the Covid-19 pandemic. Senior managers could work from home, but when workers were furloughed, quarantined, off sick or at home looking after kids, large parts of the economy struggled. Strikes can cause a crisis for an employer and sometimes for a government. The ability to cause a crisis for those in power is essential for achieving change.

When talking about organising at work, it is important not to narrow our view. The working class is more than just those of us in paid work (whether working legally or in the underground economy) at any time. It includes people too young, old or sick to work, those too busy with unpaid work in the home or caring for others, and all those who would be working if employers didn't judge it more profitable to prevent us doing so. We are strongest when we bring together the power of organisation at work and in the community.

Even those of us in paid work aren't only concerned about work issues – we and our families, friends and communities are affected by all the issues in wider society. For example, rising housing costs can easily offset a pay rise; winning longer holidays hardly resolves racist violence. To improve our lot, working-class people need to win on issues inside and outside work. If we only organise around 'work issues', we will often neglect the issues that most motivate many workers – particularly migrant workers, women and other groups who suffer discrimination. Because people often work with a more diverse group than their family or friends, united struggles at work create opportunities to challenge and undercut prejudice and division. If we fail to tackle everyone's issues, we fail to involve everyone and limit our power – a problem I explore further in Chapter 7. Another way to think about this is that struggles at work are almost always about quality of life. Even when we fight over the narrowest economic issues such as pay or hours, we are really fighting to have the time and money for us and our families to pay the bills, bring up the kids, rest, recuperate and enjoy life – the quality of what is sometimes called our 'social reproduction'.[2] It makes no sense to ignore other ways to fight for the same things.

Another common mistake (all too often encouraged by union officials) is to see organising at work as meaning union organising. Unions are important – they provide a structure for workers to sustain organisation over time and on a large scale. But organising at work means building workers' power even in jobs that don't yet have any union presence. It also means recognising that being a union member – or even getting your employer to bargain with workers through your union – isn't enough. There are many workplaces where union members don't stick together and don't stand up to the boss. And there are some workplaces where workers act collectively without ever filling in a union membership form. This book argues that unions are an imperfect tool – they can help, but they are neither a substitute for organising nor the last word on it.

POWER

Working-class people desperately need more power. Previous generations assumed that their kids would be better off than them. Now, many young people are saddled with unaffordable housing costs and student debts, while work often feels more intense and less secure, public services have been deliberately underfunded and an adequate pension seems an unrealistic dream. We face an accelerating climate catastrophe and the growing risk that the trade wars and endless wars of recent decades will escalate into direct conflict between major powers. Whenever something goes wrong – from a financial crash to a pandemic – the rich are bailed out, the majority are expected to foot the bill, and employers seize any opportunity to erode pay and conditions.

Though workers usually win at least something when we fight, this has not been enough to reverse the overall deterioration of work – let alone resolve wider social and environmental issues. The gap between the unions we need and those we have is huge. It's no mean achievement that despite all the union-busting by employers and government, despite all the repressive legislation, there were 6.56 million employees in unions in the UK in 2020 (Bishop, 2021). But over 75 per cent of employees aren't in unions – and the picture amongst workers who lack employee status (see Chapter 7) is probably even worse. Only 16 per cent of employees under 35 are union members. Unionisation has largely been forced back into strongholds in the public sector, privatised industries and certain parts of manufacturing, making little dent in growing parts of the private sector. There are over 17.5 million private sector employees not in a union, as shown in Figure 2.1. In the private sector, 67 per cent of employees are in workplaces with no union presence at all, and 86 per cent are in workplaces where the employer doesn't negotiate with a union.

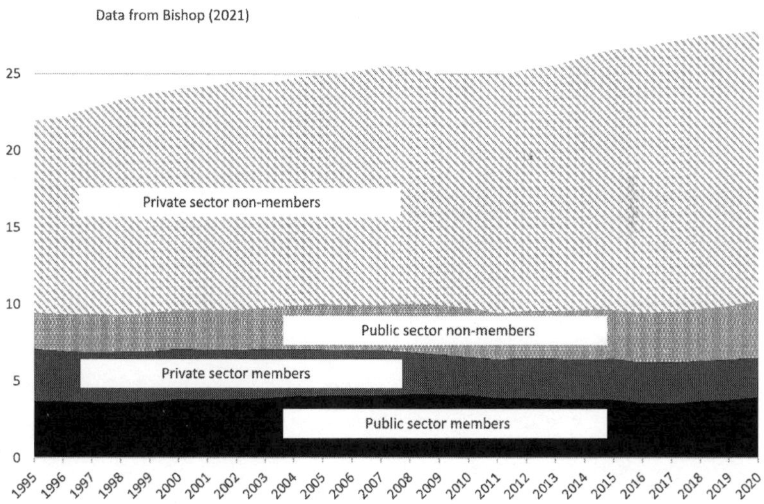

Figure 2.1 UK employee union membership and non-membership by sector 1995–2020 (millions)

The growth of un-unionised jobs is linked to the exceptionally low level of industrial action since the early 1990s. Workers join unions in large numbers when there is action. Our current weakness shouldn't make us lose sight of what workers have won. Without the workers' movement, we'd have no democracy at all, hours would be longer, pay would be lower, work would be as lethal as it still is in many poorer countries, and managers could hire and fire based on any whim or prejudice.

LIKE PUBLIC TRANSPORT, UNIONS ARE MORE ATTRACTIVE WHEN THEY ARE ON THE MOVE & GOING SOME-WHERE

We shouldn't write off the millions of workers already in unions, even when they are passive and the unions behave like companies providing services to individuals. Union membership implies, at a minimum, a recognition that workers have different interests from employers and that we need collective organisation to protect and advance those interests. However, if we want to turn the tide in favour of working-class people, higher union membership isn't enough. We need to take collective action, which itself builds union membership – particularly when we win. Collective action is crucial for turning potential power into victories.

Some years ago, I ran a training and planning session for reps, in preparation for our first national strike. One speaker was a union activist from a large oil refinery where workers had recently won a dispute over similar issues. They joked that 'it was easy for us, we had an oil refinery to play with'. What they were driving at was that their potential power was obvious to all the workers. They knew that if they stopped work, fuel supplies would be cut off across a wide area, creating a social and political crisis as well as costing their employer a fortune. They had power and they knew they did – much more clearly than most workers – and this really helped their campaign.

Many groups of workers have huge potential power but are far less aware of it. Supermarket checkout staff pass millions of pounds of perishable goods across their tills. Bar staff rake in fortunes for breweries and pub chains during major sporting events or on sunny bank holidays. IT workers control systems without which organisations simply can't function. Covid-19 helped make more workers aware of their essential roles.

Power is *the ability to achieve the outcomes you want, irrespective of opposition from your employer or others.* It's pretty obvious that most workers in Britain don't have much power at the moment – even if we have plenty of potential power. One missing ingredient is awareness of that potential power. The refinery workers had this, but many workers never think about their potential power. It's great to get workers discussing what the impact would be if we collectively stopped the job. But even awareness of your potential power isn't enough. With very few exceptions, workers need organisation to be able to wield that power – and some need more organisation than others. As Beverly Silver (2003) argues, in some industries, like production-line manufacturing, small groups of workers can stop a whole line and have massive impact, but in other industries you need far more people on board to have an impact. Supermarket checkout staff are a case in point. If one worker stops, the others can carry on – tills are arranged in parallel, not in sequence. Shutting one branch of a huge chain of coffee shops might in itself have little impact on the corporation. Effective action might require shutting many branches. The level of organisation required to wield power varies from job to job.

The final ingredient to turn workers' potential power into actual power is politics. I don't mean by this a keen interest in the goings-on in Westminster, Holyrood or the Senedd. Politics is about who has what power, how they use it and what for. In that sense, organising at work is all about politics – workers collectively and democratically gaining power relative to our employers. Workers have all kinds of political views that affect our ability to build power. One common idea is that workers are best off when their employer is successful. This has some basis in reality – few workers want to see their employer go bust. But it is a one-sided view which ignores the conflict of interest between workers and their employer. The employer's profitability comes from getting as much work from us as possible, for as little as possible in return. In other words, their success is at our expense rather than to our benefit. This doesn't mean that the highest profits always come from paying workers least – better paid and happier workers are often more productive.

These two ideas – of dependence on the employer and conflict with the employer – are at the heart of many arguments when workers contemplate action. Some unions promote a 'partnership' model which emphasises workers' dependence on their employer. Others stress the need for unions to be independent of the employer to advance workers' interests, whether or not these coincide with those of their employer. Where the partnership mindset is dominant it is very hard to take effective action – it's like trying to win a fight in which you are more worried about hurting your opponent than getting hurt yourself.

Winning relies on being able to threaten greater 'disruption cost' than the cost to the employer of conceding what you want. If you rule out imposing any disruption cost, you have lost before you start. The ideological and political arguments in workplaces and unions matter.

UNIONS AND BARGAINING

Another debate in the movement is about what a union is, and what it is for. At one extreme, there are those who see unions as businesses which provide services such as advice and representation to members. At the other, there are those who insist that 'the members are the union', seeing a union as a structure for workers to advance our own interests through collective action. In truth, unions, once they achieve any scale, contain elements of both – they are organisations of workers but require an institutional apparatus, sometimes called a 'bureaucracy', which can develop its own agendas and make the union seem like a remote third party to many workers.

Unions are inherently 'sectional' – representing only sections of the global working class. Workers' organisation develops around the contours of capitalist society – workplaces, employers, industries, occupations and nation states. Union mergers have often glued together many such sectional groups, but that doesn't change the fundamental pressure unions face to prioritise sectional and often short-term interests of existing members over the interests of the working class in the longer term and as a whole, particularly in other countries. We see this in the uneven response of unions to issues such as gender equality, trade wars, disarmament, war, climate change or anti-migrant racism.

The scope of issues unions should address is hotly contested. Some see their role as narrowly about 'bread and butter issues' directly relating to existing members' jobs, pay and conditions, as if discrimination, inadequate housing, struggling public services and climate breakdown didn't have big impacts on workers' 'bread and butter'. In contrast, some union rulebooks list a socialist society as one of their objectives. However, the day-to-day operation of even these unions is firmly within the framework of capitalist wage labour – trying to secure more favourable terms but leaving workers subordinated to management.

There's an apocryphal tale of a paid officer who went in to negotiate with the employer and came out delighted. He took the offer of a five per cent pay rise to the members, who rejected it, much to his surprise. He went back to the boss and came back with a seven-and-a-half per cent offer, only for it to be rejected again. When members rejected a ten per cent offer, he finally asked the workers – 'what is it you want?' 'Socialism', they said. He replied: 'The boss will never agree to that!'

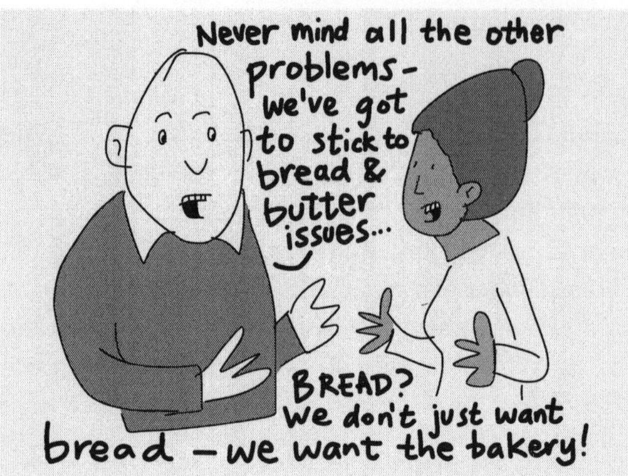

Jokes aside, negotiating an acceptable level of exploitation reinforces a commitment to the employer's success and profitability. Note that I'm using 'exploitation' in the economic sense, not the moral sense. Wealth is created when employers exploit workers and take from the environment. This commitment limits aspirations in good times but can be utterly debilitating when the employer is in trouble. During recessions, or when industries are in decline, unions can be tempted to negotiate concessions to keep employers afloat, rather than demanding state intervention to provide jobs with a future, such as in tackling climate change or improving housing and public services. Instead of propping up failing management teams, we could be insisting decisions are taken by the workers – we know better than any bureaucrat or management consultant how to make our jobs run properly.

Historically, there have been a few radical unions or parts of unions that have sought to avoid this problem by refusing to bargain with employers. They simply made demands and took action in pursuit of them, stopping when members decided to. Though this removes some of the interpersonal pressures on those involved in bargaining, it doesn't remove the central contradiction. Unless there is a challenge to the overall capitalist system, workers are still deciding their demands and when to begin or end action based on what is possible, while leaving our oppression and exploitation intact.

THE WORLD OF WORK TODAY

I have described the urgent need to build working-class power, how organising at work is key for doing this, and the huge gap in recent decades between organisation and action on the one hand, and the need and potential on the other. Can organising at work bridge that gap, or does the modern world of work make it impossible?

Nobody controls capitalism – it is an anarchic system. Even the bosses of major companies or the leaders of countries are buffeted around by competition and events outside their control. This is even more true for workers. Many union activists joke that management are the best recruiters to the union – and there's a lot of truth in that. People are primarily motivated by *issues* and it is employers and government that cause most issues that affect people in our working lives. There are times when big changes *can* prompt lots of workers to feel the urge to organise at the same time – for example, if pensions come under attack, falling unemployment makes people less fearful, there is a threat to fire and rehire workers, or rapidly rising prices threaten living standards. It's never *inevitable* that workers respond effectively to such situations, but when one group of workers do, it can inspire others to follow suit in much the same way as 'waves' of protests and uprisings sweep around the world in everything from the Arab Spring of 2011 to the #MeToo movement and Black Lives Matter. It is in such waves of strikes and social movements that mass unionisation takes place.

There's nothing special about Britain that prevents us having a powerful workers' movement. We had the first mass workers' movement in the world. In the 1970s, Britain's unions were some of the strongest. Defeating them was a major struggle, and included betrayals by a Labour government and its allies in the unions and an onslaught from the Thatcher government. That included deliberate mass unemployment, the destruction of industries and communities, mass violent policing, the defeat of major strikes, legal changes, benefit cuts and the restructuring of the economy.

We haven't seen a big wave of strikes and unionisation in Britain since the 1970s, so newer industries and workplaces are much less likely to be unionised. Few workers or paid officers have much experience of striking. We can't wish a strike wave into existence. Organising is labour-intensive and there will never be enough paid organisers to close the unionisation gap. Simon Joyce (2015) points out that workers have lost the habit of striking, and it will take a jolt to change that pattern. Kim Moody (2015) argues persuasively that the lack of effective mass resistance during decades when whole industries have closed or mushroomed has led to '"compression": intensified work, poor or falling wages, insecure employment, lack or decline in state provision, etc.' and that it is just such compression that leads to waves of class struggle.

But we can't just sit back and 'wait for the upturn' in the struggle. While we can neither cause a new wave of strikes and unionisation, nor predict what the spark for such a wave will be, what we do now matters for several reasons:

1. We can organise and win even in the current situation.
2. Organising and taking action now develops our skills and networks. It changes workers' consciousness, makes more seem possible and sows the seeds of future struggles.
3. Experimentation is required for workers to learn how to organise in current conditions and is a precondition for a new wave of struggle.
4. Organising now generates sparks of action, the prerequisite for a new wave of struggle.
5. Organising now builds networks of solidarity that increase the chances of a spark 'catching' and igniting a new wave of struggle rather than fading out.
6. Organising now can shape the character and politics of the next wave, making it more (or less) likely to succeed.

The second and third reasons are particularly important to hold onto if, like many young people, your working life involves a series of short-term jobs where building real power seems unlikely. It is still worth having a go and learning from the process.

IT'S IMPOSSIBLE IN *MY* JOB BECAUSE ...

Even if we don't set ourselves as individuals the unrealistic goal of organising the entire working class, organising just one workplace or employer can still seem daunting. It's all too easy to look at all the difficulties and decide that it's 'impossible in *my* job because ...' Of course, some places are harder to organise than others, and every job has its unique features. But workers often give similar reasons about why their work is exceptional and can't be organised. I'll look at a few of the most common objections and explore whether they really make organising impossible or whether they should just influence *how* you organise.

'Nobody's interested'

Perhaps nobody talks about unions or politics in your workplace, and when you try to start such discussions, people don't seem interested. This is a common problem, but it raises the question of *what* people aren't interested in. Lack of interest is a common reaction if you push the union like you are selling insurance. Issues are what generally motivate people, and one of our first jobs is to find out what our colleagues *really* care deeply about, which isn't necessarily what we expect or what we think they *should* care about. I will cover how to choose issues to organise around in Chapter 5. As workers talk and act, they can discover new interests too.

'My colleagues are too right wing'

In most workplaces, few of your colleagues will identify as 'left wing'. A large minority of workers vote Tory, and in some workplaces a majority will have done so, or for a party further to the right. Discovering that most of your colleagues don't share your views on everything doesn't make your job exceptional, though it might explain why this book is in your hands not theirs. Finding a few lefties can be helpful if you are starting out and trying to build a team, but most have little more interest or skill in organising than anyone else. I've stood on a picket line (where workers gather outside a workplace to prevent workers, vehicles or goods entering or leaving) alongside a UKIP member while a Labour supporter crossed it. Workers share common interests, so if you start from issues they care deeply about, you can help them work out that only collective action with their colleagues can address their needs.

'My workmates are well paid. They've been bought off'

Pay isn't the only thing workers care about. Many better paid workers may have deep concerns about bullying and stress, sexual harassment, workload and staffing levels, pensions, training or safety – or they may resent the fact that their boss is paid far more off the back of their hard work. Again, the key is to start from the issues that workers care deeply about. There are very well-paid groups of workers who are organised – and that often helps them maintain their pay and status. For example, are your colleagues really better paid than professional footballers or more professional than doctors?

'My colleagues just leave rather than trying to change things'

This is a genuine issue, but it affects *how* you organise more than *whether* you can organise. It can be rational for workers to believe that getting another job is a more realistic path to better pay than collective action. However, other issues, particularly around safety and respect and dignity at work (bullying, harassment, micromanagement), may still motivate action. Workers who expect to leave have less to lose, so may be more willing to take risks to win. If you are in a dead-end job or planning to leave anyway, the end of that 'career' holds little fear. High staff turnover (the rate at which staff leave and have to be replaced) can also help if there are influential individuals opposing organising efforts. At one branch of a pub chain, workers described just waiting for the individual to leave. High turnover does change the pace at which you have to organise though. You can't build power over months or years – you have to 'go for it' when an opportunity arises (which is not always right away!). This is one of the reasons why 'micro-unions' such as United Voices of the World (UVW) have been particularly successful at organising precarious workers – their model is to organise and ballot for strike much faster than the traditional glacial pace.

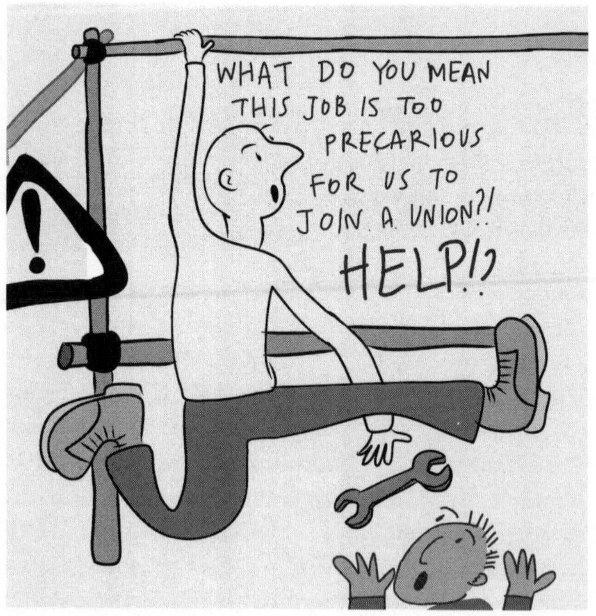

Individuals quitting jobs doesn't get issues resolved, and bad employment practices tend to spread if unchallenged – the problems follow you. On the other hand, organising in one job can help drive up standards across the labour market.

'Nobody will risk taking action as our jobs are too insecure'

Agency work, zero-hours contracts, outsourcing, bogus self-employment and the rest are widespread, particularly for younger workers. Employees with less than two years' service have few employment rights. The legal remedy for those victimised for union activity is inadequate. It's important to keep these barriers in proportion. They are not *the* reason why we don't have stronger unions in Britain. Most workers are directly employed with regular hours[3] but still aren't organised. Jane Hardy's *Nothing to Lose But Our Chains* (2021) does a great job of tackling myths about work, both in the past and today, and presents inspiring examples of 'precarious' workers fighting back.

It's worth thinking a bit more about the different forms of 'precarious' employment ('precarity'). Some relate to staff turnover, discussed above. Others deny you legal rights, which makes collective action even more indispensable. Some divide workers between multiple employers, which circumvents some legal rights. Particular efforts are required to organise across the arbitrary divisions between workers employed by different entities. Irregular hours can leave workers vulnerable to sanctions like losing shifts, but there have been examples of workers using casual status to stage 'strikes' without balloting – coordinating themselves to all say they are unavailable on particular days. For example, when members of the Independent Workers' Union of Great Britain (IWGB) at Deliveroo couldn't ballot for a strike because they didn't have 'worker' status (see Chapter 7), they simply logged off the app at the same time. Some of the most dynamic campaigns of recent years have involved precarious workers, immigrants and those in the 'gig' economy. Those in rotten jobs can feel they have less to lose by fighting back. Most employers need a reliable workforce, which is why they generally prefer to confine casual status to a small proportion of their workers. Where workers have exploited casual status in their campaigning, some have ended up being offered direct employment or contracts with regular hours.

Perhaps the main concern people have relating to 'precarity' is fear – are workers too vulnerable and afraid to organise? It's worth remembering that feeling precarious isn't just about the risk of losing your job. I can confidently walk along a six-inch-wide line painted on the ground. Put that line 50 feet up in the air and I will feel distinctly precarious. The consequences of falling have a big impact on your feeling of precarity and your perception of risk. If there are few alternative jobs, those available seem unattractive, and welfare benefits are inadequate and punitive then we are bound to feel more afraid of dismissal. This means that fear isn't something that only affects those at the bottom of the labour market – well-paid workers have 'further to fall' economically and often less experience at coping on benefits. Fear, whether of dismissal, loss of shifts, being allocated crap work or hours, blocked pay rises, bonuses, training, leave requests or promotions, is central to how managers control workers. Fear is a major barrier to organising, but it can be overcome. Let's not forget that even workers as precarious as dockers, who, in the past, used to physically fight each other to get a shift, have organised, just as organising efforts today are making headway against Uber and Deliveroo. Anger and humour are often the best antidotes to fear.

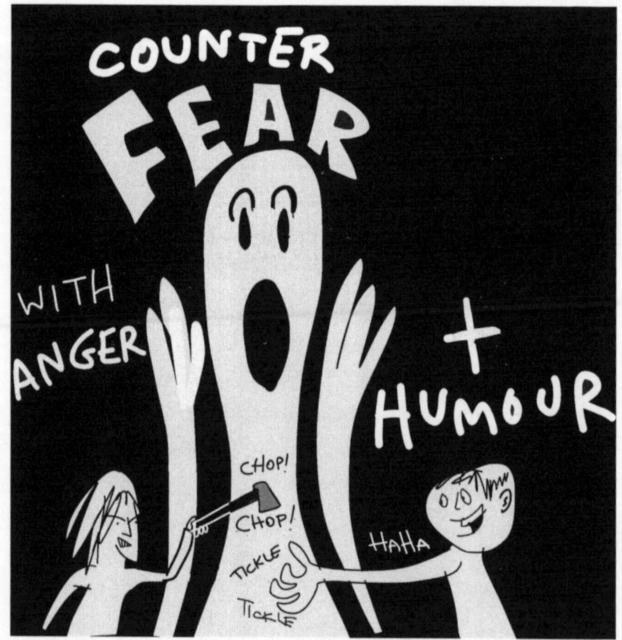

'We all work alone or on the move'

These are barriers to organising, but they can be overcome. Nearly all railway signal workers used to work alone, and train drivers still do. Few workers are as mobile as British Airways (BA) cabin crew, who work with different teams on every trip and are scattered across the world. These are well unionised groups – it's a matter of adapting organising methods to suit each group of workers, rather than giving up.

'We are all divided between different unions'

Some industries, such as healthcare, have many different unions. Workers often feel this makes it impossible to get united action. There's no doubt that if you have the choice, organising every worker involved in a (physical or virtual) workplace in one union – irrespective of employer, occupation or employment status – is the best option. In the USA, this is called 'wall-to-wall' organising. But sometimes there are already multiple unions, so that isn't an option. In a situation where organisation at work is weak, a multi-union environment may mean none of them really organise. It can mean many important decisions get taken by a few key individuals at the top of the various unions, with workers often having little influence. It's easy for each union to blame the others for anything unpopular, or to use them as an excuse for inaction.

The best response to having multiple unions is to double-down on organising the workers, and to do it across union boundaries. The classic example in Britain used to be the engineering industry (Hinton, 1973), which had separate unions for every craft (pattern makers, sheet metal workers, boiler makers, etc.). Workers responded by creating workplace structures – Joint Shop Stewards Committees – that spanned across all the unions. In this context, multi-unionism often actually benefited workers – key decisions were taken at workplace level by workers themselves and it was hard for paid officers of particular unions to interfere. We still have some unions based on occupations rather than industries (teachers, journalists, train drivers and many health professions, for example) and real efforts are required to build wall-to-wall organisation that includes everyone.

'Our union is a barrier to organising'

Sadly, many workers see their own union this way – sometimes due to inaction, incompetence or inaccessibility, and sometimes due to active obstruction or sabotage of organising efforts. It can be tempting (and very occasionally necessary) to switch unions, but if our interest is organising workers then the union most of your colleagues are in is nearly always the place to be. There are no shortcuts to winning them over to collective action. A useless or obstructive union, at workplace level or higher up, can be a real barrier, but there are ways to work around or overcome this, which I will cover in Chapter 11.

SEEK ADVICE; EXPERIMENT

Hopefully, the examples in this chapter have illustrated that you have to think about your specific situation and work out how to apply or adapt good organising practices – and occasionally make up new ones. It's a big help if you can build a network of people inside and beyond your own work that you can discuss organising problems with. You will undoubtedly get conflicting advice, have to make up your own mind, try something, and learn from it. Not everything will work, but there's no shame in that.

While different people won't give identical advice on organising techniques, effective organisers share a belief in the potential of workers. This doesn't mean pretending that workers are all saints or hyper-radical. It means confidence that if workers are confronted with choices that really matter to them, expressed in ways they understand, they will usually make good decisions. The organiser's job is to work out what really matters to workers and how to help them work out that collective action is the best way to achieve their goals.

Key points

- Employment generates conflict because bosses need to manage workers to get as much effort from us as possible.
- Work is a collective experience for the vast majority in Britain, creating a bias towards democracy when workers organise.
- Workers are concerned about issues beyond the workplace too.
- Organising is about building workers' collective power, not just union membership.
- The pool of un-unionised workers has been growing in Britain since the early 1980s. There are still around 6.5 million employees in unions, and things would be much worse without that organisation.
- Power is *the ability to achieve the outcomes you want, irrespective of opposition from your employer or others*.
- Using potential power requires being aware of it, having the organisation to wield it, and a political willingness to inflict costs on your employer rather than a partnership approach.
- The role of unions is contested – they resist employers and make accommodations to them.
- There are many reasons people think it's impossible to organise their workplace.
- We can't wish a major revival of unions into existence, but what we do now makes a difference.

Discussion questions

1. Why might your work colleagues think building a strong union at your work is impossible and how might you respond?
2. How aware of their potential collective power are your workmates?

3
Starting out

You may be working somewhere with no organisation at all or trying to strengthen existing organisation. In this chapter, I will look at some initial steps you can take. I will cover building relationships with other workers, avoiding victimisation and finding the resources and support you need.

TALKING, LISTENING AND FINDING ALLIES

It's harder to organise if workers barely talk to each other. For example, some open-plan offices and workplaces with intimidating management can be depressingly silent. With a bit of effort, it's often possible to gradually change this. Asking people work questions verbally, rather than using electronic communications, can break the silence and normalise people moving about. Starting conversations about harmless non-work topics can be the next step. If people are generally scared to talk, is anyone in before the supervisor, or still there when they've gone? Then perhaps ask people what they think of some story in the news, which may give you a feel for people's attitudes. As you get a bit more established, don't be afraid of raising bigger questions, like who decides what work gets done, who does it, how it's done or who benefits from it. When there's so much useful work in society that doesn't get done, why do we spend so much time on pointless and boring work?

Even if you are starting with a small group who are willing to act, you're aiming to get the vast majority of workers to unite together, so try to avoid involvement in gossip or 'office politics', let alone siding against people who may not fit in. Quite apart from being divisive, you never know whether the team odd-ball might turn out to be really committed or have skills or connections that will prove valuable.

Are there opportunities to talk away from your workspace? Where do people go on breaks? Who smokes – when and where? Does anyone go for a walk on a lunchbreak? Can you get people together outside work for a bit of fun, like a quiz night, if there isn't a tradition of socialising? One activist I know organised a work (not union) quiz night and included the odd question mocking management, which got people talking while being hard for management to complain about.

Are there WhatsApp groups or other social media connections between workmates? Take every opportunity to communicate with your workmates but remember to assume anything written down will be seen by the person you least want to see it, even if it is a 'private' message.

Getting people talking helps dispel one of the biggest barriers to organising: 'pluralistic ignorance'. This is the term for when a majority of people think something but assume that most other people disagree with them.

The key when you are starting out is to encourage workers to talk to each other and to *listen*. In a conversation with a worker, spend twice as much time listening as talking. Active listening is a skill. It's not just about not interrupting someone else when they are talking. You can't really listen if you're thinking ahead to how you will respond. Allowing a few moments' silence after they stop talking gives them space to let their thoughts unfold, helps them feel heard and gives you time to think. You know what it feels like when someone is really listening to you and how they show it – try to be an empathetic person who workers want to talk to.

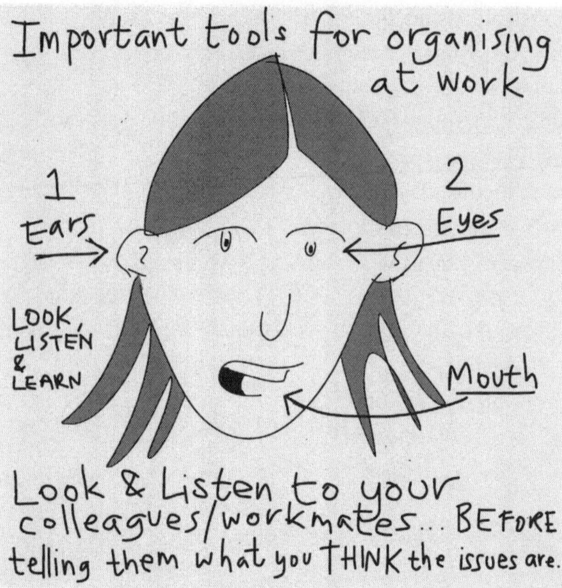

Important tools for organising at work
1
Ears
2
Eyes
LOOK, LISTEN & LEARN
Mouth
Look & Listen to your colleagues/workmates... BEFORE telling them what you THINK the issues are.

Effective organising is a collective effort, and it's important to find an ally or two from an early stage. All your listening not only means you have a better chance of working out who might be supportive and who you can trust, it also makes it safer to broach riskier questions – people are less likely to grass up someone they have more of a relationship with.

When the employer does something bad, it's good if you can say at least something to workmates (not necessarily in front of the manager!). You may get a reaction from someone that you can build on. Even if you don't, you make it more likely that when a colleague is unhappy about something in future then they will talk to you about it.

Sometimes you can find allies in unlikely ways. When the 2003 Iraq War kicked off, one activist I know worked in an un-unionised workplace for an arms company. A few of the workers campaigned against the war, which, while not very popular in that workplace, meant they built trust with each other and got used to campaigning together. It took courage, which made them more confident to build a union. This group then became the kernel for an organising effort that later won union recognition.

Activists are often afraid of talking politics at work, but bear in mind that your employer is likely to perceive this as *less* of a threat than talking about work-related issues. Also bear in mind that having leftie politics on other issues doesn't necessarily make someone a good organiser – or even someone committed to organising at work.

It's important not to mistake the first allies you find for the future 'leaders' of the workforce. This is rarely the case. The most influential workers tend to be cautious. In nearly all cases, you and your first allies need to act as organisers rather than leaders. In Chapter 6, I will explain the difference between leaders and organisers, as well as the different sorts of leaders and how to identify them. Building a team or committee is a vital part of the process of organising at work. An effective organising committee can't just be made up of those who initially support the union. Nonetheless, you start with the allies you find rather than the ones you wish you had. You will want to bring the most influential workers onto your committee and make sure it represents the full diversity of the workforce.

STAY SAFE

If you get fired, not only will it be much harder for you to organise on that job, but other people will be more reluctant to step up and play an organising role. There may be times where you decide on principle that you have to act or to take a calculated risk and 'go for it', but your default approach should be to protect your own job. Exceptions should be rare and decided with a cool head.

You need to be respected by your workmates, and that means doing your best to be good at your job, which also makes it harder for management to pick on you. But don't go too far. Part of the informal struggle in any job, organised or not, is over 'effort norms' – how hard people are expected to work. You don't want to appear brown-nosed or give management ammunition to increase workloads or pile extra duties on other workers. Focus on trying to be competent in the eyes of your workmates rather than taking on huge workloads or work outside your normal job. Knowing your job well can also help you identify ways to ease the job – sharing these with colleagues can earn you respect.

By organising, you give your employer a reason to want to get rid of you. There is legal remedy (compensation) for dismissal or detriment[1] for trade union activity as long as it is carried out 'at an appropriate time', which means either in your own time or when the employer has agreed to it. There is a Supreme Court appeal in the pipeline against the Court of Appeal overturning case law[2] that participating in industrial action is covered as union activity. Employers usually try to find another excuse when they want to victimise an activist. This means if you are going to organise then you have to be 'squeaky clean' – give them no excuses.

Many employers monitor internet use, emails and messaging systems, and even private messages outside work can get back to the wrong person. Be very careful in your use of social media. Encourage everyone you are organising with to adopt safe practices.

If you are reading this, then you are probably more committed to challenging injustice than most of your workmates. It can be tempting to shoot your mouth off at management. This can sometimes be popular, but if you are doing it on your own then your colleagues may feel they don't need to speak up because you always do. This won't build collective strength. Focusing on discussing issues with your workmates more than rowing with managers is more effective and keeps you safer.

You'll spend a lot more time thinking about the issues, their causes and solutions than workmates who aren't trying to organise. If what you say and do isn't one step ahead of them then you aren't moving things forward. But if you are a hundred steps ahead you won't connect – start from where workers are, not where you wish they were. You need to take people with you and that means lots of listening, discussion and democratic decision-making.

Democracy is vital for your protection once you've got a little team together. People are much more likely to back you up if what you do flows from decisions they helped make. Once you get more organised, it can also deter management action. I was once distributing a union leaflet in a different building at work when a manager told me I couldn't and threatened to call security to have me thrown out. It was already clear that workers in this building were afraid to take leaflets. Instead of escalating the confrontation with the manager, I went back to union members, who voted to instruct *all* the union reps to go and leaflet that building. We made sure management knew about this. We also checked that we'd recruited the security guards. We never had any more problems leafleting there – the manager knew he'd be picking a fight with everyone, not just one individual. This raised the confidence of the workers too.

As well as using democracy and collectivity to cover your back, use paid officers too. If you feel under threat, keep them informed. It's good practice to keep a log of any management action you feel is threatening or pressuring you – with dates, times, names, witnesses, what happened and how it made you feel. Hopefully you'll never need it, but you shouldn't rely on remembering or being able to find all the information from scratch if you ever do. If things escalate, some managers back off if the paid officer contacts them directly to make clear you have the backing of the union.

It's worth thinking about whether there's any information about you that management might spread around to undermine support for the campaign. For example, 'red baiting' against leftists – trying to demonise them by 'exposing' their politics – is not uncommon. If there's anything you feel might be used against you, consider being very open about it with your workmates. For example, whenever I stood for election as a union rep, I always included the information that I was a socialist in my election statement. If management had ever tried to make an issue of my politics, my colleagues would have been unsurprised and uninterested.

BUILDING UP RESOURCES, SKILLS AND SUPPORT

In this section, I'll cover gathering information about the organisation you work for, choosing a union and getting its support – including training, acquiring resources and building up networks you can use for advice, support and solidarity. I'll use the term 'employer' as shorthand, irrespective of whether you are technically an employee (see Chapter 7).

You will know quite a bit just from working somewhere. But there will be lots you don't know, and some of what you think you know won't be right. Gathering information can make you a more effective organiser and help avoid mistakes.

If your employer has a public website, have a good look around to see what they say about themselves. Many have information about other workplaces and make ethical claims, and some include policies that aren't promoted internally. Just knowing how the employer likes to present itself can help you work out what buttons to press in campaigning.

Search the web for the name of your employer and see what you find. Is there news coverage? Are workplaces listed? Try searching for their name and 'union' – you may find that other people are trying to organise too, or that other parts of the organisation are already unionised. You could set up an automated Google alert[3] so that you get an email when new material appears online about your employer.

Via Companies House[4] you can find information about many businesses and not-for-profit organisations, including accounts and details of directors. Reading company accounts can be daunting, but they usually include profits, and for larger organisations numbers of workers, pay, pensions – and the packages of company directors – campaigning dynamite. Look out for the information about subsidiaries and owners – many employers have multiple legal entities. You can 'follow' a company via the website, so you get an email about any updates.

Get to know your employers' policies. This can help you avoid falling foul of them, enable you to give good advice to colleagues, and spot if your employer isn't following its own policies. When I started work, a group of us got holidays we'd been told we couldn't have because we uncovered that management hadn't read their own annual leave policy – and I did. These can be easy wins. Becoming known as someone people can ask for advice is useful.

Gather the names, contact details and other information about as many of the workers as you can. Once the employer knows workers are organising, they may make it much harder to get this information. Many companies have email systems or internal websites that include a directory or Global Address List. Having a nose around these can give you lots of information. Often you can see which distribution lists you or someone else is a member of, then see who else is in the same ones. You may be able to work out what other workplaces there are and get a feel for how big they are. Quite often, managers send round emails without 'blind copying' workers, so you can see the whole list of recipients. Fire marshals may have access to staff lists. Other good sources include shift rotas and holiday booking systems. Admin staff may give you a list to take round a leaving or birthday card.

Employers with 250 or more employees have to publish information about their gender pay gap.[5] If your employer is in the public sector, you may be able to get someone who doesn't work there to submit a Freedom of Information request[6] (best not to do it yourself to avoid the spotlight). You can search for legal cases involving your employer using the BAILII website.[7]

Finding out about competitors can also be useful, particularly examples of them treating workers better. Trade press and networks within unions can help. The Labour Research Department (LRD)[8] maintains a PayLine database which you may be able to access via your union. Some unions have their own databases, notably Unite's 'Work Voice Pay'[9] system, which can produce employer profiles, collective agreements and details of workplaces with Unite members in.

Mark Bergfeld has collated some useful research resources for trade unionists.[10]

But don't get too obsessed with gathering information online – the most important source is the workers themselves.

It's common to see people discussing online which are the 'best' unions, but this generally reflects a prioritisation of the union as an institution – its policies, leadership, structures, etc. – over the union as a collective organisation of workers. If you are in a job where some workers are in a union, or where a union is already recognised by the employer, then it's nearly always best to join the one with most members amongst your workmates. If there are no union members in your work, look for a union which organises in other parts of your employer, or at least in the same industry. The Trades Union Congress (TUC) has a 'union finder' tool[11] to help you find an appropriate union to join. However, this only includes TUC-affiliated unions. There are a number of smaller unions which aren't affiliated to the TUC which are doing some great work, particularly amongst very precarious workers and migrant workers. The main 'micro-unions' are United Voices of the World (UVW), Independent Workers Union of Great Britain (IWGB), Industrial Workers of the World (IWW), the Cleaners and Allied Independent Workers Union (CAIWU) and the App Drivers and Couriers Union (ADCU). There are some big unions that aren't TUC-affiliated too, such as the Royal College of Nursing (RCN) and the British Medical Association (BMA), often because they are also professional associations and don't fully see themselves as part of the wider workers' movement. Do join a union right away – you don't have to wait for others to join and you can always switch if you picked the wrong one.

Ultimately, if you want strong organisation at work, there is no shortcut to winning over and organising all your workmates. Joining a more radical union while colleagues are in a more conservative one is usually a mistake. It isolates you and leaves them under the unchallenged influence of conservative leaders. If the employer bargains with the bigger union, you make your actions and arguments less relevant. Some activists 'dual card' by joining a second union. This can offer protection if you can't rely on the main union that organises on your job to back you, but your organising efforts need to go where they are most effective, even if that seems hard. Remember that all unions of any size are very uneven. You will find great organisation in some workplaces even in the 'worst' unions – and workers there will have a positive view of their union. Similarly, even the 'best' unions will have workplaces with weak organisation served by lazy, incompetent, right-wing or even corrupt reps and paid officers.

None of this is to say that the nature of each union as an institution is irrelevant, even if it isn't of primary importance. If you are left with a choice between two or three unions after investigating your workplace, employer and industry, pick the one that will make it easiest for you to build a strong and assertive organisation. Because unions are uneven, don't just go off their reputation. In most unions, branches are the basic groupings of members, often based on an employer, industry or area. Branches typically have meetings, lay officers and sometimes funds. Find out which branch you would be in and which paid officer you would be dealing with, if you joined. Ask around about what they are like. Give them a ring, explain that you want to organise where you work and ask what advice, training and support they could offer. If you already have a group of workers who are interested, you could invite each potential union to come along and speak to the group, then decide collectively which one looks best. A good branch secretary or paid officer can make a big difference, particularly when you are first starting out.

Unions are nearly always delighted to have new activists come on board. While sometimes union structures and processes can be opaque, people are often happy to help and advise if you ask. One barrier can be if people from the union structure think you are just looking for help with an existing individual issue, so always emphasise that you want to get involved and organise your workmates.

Most unions provide free training for their activists, though in some cases you have to be elected as a rep or to some other position first. Ask through your union about what is available and search their website. In addition to what your own union provides, you can find online and in-person training via the TUC[12] and the General Federation of Trade Unions (GFTU).[13] Independent unions often organise training sessions. Groups of activists increasingly do too, and there is free online training from organisations such as Labor Notes, the Rosa Luxemburg Stiftung and the Ella Baker School of Organising. Union training ranges from the inspiring to the dismal. Don't be put off by a bad experience – look for something better.

If you are creating a new structure or changing an old one, a key decision is whether elections for reps should treat the whole (physical or virtual) workplace as one constituency with all the members electing all the reps or whether it should be divided into multiple constituencies (e.g. for departments), each with their own reps. At early stages, candidates will probably come disproportionately from a few areas that are better organised, so a single constituency helps involve everyone who volunteers and is approved by members. But as your organisation develops, having separate constituencies creates a closer link between reps and the workers they represent. It makes it easier for reps to consult 'their' members and hold relatively informal 'section meetings' to discuss issues before any decisions at reps' committee meetings. Some unions (e.g. Unite) have rules to promote the election of reps who reflect the gender and ethnic diversity of members. Strong unions typically have one rep for every 10–20 workers. Recognition agreements (see Chapter 7) often limit the number of reps that the employer recognises, but there's nothing to stop members electing more reps – they just won't be treated as reps by the employer or be allowed to carry out reps' union duties in work time.

Sometimes you need to recruit one or more reps from a particular group, to ensure their issue is addressed. If you don't know the workers and their relationships well, it is tempting to ask the group for volunteers, but this rarely works. Much better to ask the group which of them they think would be the best reps. Generally, all the workers point at each other and it's clear who most people want. This is flattering, gives those individuals a confidence boost and puts them under a little pressure to step up. This often results in candidates and new reps.

If you are in a job where the employer recognises the union (see Chapter 7), there is a legal right for reps to take reasonable paid time off for appropriate training, and a right to reasonable unpaid time off for all union members. There's an *Acas Code of Practice on Time Off for Trade Union Duties and Activities*.[14] If you don't yet have union recognition you will be reliant on their goodwill (!) or, more likely, using your own free time. This can make accessing training quite difficult – many courses are organised to be in work time, to suit reps in organised workplaces.

As well as training, there are many resources that can make you a more competent and confident organiser.

Spend some time exploring your own union website. Many make it hard to find information and could be better designed. There is sometimes a 'site map' link at the bottom of the home page. It can often be easier to find what you are looking for using Google or an alternative. You can restrict your search to a particular website. For example, if you only want information about training from the Unite website, you could Google 'training site: unitetheunion.org'. Many union websites have areas that are restricted to members or reps, so find out how to log on.

The LRD is a long-established organisation which provides authoritative but readable information about work issues, the law, state benefits and more. Many union branches affiliate to the LRD to get copies of their publications or access to their online publications database. If you want to keep on top of employment law, several of the law firms who work for unions (e.g. Thompsons[15]) produce free newsletters that you can subscribe to. The TUC website allows you to selectively subscribe to email updates.[16] Many unions have a variety of electronic and printed publications. Remember not to use a work email address!

Other websites with useful information include the Advisory, Conciliation and Arbitration Service (Acas), the Equality and Human Rights Commission (EHRC), www.legislation.gov.uk for legislation, www.bailii.org for caselaw, www.ier.org.uk for employment law, the Health and Safety Executive (HSE), www.hazards.org for health and safety, the Office for National Statistics (ONS), the Pensions Regulator, and www.ewc-news.com for European Works Councils.

No guide, training or website can answer all your questions. Everyone trying to organise needs to build a network of people they can turn to for information, advice and ideas. This is one reason why those who focus entirely on their own workplace and ignore the wider union structures and labour movement are rarely the best organisers. Keep your main focus on organising with your workmates but have some involvement in the wider movement.

Although many union meetings can be fairly dull and lifeless, take the opportunity to look out for anyone who can help. Swap contact details with lots of people so you don't have to wait for a meeting to pick someone's brains. Get advice from several people, make your own mind up, see how it goes and learn whose advice was best. You might want these contacts for more than advice too, for example, if you need a speaker or solidarity.

The TUC has a unionreps.org.uk portal which reps from all TUC-affiliated unions can sign up to. The bulletin boards part of it allows you to post questions or ideas and join in discussions. You can set up email alerts for new content. There are also lots of social media spaces and real-life organisations, including trades councils[17] (umbrella groups for unions in an area), left groups and rank-and-file networks which connect union activists.

This chapter has covered some key points for starting your organising in a particular job. Before we get into the practicalities of how to organise, we need to take a step back and consider what people mean by organising and their different approaches to it.

Key points

- Get your work colleagues talking and listen to them.
- Find some allies.
- Earn the respect of your workmates.
- It's much harder to organise if you give your boss an excuse to fire you.
- Assume everything you write down will get back to the worst person.
- Use democracy and the wider union to help keep you safe.
- Research your employer.
- Choose the union best able to build collective power, not necessarily the most radical one.
- Get training, gather resources and build your networks.

Discussion questions

1. What do you need to find out about your employer and the workforce?
2. If you aren't already in a union, what are your options and the pros and cons of different unions?
3. What can you do to build your networks beyond your physical or virtual workplace?

4
Servicing, advocacy, mobilising and organising

The word 'organising' is used and misused in many ways. One thing to get clear from the start is that organising workers isn't the same thing as recruiting them to a union. A group of workers can have unbreakable solidarity without filling in membership forms, while many workplaces have plenty of members on paper but little sense of collectivity. Your priority should be organising workers. Getting them to join a union is usually part of that process, but it is not the goal. We organise to win change, to make our lives better, to challenge injustice and protect our environment – those are our goals.

In this chapter, I contrast different models of trade unionism and views of union purpose. While real power comes from collective action rather than handling cases through legalistic processes, casework is sometimes necessary and can help you organise. I discuss the potential of casework and two of the issues activists in unorganised workplaces are most likely to meet: non-payment of wages and dismissal. I then cover the pitfalls of casework and conclude with examples of 'non-work' issues likely to affect workers in non-unionised workplaces.

MODELS OF TRADE UNIONISM

You will often hear trade unionists contrasting what they call 'servicing' (or business unionism) and 'organising' models. A servicing model sees the union as a third party, like an insurance company or the Automobile Association (AA), which provides services to members in exchange for their membership fees or subs. After the terrible defeats of the 1980s, many unions shied away from collective action in favour of a servicing model. It was often mocked as 'credit card unionism' after the way unions tried to recruit people using offers of credit cards or free wills. This wasn't even effective at propping up unions' membership and subs income (there are plenty of places you can get consumer offers), let alone at enabling workers to resist the onslaught from employers and governments. Nearly all unions claim to have abandoned the servicing model, but elements remain – particularly an emphasis on individual 'casework' and legal representation. A servicing model has little appeal to workers who feel they don't need such services. It helps management portray unions as organisations for bad workers. It encourages individualism, which undermines workers' power.

One step up from a servicing model is 'advocacy', which still sees the union as a third party. Under this model, union staff skilled in negotiation, lobbying and media presentation would advocate on behalf of workers. At least advocacy recognises that workers have collective interests rather than just individual needs. But workers' role in an advocacy model is little more than providing numbers to support their representatives by signing petitions or sending letters. Sometimes a few workers are trained as 'authentic messengers' to talk to the media, but an advocacy model has no place for collective action.

Most unions now claim to have an 'organising' model, but this can mean anything from using a partnership with a big employer to recruit lots of passive members, through to building real power. Jane McAlevey makes a useful distinction between 'mobilising' and organising. Mobilising is about identifying people who agree with you, or can be easily persuaded to do so, and getting them to take action together. This is much better than servic-

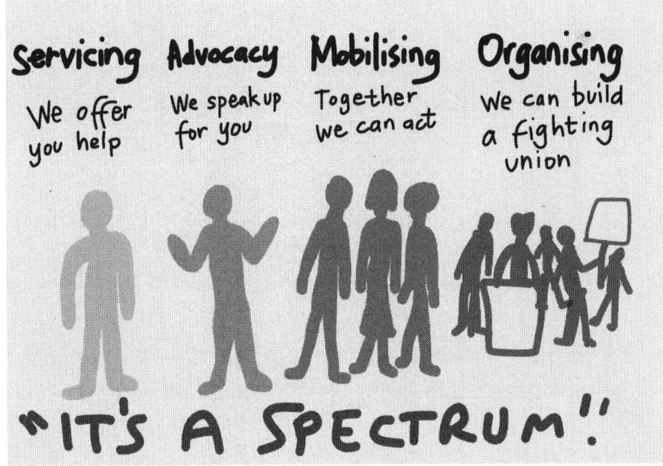

ing or advocacy. It makes collective action central and sees workers as the union rather than being its customers. It can be very militant. Organising goes further – winning over new people, building our movement's power rather than just skilfully deploying it.

While it's good to push the balance of what we do as far along the spectrum (servicing, advocacy, mobilising, organising) as we can, we do need a mix (and all unions have one). There will be issues that aren't suitable for organising around, sometimes we tactically need to use the law or lobbying, and we often need to mobilise our existing supporters during a campaign.

WHAT IS A UNION FOR?

The different models raise the question of what a union is *for*. What is its *purpose*? Some people see this very narrowly, as about advancing the interests of a particular group of existing members in direct connection to their job. The attraction of this approach is that it appeals to a lowest common denominator and avoids contentious issues that might put people off. But, in reality, it means ignoring many of the issues that are most important to people, prevents the union growing into new groups by ignoring their issues, limits power by failing to build solidarity and leaves workers unprepared by preventing them learning from others beyond their group. A narrow approach is often accompanied by short-termism. It discredits unions in the eyes of those with a commitment to social justice or the environment, for example, by justifying harmful industries in the hope of short-term job security rather than demanding useful jobs with a sustainable future. It feeds into the employers' narrative that unions are about selfish workers.

The strongest unions have always taken an expansive view of their role and seen themselves as a key part of an international movement for social justice. This isn't without its pitfalls though. Some union leaders bankroll remote radical causes to buy 'left cover' against criticism from activists, while doing little to educate or involve members in them. If workers perceive that the union is less concerned about their own issues than about others that don't directly affect them, they can become cynical, and their resentment may even feed opposition to those causes. As an activist at work, you have to make sure people can see that the bulk of the union's energy is going into helping them tackle their own issues, at the same time as educating and involving them in the wider movement.

THE POTENTIAL OF CASEWORK

In this book, I'm arguing for an organising model of trade unionism, but there is still a need for some servicing, advocacy and mobilising within that overall approach. Even when issues are suitable for organising (and not all are), focus those efforts on a limited number of issues at a time. If a worker is having to engage with an individualised process like a disciplinary, a request for flexible working or a sickness return to work meeting, it's natural that they turn to their union for support. They face managers, sometimes backed by Human Resources (HR), who deal with the processes more often than workers do, and they are better off with support, ideally from someone who knows the ropes. Just having a supportive witness can be a big boost, let alone a rep who can speak out against injustice more easily because they aren't so personally involved.

You may get involved in casework at an early stage in organising because many of the individual issues workers raise can be resolved with a bit of advice and support, without any formal process. Workers also have a right to be accompanied[1] in certain meetings irrespective of whether their job is unionised. The right to be accompanied only applies in disciplinary meetings where a formal sanction could result, appeals against disciplinary sanctions, and grievance meetings where a worker is complaining about a legal duty their employer owes them. Later in this section, I explain how this right works and some basics about how to use it.

You achieve a successful outcome to a case by convincing the decision-maker to do what the member wants. You may be able to persuade them that doing so is in their interests, for example, to uphold a policy or demonstrate consistency or compassion. Often, a degree of pressure is also required, either from campaigning or by demonstrating that the member could bring a legal claim with reasonable prospects of success. Employers aren't only concerned about having to pay compensation from a legal claim, they often worry about the time and money involved in contesting cases, the reputational damage of losing a case, and the risk that the public nature of a case might lead other workers to follow suit.

Helping individuals with cases (casework) can help you organise. Managers whose workers aren't unionised get used to doing what they like, without challenge. This can make wins possible despite how limited workers' rights are. As workers learn that managers have been taking advantage of their lack of awareness of their rights and their lack of organisation, and that they can be challenged, this creates organising potential by educating workers about management behaviour and showing the benefits of collective organisation. Towards the end of this chapter, I discuss the pitfalls of casework and how to manage them. Chapter 7 discusses in more detail the problems arising from relying on 'rights' rather than collective power.

A worker can choose their companion (though the companion can refuse) – either a paid union officer, a rep whom a union has certified as competent to accompany workers, or a work colleague. If you are at a very early stage of unionisation, workers may prefer to have you along as a 'colleague' even if you are a trained rep, to avoid disclosing their union membership to the employer. On the other hand, some employers with no experience of union representation are afraid of dealing with a union and give a lot of ground. If you are accompanying someone who works for the same employer, you are entitled to reasonable paid time in working hours to prepare for and attend the hearing. A companion can address the hearing and confer with the worker if they wish, but they can't answer questions on behalf of the worker. Employers may agree to accompaniment beyond these circumstances, such as in formal investigation meetings. There's an *Acas Code of Practice on Disciplinary and Grievance Procedures*[2] and it's important to familiarise yourself with this and the employer's own disciplinary and grievance procedures before accompanying anyone. The LRD has a useful *Disciplinary and Grievance Procedures* booklet too.

Some unions have guides for casework. Here are some basic tips:

- Workers' information is confidential unless they consent to you sharing it.
- Get all the worker's contact details – this is particularly important in case they go off sick or are suspended.
- Check whether the worker is a union member at the outset.
- Check whether the worker needs any reasonable adjustments for disability.
- Take notes, with dates and times, and keep them safe.
- Explain your role to the worker.
- Spend time actively listening and asking the worker questions to flush out *all* the issues and get their story straight in your head.

- Unless there's a good reason not to, validate the worker's sense of grievance and injustice.
- Explore whether they have attempted to resolve their issues informally, and whether such an attempt would be appropriate.
- Try to understand any underlying issues and whether other workers are affected. Can the issue be made more collective?
- Get the worker to specify what outcome(s) they want. Discuss what is realistic and what they will need to do to achieve them.
- Remember that it's the worker's case, not yours. You can explain their options and express opinions about what might work, but they should decide how to proceed. If they decide to do things you believe are unwise, ensure there is a paper trail of your advice.
- If you are going to campaign around the case, consider getting a photo and a quote about the impact on the individual.
- Agree what role you will play in any hearings.
- Never discuss the case with management without the worker's agreement.
- If they need support, for example with their health or mental health, signpost them rather than taking this on yourself.
- You and/or the worker should look up policies and any relevant law.
- Collate any relevant documents.
- Support the worker as much as possible to be involved in preparing and dealing with their own case, and agree what each of you will do.
- Be aware of time limits (typically three months minus one day from the incident) for the worker to bring legal claims. If they might have a claim, you should draw this to the attention of your union's legal team (probably via the paid officer) *well before* the deadline and clarify.
- If you aren't sure, ask for advice (while respecting confidentiality).
- When the case is over, will the worker provide a quote (possibly anonymised), explaining how the union helped them, that can be used in campaigning?

In Britain, law comes from several main sources.[3] 'Primary legislation' mostly consists of Acts passed by the UK, Scottish and Welsh parliaments, which are sometimes known as statutes. 'Secondary legislation' is made by ministers or others using powers set out in primary legislation and includes Regulations. A vast proportion of law is created by unelected judges through court judgements, which are used as precedents that other courts must follow. This is known as 'case law'. Brexit meant that a large volume of law from the European Union (EU) is now part of UK domestic legislation.[4]

There is a wide range of issues that workers may bring up as individuals and which may require an element of casework. Chapter 7 covers some of the rights that are useful specifically for organising, but can't cover all the issues likely to come up in casework. The LRD's annual *Law at Work* booklet is a good, readable reference. Next, I summarise your rights around two of the most common issues for workers in unorganised workplaces – wages and dismissal – because you may have to use casework as at least part of how you deal with these at an early stage in your organising.

NON-PAYMENT OF WAGES AND THE MINIMUM WAGE

For many workers at the bottom of the labour market, being paid less than you are entitled to, or not at all, is a common experience, which can be challenged using a combination of casework and collective action. Unauthorised deduction from wages made up 14 per cent of all Employment Tribunal (ET) claims in the ten years to 2021 (ONS, 2021), despite the fact that many workers lack the time and resources to pursue a case. Add to this the fact that 22 per cent of ET claims are under the Working Time Regulations, some of which are actually about holiday pay, and you get a picture that many employers are frequently cheating workers out of wages.

The rights around wages are individual, not collective, but if lots of workers are having the same problem, you can still organise collectively around them. One individual may be afraid to lodge a legal claim for fear of victimisation, despite it being unlawful to penalise a worker for bringing a claim. But a group of workers will feel safer taking a claim at the same time or threatening to do so. Almost all unions will pursue claims for members free of charge if they believe the cases have reasonable prospects of success, though most require you to have been a member for a certain period before the issue (e.g. four weeks in UNISON and Unite). An ET can award you up to two years' back pay, but the claim must be brought soon after the most recent in a series of deductions. For these purposes, wages include fees, shift allowance, bonuses, commission, holiday pay, guarantee pay, sick pay, maternity, shared parental and adoption pay, as well as notice pay if you worked your notice – but not employer pension contributions. Unlawful deduction claims can sometimes be used to claim your original pay despite the employer imposing a cut in rates or hours.

If your employer pays you less than the National Minimum Wage (NMW), enforcement is via HMRC. Anonymous complaints are possible, and HMRC have powers not only to recover arrears of up to six years but to name and shame non-payers and bring criminal prosecutions. Bear in mind that it is an average hourly rate[5] that is set under the National Minimum Wage Act[6], so workers may fall below it if working additional unpaid hours, including some categories of travel time. Pay rates above the 'basic', such as for overtime or unsocial hours, don't count towards the NWM. Employers are required to keep adequate records to prove they are paying the NMW, and workers are entitled to inspect them.

Not everyone is entitled to the NMW. For example, self-employed people aren't treated as 'workers' and are denied it. Some of the new, independent, micro-unions follow a strategy of taking test cases to win worker status and then enforcing the NMW.

DISMISSAL

Sadly, dismissals are not rare, particularly if your job isn't yet unionised. It's not just that managers have reasons for wanting to get rid of particular individuals. The threat of dismissal, whether spoken or unspoken, is a key mechanism of managerial control. Even if you aren't strong enough to prevent a dismissal, there are lots of low-key ways workers can show solidarity with someone sacked, from taking round a leaving card and a collection to presenting a massive bunch of flowers under the manager's nose. One collection I organised for a sacked worker raised what would be well over £2000 in 2022 prices – quite a message!

The ending of a fixed-term contract counts as a dismissal. In rare cases, a resignation under duress can too. Some workers have some legal rights in relation to dismissal, such as the right to bring an unfair dismissal claim to an ET. The right not to be unfairly dismissed is set out in sections 94 to 98 of the Employment Rights Act 1996. Normally, only employees (see Chapter 7) with at least two years' continuous employment can make a claim, but there is no qualifying period if the dismissal is the result of a business transfer or discrimination.

A dismissal is unfair unless the employer can satisfy two tests:

- The dismissal was wholly or mainly for one of five 'fair reasons':
  - capability or qualifications
  - conduct
  - redundancy
  - to comply with a legal duty or restriction (e.g. loss of driving licence, immigration status)
  - some other substantial reason (e.g. breakdown in trust and confidence, and sometimes including ending a temporary contract, pressure from a third-party client or refusal of changes to terms and conditions through 'fire and rehire').
- The employer acted 'reasonably' by dismissing the employee for that reason. When assessing reasonableness, the tribunal must consider all the surrounding circumstances, including the employer's size and administrative resources, whether there was a 'fair procedure', consistency, and factors personal to the employee. They must decide fairness in accordance with equity and the substantial merits of the case.

Employees with at least two years' service have a right to written reasons for dismissal within 14 days of requesting them. Employees dismissed while pregnant or on leave for maternity or adoption must be given written reasons irrespective of service. Other than in cases of gross misconduct resulting in summary dismissal, employees are entitled to notice pay based on their length of service and their contract, subject to statutory minimums. There is no qualifying period to claim Wrongful Dismissal if the employer fails to give full notice when they should.

In disciplinary cases, when the employer is complaining about an employee's conduct or capability then a dismissal will normally follow one or more stages of a disciplinary procedure. Employees wanting to challenge a dismissal or other sanction should follow their employer's appeal or grievance procedures, raising all the issues they might later want to raise at a tribunal. For example, if an employee believes discrimination is the reason for the sanction, it is vital to say so. A disciplinary sanction cannot be increased on appeal. Some employers have specific procedures for complaining about issues such as bullying or harassment. The employee should also ensure they follow the Acas early conciliation process[7] in good time before the deadline and are aware of deadlines for submitting an ET claim[8] too. This is usually three months less one day from your employment ending or the problem happening. Get advice – and, if possible, representation – via a union as early in the process as possible.

When an employee believes the main reason for dismissal was for lawful union activity, they need to act even more quickly. The union may be able to apply for 'interim relief', which needs to be claimed within seven days of dismissal. If the ET decides that the employee has a 'pretty good chance of success' of winning an unfair dismissal claim for automatically unfair grounds (for acting as a health and safety rep; lawful trade union activities; acting as a trustee of an occupational pension scheme; acting as a rep for collective consultation over redundancies or TUPE; or whistleblowing), the interim relief order means they get full pay, and in some cases reinstatement or re-engagement until the case is dealt with.

This has been a very brief overview of a complex topic, and no substitute for doing your homework or getting proper legal advice if you face these issues. A fundamental point to grasp is that the law can't force an employer to give a worker their job back, no matter how outrageous the dismissal. In the vast majority of cases, the most the worker gets from a long and stressful legal process is some money. No wonder most trade unionists view legal cases as a sign of failure. Collective action can be far more powerful – it can and does prevent and reverse dismissals. Our focus must be on organising to build collective power. Casework can help us do that, but it's no substitute for it.

THE PITFALLS OF CASEWORK

Many unions push their activists heavily in the direction of individual casework. This is partly out of weakness – if you have little power, you are left trying to enforce employer policies and legislation that generally favour those in power. This turns our rights into a ceiling we fight to reach, instead of a floor we build up from. Sometimes paid officers want you to take on this work instead of it soaking up their time. Years of recruiting union members on the basis of a servicing model have also created expectations from members that 'the union' will solve their problems through skilful representation.

How can you avoid getting so overloaded with casework that you have no time to organise and build power? Individual cases are almost invariably

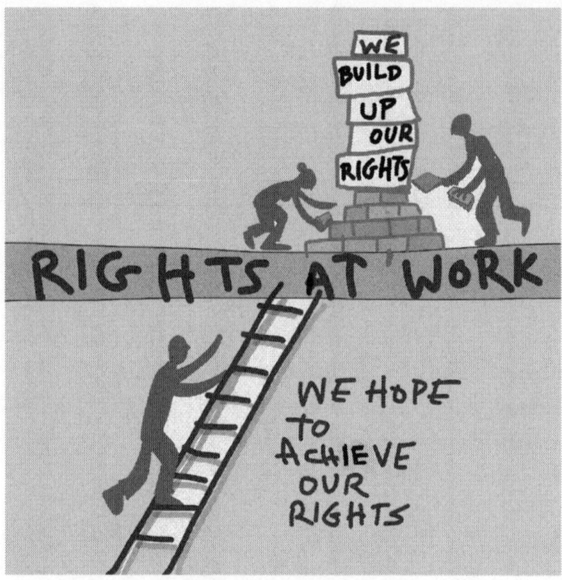

symptoms of collective problems. For example, the worker who is frequently late – is that because of inadequate public transport, long hours, low pay that means they have two other jobs, problems with childcare, or dreading coming to work because of boring work and a bullying manager? Are rigid hours rather than flexitime necessary anyway? Many cases come down to lack of training, understaffing, systems of work that aren't usable or excessive workload. How many workers are affected by the underlying issues? Can you turn the case, or at least part of it, into a collective issue and get other workers involved in pushing for change? This isn't always possible. Sometimes issues are highly sensitive and confidential for the worker, or the worker is so unpopular that it's hard to win support even if they are right. But you should always ask yourself whether a case can be made collective and whether collective action could get better results than only going through a grievance procedure.

If you do decide that a casework element is the right way to go, remember the iron law of organising: never do for others what they can do for themselves. This isn't about being lazy. If you can involve the worker in researching and preparing their own case, they will end up with a better understanding of their rights and their limitations, and how to exercise them, as well as a better understanding of the relationship with their employer. If you get this right, the member who started out looking for you to rescue them may become a committed activist herself.

As with most 'iron laws', this one does need qualifying. For example, some cases involve traumatic experiences such as sexual violence or harassment. If a worker has trusted you to disclose their experience to, this is a big responsibility. You need to give it careful thought and probably seek advice, without disclosing who is involved or the specifics of the issue to anyone without the worker's explicit permission. Avoid getting so angry about the issue that you disempower the worker by taking decisions for them, for example, reporting or escalating the issue in ways they don't want and adding to their trauma. Too often people prioritise the short-term interests of their organisation over the needs and wishes of the survivor. The opposite mistake is a 'survivor-led' approach, which leaves all the responsibility for deciding how to deal with the issue to them. Some survivors may want that, others may not, and of course you have a responsibility to act ethically yourself. Instead, aim at a 'survivor-centred' approach[9] that prioritises survivors' needs and wishes.

Cases where a member is accused (sometimes by other members) of unacceptable behaviour, such as bullying, violence, harassment or discrimination, can be particularly tricky. Members accused are entitled to be accompanied in any formal process, but this should never be by the same person supporting the victim and it's good practice to give the victim first choice of who supports them. It's important that you and the union aren't seen to be defending oppressive behaviour or its perpetrators when helping ensure the employer applies fair process and minimising further harm to the victim. These can be varied and complex situations that need careful thought.

Unions are generally cautious about providing support to workers who join with existing problems, fearing that this will soak up limited resources and the worker might leave once their issue is resolved. This can undermine a key benefit of membership, creating resentment from existing members. People often over-state unions' rules on this though. Formal requirements for prior membership often only apply to legal representation, which is rarely what workers first need.

If you are organising at work and a non-member approaches you for help, you need to apply some judgement. It's hard to imagine circumstances where it would make sense to accompany someone who refused to join. You'd be reluctant to help a worker in a well-organised workplace who had left again after being helped with a previous issue and who had been a vocal opponent of the union. At the other extreme, you'd be more supportive of someone who had never been asked to join and was from a group of workers with little or no union presence. The nature of the issue may be a factor in your decision too. Someone joining with an issue can help you establish a foothold in a new area. If you do decide to offer immediate representation, it's good practice to agree some actions they will take to build the collective in return, such as talking to colleagues and signing some up.

ISSUES BEYOND WORK

Workers may also face issues that aren't directly work-related but which may require an element of casework to resolve. Two common examples, particularly in unorganised workplaces, relate to immigration and state benefits, but there are many others.

Successive British governments have created a 'hostile environment' for immigrants which often extends to those perceived to be immigrants, whether they are or not. Part of the hostile environment is the extension of immigration enforcement from borders into every aspect of our lives, including work. Landlords are required to check the citizenship status of potential tenants. Employers are required to check applicants' right to work before hiring anyone. Some workers are also expected to check the citizenship status of people trying to access services, turning public service workers into border guards. The Windrush scandal and the Brexit process both showed how people can suddenly lose their rights due to administrative issues. There are some great campaigns, many with union backing, against the hostile environment. The hostile environment has made migrant workers who don't have the right paperwork more vulnerable and often deters them from accessing advice and information, let alone legal remedy. This has been a recipe for abuse. Though unions don't generally train reps in how to support members with immigration issues, several now have helplines for immigration advice, and the University and College Union (UCU) published advice for migrant workers about taking industrial action.[10] Immigration cases have very high stakes for the workers affected, so be sure to handle them with discretion and signpost them to good advice and support, whether from your union or other organisations.

A large proportion of those in receipt of state benefits are in work, so many workers have issues with the welfare system from time to time. Some unions are geared up to provide advice and support on state benefits, others aren't. For example, many of Unite's community branches have lots of expertise. The LRD booklet *Universal Credit and Other In-Work Benefits* is helpful, and you may be able to access help via Citizens Advice or a Law Centre. Dividing those in and out of work is a key tool for driving down pay and conditions, so we ignore these issues at our peril.

Helping workers win on all their issues, whether work-related or not, contributes to building engagement and power, and promotes a vision of trade unionism that doesn't limit itself to changing things at work but aims to change society for the better too.

Key points

- There are various models of trade unionism, from servicing, through advocacy and mobilising, to organising. You will need a mix, but as much organising as possible.
- If you only take up issues that everyone can see facing them already, you fail to prepare people and let down those affected by other issues. Ensure all the workers can see issues they care about are being taken up.
- Workers have the right to be accompanied in grievance and disciplinary meetings even before their job is unionised.
- Casework can help you organise, but can also overwhelm you and prevent you tackling the underlying issues.
- Remember the iron law of organising: never do for others what they can do for themselves. But don't pile all the responsibility onto someone who has been through trauma.
- Some of the most common casework issues in unorganised workplaces are non-payment of wages, the National Minimum Wage and dismissal.
- Workers may want support with non-work issues such as immigration and state benefits.

Discussion questions

1. Are there issues some workers care about that you'd worry about raising with others? How might you address this?
2. What issues face individual workers on your job? Are any of them symptoms of bigger issues? Could they be resolved collectively?

5
Choosing and communicating about issues

This chapter and the next one set out some tried and tested principles and techniques for organising, but you will need to adapt them to your own situation. There isn't 'one best way' to organise that fits in all circumstances. You have to try things, some will work better than others, and some won't work at all. That's fine, as long as you avoid taking ill-considered risks and you all learn from what goes wrong. But you can save yourself a lot of trouble by learning from other workers' successes and failures as well as your own.

Effective organising is around *issues* that workers care about. In this chapter, I discuss the role issues play in organising, how to choose good issues to organise around, and how to communicate effectively in one-to-one organising conversations and in writing.

It is helpful to think of an 'organising cycle' which you go round repeatedly, building power each time. There are different versions of the organising cycle, but the one given in Figure 5.1 is fairly typical.

The *issue* stage is about identifying an issue to organise around. *Organisation* is about establishing organisation and using it to engage people about the issue. This includes teams and committees, communication channels, mapping and charting the workforce, and identifying and testing leaders. You use *education* to improve workers' knowledge, such as how organising through a union can help achieve their goals and how the campaign plans to win. The *action* stage involves one or more collective actions. I explain in Chapter 8 that actions aren't just about achieving your campaign goals, they should also have objectives to mobilise people and to build power. If the action wasn't enough to win on the chosen issue, you may need to go round the cycle again. Each time round the organising cycle you build the capacity of your organisation and the workers' knowledge, skills and experience.

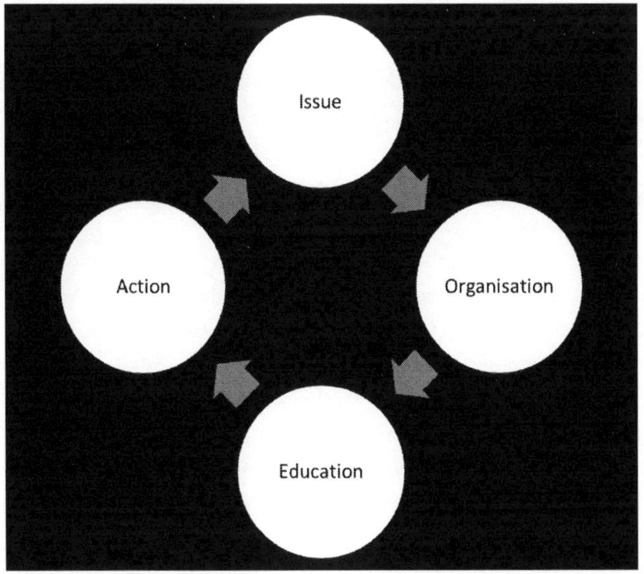

Figure 5.1 The organising cycle

CHOOSING ORGANISING ISSUES

Some issues are better than others to organise around. That doesn't mean you never tackle other issues – sometimes they are too important to ignore, or best addressed using a servicing approach so that you can direct your organising energies elsewhere, and sometimes you need to build more power before you can tackle an issue. Occasionally, you should even say things that are unpopular now, to avoid paying the price later for being unprincipled.

Arnie Graf (2020) makes a useful distinction between *problems*, which can be quite general, and *issues*, which are specific, can polarise people, and which can be winnable. There may be many issues relating to one problem. You can tackle a problem by winning on a series of issues, but a win on the problem itself would be hard to define and mobilise around.

Just because you are organising at work, that shouldn't mean that every issue you organise round will be a 'work issue'. Sometimes issues beyond the job are vitally important to workers, and the power and experience gained at work can make a difference in the wider community. Neither should you think only of 'economic' issues like pay or hours. Issues such as workload, stress, safety, the working environment, management behaviour, work allocation, bullying, harassment and discrimination can be just as important to workers. It can help to think of work issues as either to do with 'market relations' – the things that get written down in a job offer – and 'managerial relations' – the things dealt with between you and your manager (Fox, 1966). A broad range of issues is particularly important if you work in a large organisation where bargaining is centralised in the hands of a few reps or paid officials. They are likely to deal with the big, simple, market relations issues. It's hard to organise if you're left with nothing but casework – you need to find other issues at a lower level to organise around and achieve some collective wins.

If someone brings an issue to you, check the facts. Sometimes people have the wrong end of the stick or only tell you half a story. You could do a survey of workers (*not* just union members – you are trying to win over the so-far unconvinced!), or a bunch of you could get together and make a big list of possible organising issues, then assess them against these criteria:

- *Widely felt*: *who* cares about the issue? Unless it is a significant proportion of a workgroup, team, department, workplace or occupation it will be hard to organise around successfully.
- *Deeply felt*: *how much* do workers care about the issue? There are plenty of issues that workers moan about. Which are they prepared to do something about?
- *Winnable*: one of the biggest barriers to organising is feeling powerless. Every win builds confidence. Starting from where you are, not where you wish you were, could you make a plan to win that workers could believe in? But don't aim too low – you want to raise workers' expectations. Nobody will make much effort to win something that seems tiny to them.
- *Visible*: some wins are visible to everyone, some more private. Some are quickly forgotten, while people are reminded of others all the time. Visible wins do more to build confidence.

While most issues relate to long-standing problems, it's worth looking out for issues relating to any disruption to 'business as usual'. Employers never let a good crisis go to waste and neither should we. If there's less work for a while, is it a good time to push for a shorter working week or more holidays?

If there's understaffing, would pushing for pay rises or better conditions or more secure contracts help attract more staff? What about providing help with childcare? If management are struggling to get people to work at certain times, why not introduce premium pay rates for unsocial hours? Look out for management asking for temporary changes they will want to make permanent. On the other hand, if temporary arrangements are good for workers, can you keep them?

When you think you've identified one or two potential issues to organise around next, it's usually worth *testing* the issues to check workers agree with your assessment before going too far. This might involve doing a survey, talking to a sample of workers or asking workers to undertake a low-visibility task and assessing their response.

COMMUNICATING ABOUT YOUR ISSUE

How you 'frame' your issue is jargon for how you describe it. Good framing can help position a grievance as an injustice, strengthen a collective identity ('us'), bring workers on board, as well as potential supporters or allies, and make it harder for opponents to mobilise. As Srdja Popovic and Matthew Miller (2015) point out, you want to create a line of division with the vast majority on your side and a tiny group of opponents in the wrong.

Eric Batstone, Ian Boraston and Stephen Frenkel (1978) describe some of the 'vocabularies of motive' workers use when discussing conflict at work. Workers complain of management breaking agreements, conning workers, taking a hard line and ignoring workers' effort, goodwill or intentions. We sometimes make appeals to fairness, make comparisons with better treatment, refer to what is in our job description (if we have one!) or cite rules and precedent. We can appeal to social norms such as reasonableness or responsibility. There can also be more specific issue-based justifications, for example around money or safety, which may link to the customary balance between reward and hardship in a job. Sometimes workers draw on what might be seen as 'union values' such as avoiding a negative impact on other workers.

Peter Armstrong, Jeffrey Goodman and Jerahn Hyman (1981) describe the 'resistance principles' that workers draw on to justify resistance. Sometimes we draw on ideas from managerial ideology (the ideas that justify managers' power), trying to turn them to our own advantage. For example, management justify their control by claiming they are acting in the interests of society, that what they want is in the interests of efficiency or customer needs, or that they have special management expertise in a division of labour between managers and workers. Workers can turn all these against management – but at the price of strengthening these ideas, which generally work against us. As the black feminist poet Audre Lorde (2007) put it 'the master's tools will never dismantle the master's house. They may allow us temporarily to beat him at his own game, but they will never enable us to bring about genuine change.' Other resistance principles, such as fairness and consistency, are more neutral. Less often, workers can deploy principles not derived from managerial ideology. Examples include the right to autonomy in the labour process or defence of the customary effort–reward ratio (how hard we work, for how much in return). Workers sometimes claim 'property rights' over jobs or the equipment we use with arguments like 'that's my job, you can't give that work to him' or 'this is my desk, I'm not moving there.'

Other arguments you often hear workers use to justify action are demanding management act in line with their words, as well as arguments based on dignity and respect – which can cover everything from privacy and opposing micromanagement to decent wages and the absence of bullying and harassment. It's worth checking whether management actions contradict their policies or the statements they make to the public, shareholders or customers.

The framing of issues usually draws on four overarching 'master frames': injustice, democracy, protection and rights. According to Peter Gahan and Andreas Pekarek (2013) framing can provide three key elements:

- *Diagnostic*: identify the source of the grievance, its causes, who is to blame, who is on our side and who are our enemies.
- *Prognostic*: set out the solution and strategies to achieve it.
- *Motivational*: provide the rationale for someone to participate.

What to include or emphasise will depend on the particular circumstances and issues. For example, messages about corporate power and the general injustice of capitalism are likely to be more central if you are organising in a job with high turnover, or in corporate giants like Amazon or McDonald's rather than in a small business or the public sector. But in either case you are trying to connect injustice, democracy, protection or rights to the specific issue on which you aim to win. Showing your understanding of the issues gives you credibility. However, the more you can frame your campaign in terms of general principles of social justice rather than detailed specifics of your job, the easier it is to find allies beyond your job and the greater the potential for your win to 'spill over', inspiring people in other workplaces to organise.

There are some important principles for communicating about your issue or other topics:

- Keep it clear, simple and jargon free. It can help to imagine you are explaining to a specific person you know, who isn't well informed.
- Keep focused on what the workers care about; don't get side-tracked.
- You are helping workers build their power. That means being honest with them, not manipulating them.
- You need to earn and keep workers' trust. Don't share personal information about workers without their agreement. Check your facts. Resist any temptation to exaggerate or speculate. This also helps protect you from employer complaints.
- Use inclusive language which doesn't assume everyone is male, white, able bodied, etc.
- Avoid 'passive' language – this is not only boring but hides who is doing what to whom. For example, 'Senior management propose to

cut your pay' is much better than 'It is proposed to cut workers' pay' and '30 workers protested outside the gate' is better than 'a protest of 30 workers took place outside the gate'.

- However frustrated you may get, never blame the workers. It is off-putting and diverts attention and energy from what needs to be done.

Consider how your opponents might try to frame your issue alongside the options for how you could frame it. Again, you can test out your thinking with some other workers before your campaign gets going.

WORDS MATTER

When you are interested in a cause it is easy to forget that most workers aren't familiar with its terminology and jargon. On top of this, some struggle with literacy and many don't have English as a first language. Keep things simple and direct, avoid jargon, but don't talk down to people. If that isn't enough, can you get material translated into workers' other languages? Not only does that help get more people involved, it can terrify management.

Millions have never been in a job with a union, particularly younger workers, so they may not have a clear idea what one is, never mind jargon like motions, branches, recognition, strike and picket. This situation has been made worse by unions that have spent years promoting themselves as responsible partners and advisers to government, providers of financial and legal services, and as third parties providing insurance against something going wrong at work. As well as misleading workers, this helps employers present unions as parasitic third-party businesses that take our money, aren't interested in our issues, boss us around, cause conflict and deliver little.

If workers want the power to improve our lives, the key is our own collective activity. Fundamentally, a union is a club for working-class people who agree to back each other up and stick together to improve our lives. I will discuss in Chapter 11 how this isn't the whole story, but it is the foundation.

If you are organising at your work, the way you talk about organising and unions will have a big influence on how other workers think about them. Unfortunately, it is spectacularly difficult to free ourselves of widely used language that is unhelpful to our own organising efforts. The words we use and what they mean (semantics) are vital for organisers. We have to practise saying and writing things in ways that convey what we really mean, rather than reinforcing employer propaganda. Jane McAlevey calls practising this

'semantic drill' and recommends doing it every day with the people you organise with. The aim is to get good at avoiding treating the union as a third party, making clear that workers' own activity is the key, and linking everything back to issues that the worker cares deeply about.

Some examples might make this clearer (see Table 5.1). Some of them assume you are talking to a worker in a different department.

Not saying 'thank you' comes hardest to most people. For the avoidance of doubt, I'm *not* saying you shouldn't show your appreciation for someone's contribution. On the contrary, recognising each other's work helps us build confidence, develop and feel part of the campaign. Look for ways to do this even with small tasks – they may still be big for the worker who did them. The point is to avoid thanking people in a 'transactional' way that implies their contribution was for you rather than for the cause they are fighting for.

If you want to do a semantic drill exercise, you can think of conversations you've had or heard, or take text from a union leaflet, website or newsletter. There's no 'right' answer – the point is to get the people you are organising with to think about different ways of saying things, the pros and cons, and to come up with the best alternative you can. Keeping working at this will make you better at having conversations with workers and producing written material.

Table 5.1 Semantic drill examples

Commonly used phrase	*Problems*	*Alternatives*
Thank you for coming.	Implies that people are doing you a favour, not acting for themselves.	It's great to see you here today.
Unless you join, the union can't offer you much support.	Union as third party. Worker as passive.	If you want to resolve [your issue], you need to join with your workmates in the union so that you have power and resources.
Unions won the weekend.	Unions as third party. Did workers do anything?	Workers won the weekend by organising in unions.
The union has lots of resources which can protect members.	Union as third party. Members as passive.	By joining together in a union, workers have the resources to protect ourselves.
Could you hand this leaflet round your area for me?	Implies that people are doing you a favour, not acting for themselves.	If you want to resolve [your issue], you need to get your colleagues on side. Are you willing to give this leaflet to workers in your area?
That's awful – you should contact the union.	Union as third party. Worker as passive.	That's awful – you should discuss how you can tackle it with workers, union members and reps in your area.
You say you have no problems now, but you might need the union if you get a bad manager tomorrow.	Union as third party, and only there for individual protection, not to make things better.	I understand that you get on well with your manager, but there are lots of things they don't control. If you had a magic wand, what would you change?
The union believes strikes are a last resort and works hard to avoid them.	Union as third party. Workers as passive. Reinforces negative view of strikes.	There will only be a strike if you and all our workmates democratically decide it is necessary. Sometimes strikes are the only way to resolve your issues.

Commonly used phrase	*Problems*	*Alternatives*
The union can achieve much more than you can individually.	Union as third party.	If you ask management to resolve an issue, they aren't likely to listen. If you and all your workmates ask through the union, you stand a real chance.
We need all members to write to their MP about this issue.	'We' is a third party. 'All members' is not addressing the worker directly.	If you want to resolve [your issue] then you need to pressure your MP to back you. If all the workers write to our MPs, it has an impact. Will you write to yours?
That's legal and in line with the employer's policy so there's nothing we can do.	'We' as third party. Assumes only legalistic individual action is possible. Worker as passive.	They think they can get away with that because the law and their own policy allows it. To stop it you will need your workmates' support. As a first step, will you talk to them about it and find out what they think?
We need someone from this department to join the negotiating team.	'We' as third party. Doesn't address the worker directly.	If you want your views represented in the negotiations and to be kept fully informed, you and your workmates need to elect someone from your department to join the negotiating team.
How can I get you to join the union?	Union as third party.	If you want to resolve [your issue] you will need to join a union with your workmates. Are you ready to do that?
You are right, the union didn't handle that well.	Union as third party. No way forward.	You are right, that's not good. You need more people in your area to get more involved to avoid mistakes in future, and a stronger union to address it.
'Thank you' as a way to end a conversation.	Implies they have done you a favour rather than that you are working together.	That's been really useful – you're making a real contribution to resolving [your issue].

TECHNIQUES IN DETAIL #1: ORGANISING CONVERSATIONS

The one-to-one conversation is the most powerful tool in your box. It allows both of you to talk relatively freely and build a relationship. It helps you to find out what a worker thinks and allows you to adapt what you say specifically to them. It avoids the risk of other people derailing the conversation. It minimises the risk of management getting wind of your campaign prematurely. It maximises your chances of a worker agreeing to do something for the campaign.

If you are starting small in a big workplace or employer, it can be tempting to skip over one-to-one conversations because the scale of what's needed seems too daunting. This isn't a shortcut, it's a diversion that leads away from strong organisation. If you can't talk to everyone, at least talk to someone. You could start with a particular team or area, for example. You can't build strong organisation without talking to individuals.

An organising conversation isn't just a chat. It has a purpose, to 'move' the person you are talking with in some way, sometimes to shift their thinking, and nearly always includes an 'ask' – something you want them to agree to do. However, you rarely do this by 'changing their mind'. You are listening to what the other person says, reinforcing the best bits, teasing out the inconsistencies and helping them work out answers. Asking a worker to do something is a really useful way to gauge their commitment to the campaign. I will explain in Chapter 6 how you can use charting to understand how supportive different workers are.

Some people have more of a flair for organising conversations than others, but most good organisers agree it is useful to use a structure for them. There are various structures people recommend, though they all have a lot in common. Using one not only helps you get the outcomes you are looking for more of the time, it helps ensure you are giving consistent messages and getting back consistent information. But don't be afraid to abandon the plan – or the conversation – for example, if it becomes clear that the worker is dangerously close to management.

Not every conversation you have will be a structured 'organising conversation' – your workmates are going to think you are pretty weird if it is. In most cases, you will have relationships with them that aren't just about organising. Relationships between people are at the heart of organising and the better you understand each other, the easier it is for your organising to succeed.

In all our conversations, we need to bear in mind the semantics – choosing our words – and remember that a structure is not a script. We are doing more listening than talking and we need to adjust what we say to fit what we hear. Nonetheless, you should plan all organising conversations to some extent – the more important the conversation, the more planning you need. For the most important conversations, with key influential workers, you may even want to practise with a colleague.

Think about when and where to have a conversation with someone. When approaching someone for the first time, talk to them then and there rather than asking if you can speak later. If you haven't already got them on board, they may not agree to talk again, in which case continuing the conversation appears rude – as if you are not listening. Only pre-arrange conversations with a worker once you know that they will be up for it, or if it's the only way to meet somewhere appropriate. If you are trying to arrange to talk individually with individuals who are already on board, it's easy to waste lots of time trying to find suitable times. Some activists put times they are available into an online tool like Calendly, then message a number of people inviting them to book a time that suits them. Tools like Doodle and When2meet are the equivalent for choosing a time for a group of people to meet.

You are unlikely to get the best response under the watchful eye of a manager. Even the presence of colleagues may inhibit some workers. In the USA, where employers routinely hire professional union-busters, unannounced home visits are more successful for initial contact than trying to talk to people inside a workplace or at the gate. Even in Britain, some people, particularly from some ethnic minority groups, find it safer and easier to do a lot of their organising in the community – even when it's to build power at work. If a worker says they are busy, you can still talk to them while they do a chore or keep an eye on their kids. Unless you know someone well, it's best to avoid meeting in bars, even if the worker uses them, and in any case, you want to have the conversation with both of you sober. You also want to avoid them mistaking your meeting for a date!

Here, I'm going to set out one model for organising conversations, based on the following steps:

1. Introduction
2. A is for Agitate
3. E is for Educate
4. I is for Inoculate
5. O and U are for Organise with Urgency and You
6. Next steps

You can download a crib sheet from workers-can-win.info/conversations.

#1 Introduction

Don't beat about the bush or pretend you're just having a chat. Every organising conversation is 'showtime' – try to show confidence and energy no matter how you are feeling, but that doesn't mean you are following a script. Explain clearly who you are and why you are having the conversation.

#2 A is for Agitate

Identify the issues that the worker you are speaking with cares deeply about. Use open questions like 'if you could change three things, what would they be?' Follow-up questions can help get their story and the details of their issues without making assumptions. But keep it friendly – not an interrogation.

Agitation is the process of helping someone get really angry about their issues. In general, try not to show more anger than they do about their issues. If you feel they aren't recognising the injustice of their situation, use questions to encourage them to think. You can ask questions about how things could be different (raising expectations), who could fix their issue, why they don't, how the problem makes them *feel* and how it would feel if the issue was resolved. For some issues – for example, pay or working hours – you could also ask about the impact on life outside work and family. As Mike Pudd'nhead (2020) puts it:

> Agitating is not about you telling your coworkers what's wrong at work. It's about getting them to tell you what's wrong at work. And you can't stop there – you also have to ask why it's a problem, figure out the emotional element. So you don't get paid enough. Why do you care? What kind of monthly expenses are you struggling to pay? What happens if your [cheque] … is short?

If you are also affected by the issue, or know others who are, it can help to talk about that. When the worker knows that others share their anger, it feels more justified.

Getting angry helps overcome apathy, inertia and fear. When they are agitated, or are wondering what can be done, it's time to move on. However, if you later feel that the worker isn't really motivated to act, you may need to do some more agitation. Every worker has reasons to be angry.

#3 E is for Educate

Without hope, anger leads nowhere useful. Return to how things could be different and start to explore how collective power is the solution. You could ask how they think the boss would respond if they raised the issue as an individual, and how they think management would respond if there was a strong union raising it. You need to help them work out that the only way to solve their issue is collective action – they don't have the power to solve it individually. This is an opportunity to learn from them – you could ask them if they have any experience of dealing with the issue or it being better, or how they think it could change (x362014, 2021). Give examples to create a vision of things being better – in other workplaces, departments, countries, with a different manager, or on that job in the past. The more you can educate yourself about what's going on at your work, about other current disputes and campaigns, and about labour history, the easier this is. If you already have a plan on the issue, explain how it can give the worker the power to win.

Most workers don't know how unions work generally, never mind how one would function where they work. Explain (a little and without jargon!) how a union would function on your job, for example, that you would build a committee with people from every team and shift, then you can work out demands together that workers can unite behind, and only take them to the boss when you have majority support.

#4 I is for Inoculate

Nearly all bosses will try to counter our organising efforts by putting out their own messages and taking action themselves. Part of how scare tactics work is by causing shock and confusion, and distracting workers from the real issues and tasks of the campaign. The first time I went on strike, management spread a rumour they were going to shut the site. The mundane truth was that the site was due to shut in a few years and move a couple of miles up the road to a new building. We hadn't prepared for the employer's mischief, so it took us a couple of weeks to calm everyone down and get the campaign back on track.

In everyday use, inoculation means the same thing as vaccination. Some vaccines (though few modern ones) work by deliberately introducing a weak form of an infection to prompt the body to develop an immune response which protects it from dangerous infections. In organising, inoculation means preparing workers for the bosses' poison. Thinking, at a time of our choosing, on our terms, about what the boss could say or do reduces the impact when they do it at the worst possible time.

In the context of an organising conversation, you want to encourage the worker to express *their* fears or doubts first. You could ask them how they think the boss will react, or what the boss might say or do to try to undermine the campaign. You want them to understand that the employer will fight back – they want to keep power and control – but that when they do, this reflects badly on the boss, not the campaign. You are trying to prepare them, not freak them out, so you need to be ready to reassure them. You could prepare by working with the people most committed to the campaign and talking through what people might come up with and how you might respond.

The two things that best undercut fear are anger and humour. Keep going back to the worker's anger about the issues they care deeply about. Humour must be used with care. You want workers to take the counter-campaign seriously but to expect management mischief and see it as proof that your campaign is having an impact, forcing them to respond.

It is vital to be honest with workers, rather than giving exaggerated reassurances about the protection available from the law or the union. There are no guarantees that an employer won't break the law to victimise an activist. Even when the law backs us up, it offers compensation after the event, not genuine protection. Though unions do prioritise defending their activists, there are no guarantees of success. However, millions of workers are in unions and there are tens of thousands of activists, and victimisations are relatively rare. Meanwhile, every worker who fails to organise is at the mercy of their boss. Many are treated unfairly or lose their jobs. Organising isn't risk free; it is a calculated risk to be balanced against the certainty that unorganised workers endure arbitrary treatment.

After the bad experience before my first strike, we learned about inoculation. Before our next strike we distributed a leaflet[1] (see figure 5.2) across the workplace which included an 'anti-union boss competition' entry form listing examples of management scaremongering. The effect was wonderful – managers were deterred from using these lies, and if they did, staff laughed at them for thinking they would be taken in. When one manager came up with a line that wasn't on the form, a worker threatened to nominate them anyway and they backed down. Even most of the managers thought it was funny. Inoculation dramatically reduced the power of the employer's anti-union campaign. You can't do inoculation online or by leaflets alone though – you need to find out what workers' own fears and doubts are, and that's why it must be included in all your one-to-one organising conversations. If workers get in the habit of not being immobilised by their fears, their confidence rises.

Many campaigns use 'buzzword bingo' cards to mock management and educate workers about what they might do. The US-based Labor Notes published an example[2] which links to a tool for making your own.

#5 O and U are for Organise with Urgency and You

Even anger and hope aren't always enough to make someone act. Without a sense of urgency, difficult decisions or unfamiliar actions can be put off until tomorrow. Without delegating tasks to other people, you will never build power. Without being clear why the worker you are talking to (the 'you' in the conversation) must take action, many will sit back and hope that someone else will do it.

When we're organising, we are usually at pains to emphasise the collective over the individual. It's easy to talk about 'you' meaning a collective group of workers. But in this step in an organising conversation, we are focused on one individual and trying to get *their* commitment and action. Without this, we risk replicating the old joke about Everybody, Somebody, Anybody and Nobody:

> There was an important job to be done and Everybody was sure that Somebody would do it. Anybody could have done it, but Nobody did it. Somebody got angry about that, because it was Everybody's job. Everybody thought Anybody could do it, but Nobody realised that Everybody wouldn't do it. It ended up that Everybody blamed Somebody when Nobody did what Anybody could have.

"Anti-Union Boss" Competition

While most line managers don't want any part in anti-union and anti-employee shenanigans, there are a few who seem to prefer spreading lies and innuendo to managing people professionally.

Do you have the misfortune of listening to someone talking like this? If so, our competition could be some consolation. The entry with the highest score returned by Wednesday 10th May wins a prize!

Entry Form

Your name:	
Name of "anti-union boss":	

Please circle the scores for all the remarks your anti-union boss made.

Silly Remark	Score
"You don't need a union because we have a forum" members play key parts in many of the forums dotted around . Some are useful, while others are little more than a joke, with company-appointed "representatives" and discussions secret from employees. Unlike a union, none of the forums can be fully independent of HR, who tend to set the agenda, censor reports and control communication.	20
"Union Reps eat babies for breakfast" Even low pay and restaurant price rises haven't made staff that desperate!	100
" will close the site because of the union" Don't tell me, the sky will fall in as well. Companies do open and close sites from time to time, but who in their right mind would close a thriving business just to stop their employees having a voice?	50
"If you join, you'll never get promoted" Can I have that in writing? Members have legal protection against discrimination. Your anti-union boss doesn't have to know you're a member. Anyway, there are masses of members at all levels within . Support and information from can help you progress your career, hopefully moving to work for a competent and professional manager instead.	30
"The union just gives your money to the Labour Party" The "political fund" is totally separate from its "general fund" and this is subject to strict legal checks. It is for much more than just the Labour Party. Any member who doesn't want to pay the "political levy" (currently 57p per month) can simply opt out.	10
"The union is not for helpdesk staff" There are members and Reps throughout . The members *are* the union – it is a very democratic organisation. Helpdesk staff have won a lot from union campaigning, including sick-pay from day one and the increase in holidays from 20 to 25 days. Current issues include pay, progression and reducing working hours from 40 to the normal 37.	25
"The union is only for helpdesk staff" Most employees are not on helpdesks, so most members are not on helpdesks. The union reflects the continually changing composition and priorities of the workforce. Current issues include pay, out of hours cover, utilisation, travel, and the lack of published pay scales.	25 [Extra 80 if this and the one above!]
"The union spends all its time representing losers" No it doesn't. But it's the job of managers, not union reps, to manage their staff. Any member can ask to be represented by their union. Why does your anti-union boss expect the union Rep to decide in advance whether the member is right or wrong? That's the manager's job, once the Rep has helped ensure the member's case is heard through a proper process.	50
" stopped me giving you a pay rise" Of course, that's what unions are for! Your workmates are organising to stop the company giving them pay rises!	30

Please return competition entries to by Wednesday 10th May.

Figure 5.2 Anti-union boss competition leaflet

In this part of the conversation, you are trying to:

1. Assess what they think of the plan and what they are willing to do.
2. Convey their role and the urgency of action.
3. Ask them to do something specific – and *wait for the answer.*
4. Deal with any objections.

The 'ask' needs to match where you have assessed they are at. When you are planning for the conversation, it can be helpful to prepare small, medium and big asks that you can choose from. All should be achievable for the worker you are talking to – setting people up to fail is counterproductive. The asks must all link to the plan to win rather than being pointless activity. You are often aiming to 'push' them one step further than they thought they could go – you can acknowledge that it will be hard for them while emphasising its importance. Nearly everyone has experienced, at some time in life, feeling good about having done something that we wouldn't have done if someone hadn't given us a little push. A lot of the time we are held back by self-doubt. Working-class kids are often punished or ridiculed for any display of independent thought or initiative. Too often this continues in work. We are told we are worthless and incapable. Sometimes we need a little push to overcome such 'belief barriers' (Lees, 2019) so that we can develop, grow and win on our issues. However, this doesn't justify piling pressure on people, which can lead to burnout, as discussed in Chapter 12.

At some point during the campaign, you are going to need to ask the worker to sign up as a union member. This is necessary because the campaign needs to fund resources, in order that the worker can be part of the wider union movement and have a vote in union elections or over industrial action. You don't want membership to be the first ask, because it sends the wrong message about what is important. But if you leave it too long then they get used to the idea of participating in the campaign without being a member and the subject gets harder to broach.

When you are asking someone to do something, remember to choose your words. You aren't asking them to do something for you, rather you are explaining what they will need to do to resolve their own issue. It's about them, not you. For example:

> If you want to stop the shift changes, you'll need to make sure the majority of your workmates are on side. The first step would be to make a list of all

the people in your department so you can approach this systematically. Are you up for doing that?

It is vital that you give them time to think and answer – the 'long, uncomfortable silence'. If they aren't responding right away, that means this is a big decision for them, and you need to respect that and give them time to think without interrupting.

Dealing with objections

If they don't say 'yes', you could ask what's stopping them and explore that a bit, to see if you can deal with their objections, but don't get into a big argument. If they are still not convinced, it's better to say you need time to think about their objection or find out more information, then skip to step #6 to arrange a follow-up.

It is easy to deal with objections badly – putting someone's nose out of joint by appearing not to listen, failing to provide a clear answer or getting bogged down in side issues. You can avoid these pitfalls by using three steps – AAR:

- *Acknowledge* their feeling without legitimising the excuse, e.g. 'so you feel that if you did X then …'
- *Answer*: concisely address their objection or answer their question.
- *Redirect*: ask a question that takes them back to *their* issues.

You shouldn't need a long speech. If you have correctly identified the issues the worker really cares about and educated them about a credible plan to win, anger about their issues will motivate them to action and overcome hesitancy. If you think the objection really arises from a lack of confidence to carry out the action, M.K. Lees (2019) suggests role playing the action so that the worker can find out whether it's as scary as they thought, and the action can be adjusted if necessary.

Dealing with objections is a great thing to practise with a partner, as well as practising organising conversations as a whole.

#6 Next steps

However your conversation has gone, it should never be the end of the organising process. Leave with them agreeing to *something specific*, no matter how small – even if it is just to continue the conversation another day or to give you some information. Connect the task back to their issues (step #1) and to the plan to win (step #3).

Make a plan to complete the task together and agree how you will follow up, including when to speak again. Make sure you provide all the information they need to succeed, and ask if they need any questions answering for them to be confident to do what they agreed to. Success builds confidence and participation. You can't take for granted that people understood *how* to successfully accomplish what they agreed to do.

It is important to check whether people have carried out tasks they have agreed to – it is a useful measure of whether you have *really* got them on board. I will talk in Chapter 6 about using charting and structure tests to consistently monitor involvement and help you plan the campaign. Whenever possible, check in person or over the phone – you don't want them to go silent due to guilt or embarrassment. Checking reinforces that the task was important. If someone doesn't do a task you need to find out why and offer more help. Getting someone else to do the task or doing it yourself are last resorts, as they show a lack of belief in the worker, undermining their confidence, commitment and participation.

WRITTEN COMMUNICATION

Even though one-to-one verbal communication is the bedrock of effective organising, there is still a place for written communication. It can be effective for getting consistent messages out to lots of people using leaflets, emails, text messages, groups in messaging apps, social media and websites. But it should never be a substitute for conversations – every time you 'broadcast' a message you aren't using, testing or developing your organisational structure and you aren't having organising conversations that move people. Written communication can help, but not as a substitute for individual conversations.

Sending written requests for 'someone' to do something to a group of people gets very poor results. We're all busy and there's a natural tendency to keep quiet and hope someone else will step forward. If someone does volunteer, the odds are it will be one of the people already very active, so you've missed an opportunity to raise participation. Worse still, the volunteer could be someone unsuited to the task, and you are either stuck with them or have to spend time and energy getting them to un-volunteer, which is pretty demotivating for both of you. You get a much better response directly asking an individual to do something. In Chapter 6, I describe charting your workmates, and this can help identify suitable people to ask for a particular task. Small, achievable tasks that clearly help the campaign are ideal.

If you do want to get a message out in written form, it's often a good idea to use multiple channels. Some people read all their emails, many don't. A leaflet may not reach people who aren't in the right place at the right time. People's use of social media and messaging apps varies wildly. Most social media platforms work best with images rather than just text. Free graphic design tools such as Canva make it easier to create attractive images. A very high proportion of people open text messages, and there are lots of online tools to send them in bulk, but they have to be very short.

Whatever communication channels you are using, make sure you build up your capacity to communicate independently of the employer. A few years ago, I spoke at a meeting of workers at a large financial services company where the union had had a cosy partnership arrangement, but that hadn't stopped the employer launching a massive attack on workers' pensions. Workers wanted to take action. A major obstacle was the fact that the union relied on management to circulate union notices and hadn't collected members' contact details. The union at another big company faced nearly as big a problem. They had members' email addresses, but they were nearly all work ones, making the union vulnerable to the employer monitoring or blocking messages. On top of this, their partnership agreement required them to show communications to management before they were sent – enabling management to bully and pressure reps not to send out anything strong. You need communication channels that will still work if workers want to resist an employer that gets nasty.

All your communication should be accurate because you need workers to trust what you say. This is even more important with written communication because people have time to consider exactly what you said, and there's no opportunity to correct misunderstandings. On top of this, there's a greater risk of the employer using any mistakes against your campaign. It can help to ask one or two supportive workers who aren't very involved to comment on a draft. As well as reducing the risk of mistakes that could land you in trouble, they can point out where you have used jargon, assumed too much knowledge or not explained something clearly.

If you are producing a newsletter that includes articles on a variety of topics, it shouldn't only look forward to what needs to be won and done; it should also look back and celebrate successes, to raise workers' confidence to fight for more. After every battle, there is another battle – for its interpretation. Making sure everyone is clear about what went well and badly, and why, shapes how people go into the next fight. Management nearly always fight the battle for interpretation – to persuade workers that they had always intended to do what you won, or that a change was thanks to senior management intervention, process or procedure rather than workers' collective action. All too often, official union communications don't help in the battle for interpretation, emphasising the role of the union's legal, press or campaigns departments, or paid officers' negotiating skills, over what workers did themselves. Sometimes a deal can restrict what the union can say about it – in which case informal and verbal ways of winning an interpretation become even more important. For example, victory parties (whatever you call them officially) can be great tools in this battle.

Good newsletters include a mix of material:

- current issues
- what the reader can do: calls to action
- celebrating successes (which don't all have to be from your own work) and fighting 'the battle for interpretation'
- basic education about the union and workers' rights
- inoculation.

It's good to include current issues and campaigns from beyond your own work, but don't let them dominate unless you are confident the vast majority of workers see them as vital. You will always face some criticism for dealing with more than 'bread and butter' jobs, pay and conditions, but remember that you want to involve everyone, and most working-class people face discrimination of some sort; nearly all of us are affected by social issues around housing or public services, a large minority have family ties around the world, and a large proportion will be disabled at some point in our lives.

Raising wider issues matters, not just because they interest some workers, but also to help prepare workers for the unexpected. For example, a few workers complained when our union newsletter covered anti-fascist campaigning, which they saw as 'political' rather than union business. One even left the union over it. But when a couple of supporters of the British National Party (BNP) started racist agitation within the workplace, the fact that the union had publicly taken an anti-fascist stance was a big help. It gave workers confidence to raise issues through the union and gave the union credibility with management when pushing for more than a narrow disciplinary response. We won time out of work for staff to attend training arranged by the union to give them more confidence to challenge racism. Almost any issue can become a 'work issue' overnight – I lost work when projects were delayed due to the start of the 2003 Iraq War.

Whenever you write, it is worth double-checking for words like I, my, we, us, our, you and your, so that you can be consistent, unambiguous and avoid 'third partying' the union. Resist the temptation for your newsletter to be consistently angry or outraged. This is the equivalent of turning up the volume, but you have far more impact if there are quiet and loud parts rather than always being shouty, which turns many people off. Someone who normally speaks quietly suddenly shouting has far more impact than someone who is loud all the time.

If you are making a communication plan for your campaign, think about who is communicating, what the message is, who they are communicating to, when, by what channels and the purpose of the communication. Even if you are primarily conveying information, you are usually communicating in order that someone will do or not do something. You should also consider who needs to approve the communication – anything in writing carries some risk, but the bigger the audience, the more public, the more official, and the more contentious the content, the greater the risk. Avoid excessive bureaucracy, but put in place proportionate safeguards.

Key points

- Organise around issues. Choose ones that are widely felt, deeply felt, winnable and visible.
- Repeatedly go round the organising cycle – Issue, Organisation, Education, Action – building power.
- Consider how to frame your issue: to portray a grievance as an injustice, attribute it to specific targets, strengthen a collective identity ('us'), bring workers as well as potential supporters or allies on board, make it harder for opponents to mobilise, and set out the solution and how to achieve it.
- Choose clear and simple language. Avoid presenting the union as a third party and make workers' collective action central.
- Use a structure to plan effective organising conversations.
- Inoculate workers against management mischief by discussing what might happen in advance.
- Deal with objections using AAR: Acknowledge, Answer, Redirect.

Discussion questions

1. Thinking about issues where you are: how do they rate as widely felt, deeply felt, winnable and visible?
2. Pick one potential organising issue: how might you frame it?
3. What objections might your workmates have and how would you briefly answer them?

6
How to organise

In this chapter, I move from choosing what to organise around and how to communicate about it, to how you organise collectively with your workmates. It covers different types of leaders and how to identify them, mapping and charting your workmates, testing your structure, communication trees, meetings and social activities, democracy and collective action.

LEADERS AND INFLUENTIAL WORKERS

Leaders have a pretty bad name amongst many workers. Bosses often call themselves leaders. People who hold positions in unions often call themselves leaders, no matter how lazy, incompetent or uninspiring they may be. The word is used to describe the people who try to tell us what to do in every walk of life – most of whom neither know nor care much about our lives or what we want. Instead of relying on a few superheroes, we need to build grassroots power democratically. However, to do that we need to understand the power relationships that exist in the workplace and unions, and understanding leadership is essential for that. Rather than simply rejecting all notions of leadership, it is more useful to break down their meanings and think about how each type of leader might help and hinder you.

- *Position holders*: even if they lack any ability or commitment, they are often gatekeepers to resources such as money, people, structures, information, contact or membership lists and passwords for online services. Their support offers visibility, legitimacy and credibility. As a result, their support or opposition can make a big difference. Workers generally assume that position holders are far more committed and competent than they actually are, so their support can give workers confidence to participate. People have to learn the reality through experience.

- *Influential workers*: the workers who have most influence with their workmates. They may not be the loudest, most opinionated or popular, but they are trusted and respected by their colleagues. Correctly identifying and winning over the influential workers is key to successful organising.
- *Anticipators*: people who are good at understanding the situation, how it may develop, how different forces may react – and working out a course of action likely to produce a favourable outcome. Quite a few leftists fit this picture, as they have spent time thinking about and learning from struggles in the past or elsewhere. Again, they have a big contribution to make – as long as they don't mistake themselves for influential workers instead of working with the people who are.
- *Activists*: the people with the most commitment, energy and time. Activists make a huge contribution to any organising effort – as long as you can persuade them to act as organisers rather than influential workers – which they rarely are. By an organiser, I mean someone who tries to systematically build workers' power, which includes correctly identifying influential workers, winning them over and training them in the skills of struggle.

Influential workers are closest to the practical definition of a leader: 'someone with followers'. People can hold as many positions as they like, be as active or articulate as they like, be an armchair Napoleon or chess master – but it is the workers most trusted and respected by their workmates who are most effective at persuading them to take action.

People use other terms to refer to influential workers. The term 'opinion leader' was coined by Eric Batstone, Ian Boraston and Stephen Frenkel (1978). Jane McAlevey has used 'organic worker leader' (2016) and 'natural leader' (2019). I prefer 'influential worker' because it doesn't carry the same connotations of charisma or hierarchy and is more understandable. Whatever term we use, the point is that not all workers have the same influence with their colleagues. Even on matters unconnected with organising, such as when to take a break or which pub to go to on a night out, there are some who are more influential in any group than others. However, the degree of influence they have can vary – for example high staff turnover can make social relationships between workers more fluid.

When workers have chosen their influential workers, this must be respected, and is centrally important to organising. An organising effort will be far more successful if it involves the influential workers rather than battling against their influence. Though they can lose their influence, this is rare, except in situations where they go against the strongly held wishes of their colleagues. The social relationships workers have formed through day-to-day contact are unlikely to be overturned by the intervention of an organising campaign. It takes a lot of work to undermine their base or get their base to pressure them, but this might occasionally be necessary. The fact that influential workers value their influence means that even ones who are quite individualistic often care about majority views. It's unusual for workers to dramatically gain influence too, but it can happen through intense periods of conflict when people are tested in the eyes of their colleagues.

It's not just that influential workers are best placed to persuade workers around them. As M.K. Lees (2019) points out, the very presence of a colleague whom a worker respects and trusts makes them far more confident to take part in actions that involve some risk.

Influential workers are central to organising success[1], so correctly identifying them ('leader ID') is a key skill. Influential workers are defined by their relationship to other workers, so they can only be identified by asking those workers, not by the opinion of an organiser. In all but the smallest workplaces, you won't know everyone's relationships well, and even if you've worked there for years you are unlikely to have been thinking about all your colleagues this way.

If you explain to a worker that to win on their issue they need to build a network of the most influential workers in each team and shift, and ask them who that would be in their area, you are likely to initially get a 'false ID'. They might offer the most pro-union, the loudest, the bully or the most popular – you have to explore why they think someone is the most respected, perhaps asking for examples of where they influenced others' actions, to get nearer the truth. They might suggest the manager – you have to explain that it is the most influential of the workers you are looking for. Neither should you rely on the opinion of one or two workers to stand a good chance of correctly identifying an influential worker.

Angry Workers' (2020) account of organising in a ready-meal factory highlights another potential source of false IDs. In a workplace where many workers faced language barriers, an individual could use his language skills to establish himself as the 'go to' guy for many workers and a key contact for management and union officials alike. This was despite consistently using the situation to his own advantage and being in management's pocket rather than making genuine efforts to help those who turned to him. Power relationships between workers can give someone apparent influence without them being trusted and respected.

It is common for activists to ignore potential influential workers who aren't supportive. When we ask for examples of workers influencing others, we naturally want to find those who influence people in a positive way. But someone can be an influential worker and deeply hostile to the union. We still need to correctly identify them.

There are exceptions, but influential workers will often be relatively skilled and experienced workers, whom others turn to for advice about work matters. They will often be cautious because they value the respect of their workmates and don't want to go out on a limb unless really convinced. And they will often have good relationships with management. This isn't just because managers value skilled and experienced workers. Smart managers also look out for influential workers and seek their advice or test ideas out on them. Influential workers will often get minor issues resolved more easily than most because managers want to keep them on side, which can lead them to feel like they don't need a union, that they can resolve things for themselves. This is one reason why a servicing model is so ineffective – influential workers are unlikely to think they need the service.

However hard you work at identifying influential workers, and no matter how skilled you become, you will sometimes get it wrong. I will talk later in this chapter about using structure tests to work out if you have correctly identified the influential workers and really got them on side. As workers take part in actions, it becomes increasingly clear who are the real influential workers.

Marianne Garneau (2021) points out that some of the common features of influential workers can be difficult to handle in an organising campaign. Some can be quite individualistic, unused to taking direction from others and prone to changing their minds or cutting side-deals with management. Every individual, including influential workers, will have helpful and unhelpful qualities, but these don't change the fact of someone having influence. You must keep checking that influential workers are on side, work to keep them there and tackle any problems their weaknesses cause.

Influential workers have an important role to play in any successful organising campaign – but it's not the only important role and you need everyone else involved too. When you first start organising, your allies are likely to be activists – the most committed workers rather than the most influential workers. You'll want to ensure as you organise that everyone willing can contribute and take part in democratic decision-making. There are many ways you can structure your organisation as it grows. You could have a single committee for everything, or you could subdivide it in various ways, but keep it simple and accountable. As you identify the influential workers and they demonstrate commitment to the campaign by carrying out tasks, you want to bring them to the heart of the organisation. Keep an eye out for diversity – your structures need to reflect the whole workforce. If not, it will be a barrier to the full participation of some groups of workers and limit your strength. Some migrant workers may have their residence rights tied to their job – someone in this position might prefer to get involved in roles not visible to the employer.

Recognising that workers have a web of existing social relationships in which some are more influential than others has implications for what you do in an organising effort.

When you think you have identified an influential worker, you need to win their support for the campaign. Winning them over is a similar process to winning over anyone else – identify what really matters to them and help them work out that collective action is the only way they will get it. But the stakes are much higher when you try to win over an influential worker. Success with them can make a huge difference because they draw others in. Their opposition can turn organising into an uphill battle.

Most people's reaction, once they think they have identified a key influential worker, is to go and talk to them right away, but this can be a costly shortcut. The outcome of that conversation really matters, so you want to be as prepared as possible. You may already talk to them on the job, but that isn't the same as having an organising conversation. In general, you want to tackle the 'lowest risk' workers first – those who you already know are supportive. Then you might move on to 'medium risk' workers – those whose support you aren't sure of, but who aren't key influential workers. Only then do you have the information to help you plan 'high risk' conversations – with influential workers who aren't already on side. As discussed in Chapter 5, the key to winning workers over is finding out what they really care about and helping them work out that collective action is the only way to get what they want. The more you know about an influential worker before you speak with them, the better your chances of winning them over rather than blowing it.

TECHNIQUES IN DETAIL #2: MAPPING AND CHARTING

If your organising target is more than a handful of people, you need to be systematic. Mapping and charting are key tools to help you. The terms are sometimes used interchangeably, but it is useful to think of them as two separate techniques.

In mapping, you draw out the physical layout of the workplace or workplaces and mark it up with information. For example, if you work for a huge company with sites all across the country, it might help you to get a map and mark all the workplaces on it, with basic information such as number of workers, number of union members, names of activists, or whatever is relevant for your campaign. If people are based at home or work from particular depots, you might try to map out where they are geographically. More traditionally, the map would be of a particular building, showing the layout, different departments, the flow of work through the building (if applicable), which workers and managers work where and any surveillance devices. Thinking physically helps avoid one of the classic mistakes – missing out workers because they are outsourced, agency workers or work a different shift to most people (cleaners and security guards, for example). Mapping can help you think about which workers interact with each other, who is supportive in each area (particularly useful if access is restricted), whether some workers have contact with lots of other groups, who has less direct supervision, or whether some work areas are strategically important because of where they are in the flow of work through the building. The process of explaining the map of your own workplace to someone else will often make you realise things you didn't know.

For example, workers organising in one major pub chain[2] found that kitchen staff were key. They were a small group who worked closely together, away from the public gaze, and their only supervision was from a kitchen manager whose status was little different to their own – yet they had contact with most of the rest of the workforce due to food orders being taken to customers' tables.

Charting, on the other hand, doesn't rely on a map or diagram of physical space. It uses a grid with a row for each worker, workers grouped in various ways, and various coloured and shaped marks to indicate different things about the worker or action they have taken part in.

A typical chart template has a section for each shift in each area that looks a bit like Figure 6.1, with a row for each worker in the group and their hours.

You need to decide a 'key' for marking up your chart. For example, you could highlight members in yellow and reps in green, have a red circle for hostile workers, a small black dot next to influential workers and a number next to each person indicating where you think they are at: 1 for supportive influential workers, 2 for supportive workers, 3 for undecided, 4 for hostile, 5 for hostile influential workers, and blank for unassessed. Whatever key you choose, be clear and consistent. In gauging support, pay more attention to what workers *do* than what they *say*.

Each time you arrange a collective action, you use one of the 'collective action' columns, putting a mark next to each worker who participates. You can see at a glance the level of participation, who has participated, whether

Hours	Group name: Location: Supervisor:	Collective actions				
		1	2	3	4	5
9 a.m.–5 p.m.	Zara					
10 a.m.–6 p.m.	Jill					
10 a.m.–6 p.m.	Layla					
7 a.m.–3 p.m.	Sandra					
11 a.m.–7 p.m.	Stan					
11 a.m.–7 p.m.	Kate					
9 a.m.–5 p.m.	Moh					
7 a.m.–3 p.m.	Pete					
7 a.m.–1 p.m.	Jaden					
12 p.m.–4 p.m.	Sally					

Figure 6.1 One workgroup in a charting template

participation is increasing or decreasing and which areas have high or low participation. I will discuss this further in the next section on structure tests.

Effective charting is visual and frequently updated – collectively. It allows you all to see easily which areas are strong or weak, both in terms of membership and in terms of participation in collective actions. If workers in one group aren't participating in collective actions, then either you haven't correctly identified their influential workers or haven't genuinely won their support. The chart can help you decide which areas to focus on next, whom to talk to and what tasks to ask which workers to undertake. It also makes members of your organising committee accountable to each other because progress, strengths and weaknesses are out in the open.

One of the key decisions to make is how to group workers on the chart. Group together the people who interact with each other most in the course of their work. This may not follow the employer's organisation structure, which might separate roles or occupations who actually work together. Nothing you decide will be perfect because life is complicated, but pick something, give it a go and change it if you need to. You'll need to re-make your charts anyway, as they get scrawled over.

In some circumstances you may need to maintain more than one type of charting. For example, junior doctors in hospitals work alongside other doctors and a mix of other medical and ancillary staff. You would want to chart whom they actually work with. But they get regularly rotated between hospitals on the basis of their specialism, so you would also need to maintain a list of the junior doctors in each specialism, across the group of hospitals they swap between, in order to maintain your organisation through frequent rotations.

It can be tempting to use a spreadsheet or database for charting. For really big campaigns this might be necessary *in addition to* the visual charts, but it is rarely a substitute for them because many people only have devices with small screens and it's hard to securely discuss and update an electronic record collectively.

A rep I know tracked which members had been at meetings when those present voted to campaign over an issue. When there was a leaflet to distribute about the issue, he made a point of asking them to do it rather than leaving it to the usual activists. By asking individuals directly, he got great results – a much higher success rate than from general appeals, where busy people generally hope someone else will volunteer. The impression on other workers was far better – seeing different workmates taking part in union activity every time rather than the same rushed and grumpy activists. It also overcame access difficulties caused by security restrictions in parts of the workplace. It shows the benefit of obeying the iron law of organising: never do for others what they can do for themselves.

The Industrial Workers of the World (IWW) also recommend 'social charting', drawing out the social relationships between workers (IWW, 2009). Social charting can help you work out who is best placed to talk with a particular worker, as well as any conflicts you might need to overcome. You would list the workers and then draw lines to show the different connections between workers, a bit like Figure 6.2.

It's important to be ethical about your mapping and charting. Don't write down anything about someone that would cause a problem if they saw it, particularly if it's a judgement about them rather than strictly factual. I was once on the receiving end of a 'Subject Access Request' from a manager, under the data protection legislation, to obtain personal information I held about them, such as emails. Fortunately, there was nothing problematic and they later joined the union. Never leave personal information lying around. Sometimes activists allow concerns about data protection to get in the way of organising. It's worth remembering what the legislation is there for. It's

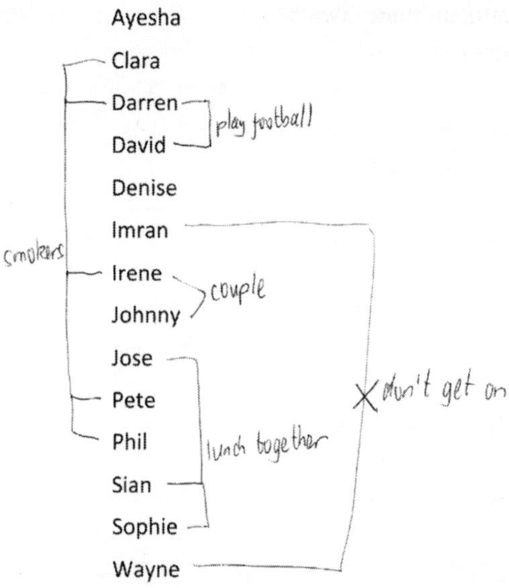

Figure 6.2 Social charting

to protect people against those in power, such as companies, intruding into their privacy or making decisions based on information they shouldn't have or which isn't accurate. You are organising to make society fairer and more democratic, challenging those who hold power. Irrespective of legislation, you aren't doing anything to harm the workers included in your mapping or charting. I've yet to hear of a union activist falling foul of data protection law over mapping or charting[3] – your employer is a much bigger threat.

TECHNIQUES IN DETAIL #3: STRUCTURE TESTS

As you organise, you are building structures, including a network of influential workers. Every time you do something, it is an opportunity to learn about how strong you are and where your weaknesses are. This can be as important for the success of your campaign as the action itself. You can do this systematically using structure tests.

As I explain in Chapter 8, actions don't just apply pressure to your targets, you can also learn and build more strength. Too often, activists put a tonne of work into getting people to a meeting or protest, but don't know who took part or what got them there. Two key things distinguish an action used as a genuine structure test:

1. You use the network of influential workers you have identified (your structure) to get people to take part, rather than centrally putting out general appeals.
2. You track who took part and record it on your chart.

There's still value in doing 'half a structure test' – where you record who took part but get people to participate using a communication channel other than your structure (the first point above). This tests workers' level of engagement with the communication channel, but not the structure you have built.

Conversations are far more powerful than leaflets, emails, social media or text messages can ever be, because they are so much more interactive and are connected with relatively strong social relationships. It is also far easier for employers, giant internet companies or the state to disrupt centralised communication channels than it is to prevent one-to-one conversations between influential workers and their work colleagues.

Once you have used structure tests to establish a solid level of participation, you can move on to 'public' structure tests. Public commitment, where a worker's support is visible to other workers, the boss or the community, helps lock in a choice to pick one side of the battle. A worker may have to justify to others why they have done so – putting their reasons into their own words and generating a social penalty for bailing out later. You don't want to rush into a public structure test without having done the groundwork to ensure a decent level of success, otherwise you can publicly undermine your campaign in the eyes of the workers – and the boss. When the boss finds out about your organising efforts, they will start making it harder, so save public structure tests for when workers are ready to back each other up in the face of the boss, not before. In general, don't go public with your organising until you can't really get much further under management's radar. Consider your specific situation carefully. Mostafa Henaway argues that going public really helped the successful unionisation of Amazon in Staten Island.[4]

Different actions involve different levels of public commitment. Signing a petition will be a big deal for some people, but for most it shows less commitment than having your picture on a photo-petition. Wearing a sticker or

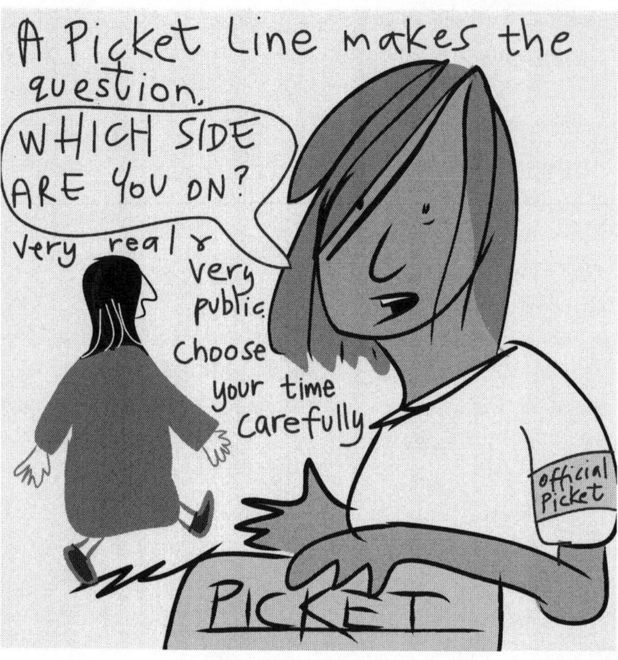

lanyard is lower than joining a public rally, which is lower than taking part in a 'march on the boss'.

When planning a structure test, it's worth setting a goal and a timescale. If you have an effective structure, with influential workers identified and won over, it should be possible to make things happen pretty quickly. Jane McAlevey (2014) sets a 48-hour goal for getting big majorities of workers to sign a paper petition, even in a large hospital with multiple buildings and shifts. If things go more slowly than you hoped, you can always extend the timescale to ensure the action is effective. You can check how far you'd got by the time of both your original deadline and the extended one.

The Trade Union Act 2016 introduced new restrictions on workers' right to lawfully strike, requiring not just a majority of voters in a cumbersome postal ballot to support striking, but requiring a high turnout too. Where unions have an effective structure at workplace level, these thresholds can be resoundingly beaten. The Communication Workers' Union (CWU) has held several national ballots across large numbers of Royal Mail workplaces since the Act came in, delivering big 'yes' votes on huge turnouts each time. Over 110,000 voted in 2017, 2019 and 2020. Part of their approach was to hold gate meetings at workplaces prior to the ballot, taking photos of workers holding signs about the ballot. In 2020, they held more than 800 such meetings on one morning. Activists could follow up any workers who didn't take part. Encouraging members to share photos of themselves posting their vote helps workers remind their colleagues to vote and enables a public demonstration of commitment.

Once you've marked up your charts with which workers participated, you can see at a glance how the structure performed in each area. This is vital information to work out where to focus. Prioritise the most important (usually biggest) of the worst areas – if you don't crack them, it can undermine your organising efforts everywhere.

Beware of the structure test concept being misused to obstruct action rather than build power. For example, some paid officials try to insist on multiple structure tests on slow timescales before authorising an industrial action ballot. In any campaign, the timescale of the issues and building rather than squandering momentum are vital considerations.

TECHNIQUES IN DETAIL #4: COMMUNICATION TREES AND DISTRIBUTION NETWORKS

It is increasingly common for workers to use group chat apps, such as WhatsApp, Signal, Telegram or Band. These are great for some purposes, particularly between people who are highly engaged. For example, this can work really well for a group of strikers from one workplace to arrange who pickets which entrance. However, whatever tool you use, some people won't use it, others won't check it and many people 'lurk' so you never know whether they have read a message, let alone whether they agree or will act on it. If groups get large, many people will turn off notifications and the less engaged will never look at them again.

If you are going to avoid relying on 'broadcast' messages as a substitute for conversations, you still need ways to get information, calls to action and sometimes physical 'stuff' out to everyone. A common approach is to rely on meetings. They can certainly be useful, but we all know that most people don't attend most meetings most of the time, so they aren't sufficient.

It's common to hear activists blaming workers who don't attend meetings and being particularly snarky towards any who ask what happened afterwards. It's more useful to think of such questions as indicating interest and being an opportunity to reach yet more people.

If you want to reach *everyone* then relying on people to turn up to a meeting or to ask about it later isn't good enough. You need to go back to your charting if you want to include everybody. Whether you start the ball rolling in a meeting or not, your charting helps you ensure someone has agreed to talk to every group of workers. Of course, the best people to do it are the influential workers, if they are available, as they will tend to get the best response from their workmates.

You might use your charting to produce a simple checklist of who has agreed to cover each group or area. For example, you could use a table like Figure 6.3 to organise distribution of a leaflet to every worker.

Task:			
Group/area	**Being covered by (name)**	**Date agreed**	**Date completed**

Figure 6.3 A distribution checklist by group or area

A more powerful version of this is the communication tree. The leaves of the tree are all the individual workers. For each (small!) group of workers, you have someone (a twig!) who agrees to contact them – ideally their influential worker, if they are supportive. You also need a substitute in case they are unavailable. If both are available, they might choose to share the contacting between them. These twigs are grouped together with someone (and a substitute) who agree to contact them. Depending on the size of the workforce, you may need several more levels to ensure nobody has too many people to contact. Each person only needs the details of the people they will contact and the people who will contact them – so they can feed back.

A communication tree can be very effective for reliably getting messages out quickly to large numbers of people, providing the people who agree to do the calling are committed to doing it promptly. You need to ensure that messages being passed through the tree are crystal clear to avoid them becoming garbled as they are passed from person to person. Communication trees fail if they aren't used regularly. On a real tree, leaves and twigs might drop off; in a communication tree, they can move around, attach themselves in unexpected places, or the twig might go missing but the leaves still be there. You want everyone in the tree to feed back when all the people beyond them in the structure have been contacted, or if parts of the tree failed, so that the tree can be updated. You could think of this as a type of structure test too.

If you have a communication tree in place, then you could still use a meeting to start multiple branches and twigs off in one go. Communication trees can be used face to face, over the phone or even by text message (though this isn't reliable unless people confirm receipt). They can be used to share information, pass on calls to action, gather information, distribute materials and much more.

MEETINGS

Almost every activist has been frustrated when they have put a lot of effort into arranging a meeting only for hardly anyone to show up. This not only means a missed opportunity to involve the people who weren't there but can be demoralising and demotivating for those who were.

It's worth thinking about what makes meetings well attended and effective – too many meetings in the labour movement are little more than rituals and serve no purpose that is clear to potential attendees. No wonder they are often only attended by the hyper-committed and those with nothing better to do.

People attend meetings for a variety of useful purposes (and some less useful ones), such as to:

- be listened to
- find out how to get involved
- get advice or help
- get other people to do something
- influence others
- learn
- meet people and network
- share experiences, ideas and concerns
- socialise or be entertained
- take decisions.

The reality is that in any meeting, people will have turned up with different expectations and mixtures of goals. The more you can make clear in advance what the meeting is for and why it would be worth someone attending, the more people are likely to come for the first time. The more you can ensure the meeting at least partially meets people's varied needs, the more likely they are to come back.

If a meeting is to take a decision on a campaign, it's worth thinking about how the proposal is worded. If it is calling on someone else to do something, be clear whom. If members are deciding on a campaign, word the proposal so that they are deciding to campaign rather than telling 'the union' to campaign. This avoids third partying the union (see Chapter 5) and sets an expectation that members will be playing an active part.

If you are clear what a meeting's purposes are, it is much easier to decide when to restrict attendance to members of a committee, or just to union members, and when to open it up to all workers in a workplace or even the wider public.

If you want to improve meetings that have been pretty dull and poorly attended, the first step is to ensure that anyone who does show up will find it worthwhile. Some things to consider:

- Does the invitation clearly explain whom and what the meeting is for, and why attending will make a difference (e.g. having a vote)?
- Does someone welcome and talk to anyone new who shows up?
- Does everyone introduce themselves, or would a newcomer feel like an intruder in a group of old friends?
- Does the agenda devote most time to the things attendees would generally see as most important or interesting?
- Is the agenda and format varied enough to meet what different people want from the meeting?
- Is the agenda and any jargon clearly explained, or is lots of knowledge assumed?
- Does the meeting stay roughly on the agenda, or can it become hard to work out what is being discussed?
- Has relevant information been circulated in good time before the meeting, and is it available in suitable formats for everyone on the day?
- Does the format give everyone the opportunity to have their say (e.g. going round the room, using breakout groups)?

- Would an outside speaker make it more interesting?
- Do a minority of people (usually older men) talk too often and for too long?
- Are new and less frequent speakers prioritised to speak?
- Is the culture friendly and supportive, antagonistic or competitive?

Successful meetings require planning and preparation – better to have fewer good quality meetings than a treadmill of frequent, frustrating, poorly attended and unproductive ones. However, some meetings can set the 'pulse' of an organisation. Many years ago, reps in my workplace increased our meeting frequency to weekly. This meant we were less likely to forget we were supposed to have done something and people didn't feel as left out if they couldn't make one meeting. Meeting notes could be less detailed without us forgetting what they were about and could be sent out sooner. It set an expectation that actions would be done quickly, so the pace of organising increased dramatically. A regular pattern of meetings is helpful, people can plan around it and are less likely to forget when the meeting is. But, as with any routine, be prepared to change it or break from it if something significant happens.

If the meeting itself is looking good, you should also think about what else might exclude people. Is the day or time suitable? Consider shift patterns, caring responsibilities, mealtimes and prayer times. Do you need to provide childcare or at least offer to pay for workers if they want to arrange their own? What about the location? Consider accessibility for disabled people, public transport and personal safety. Not everyone wants to meet in a pub, for example, because of religious reasons or because they had a drink problem.

In some cases, it can be worth organising multiple sessions of the same meeting – for example, to cover different shifts or at different locations. This has some disadvantages, particularly if the meeting is taking decisions, because all the sessions have to vote on the same things, so there's little room for people to make proposals in response to discussion. But it can dramatically improve participation.

Before the Covid-19 pandemic, relatively few workers used video conferencing to meet up and organise. Its use in Britain was generally confined to groups of workers with good access to the technology and the skills to use it. In some cases, workers in multinational companies found it the only way to regularly meet internationally without spending too much time and money.

Now, video conferencing has become widespread, and there will be no going back. The National Education Union (NEU) made the most spectacular use of the technology, with around 400,000 watching one Zoom call in January 2021 and tens of thousands at others. Many people who struggle to attend physical meetings for reasons of health, geography, travel, cost or caring responsibilities found it easier to participate when meetings moved online. But that wasn't true for everyone – many lacked the equipment, connectivity or skills to participate online. Many organisations failed to make online events accessible (for example, by providing a live transcript of closed captions or sign language interpretation). It's hard to enable much participation in large online events, and some of the platforms don't handle voting well. Online meetings are great for sharing information and getting explanations out to workers who are geographically dispersed. If managed well, they can also enable a few people to ask questions or raise concerns. But they aren't great for building relationships or genuinely participatory discussion. Big online meetings aren't great for decision-making either. Organisers who want to maximise participation are going to have to learn to combine online and in-person meetings effectively and cope with the different demographics of who participates in which.

SOCIALISING

Organising is tough, but it will be most successful if it is also fun. When a campaign is intense, there is even more need for people to have time to relax, chat informally and let their hair down. A social event could involve workers' families or community supporters, strengthening their relationship to the campaign. Being together, whether while taking action, at a meeting or socially, breaks down feelings of isolation and gives people confidence that if they take action, they won't be doing it alone.

In most groups of workers, there are people with all kinds of interests, hobbies and connections – there is nearly always someone up for arranging a quiz night, gig, picnic, barbecue or trip to the zoo. Try to make your events inclusive and accessible. It's best to vary who organises such 'morale and motivation' events – whatever you do, it won't be to everyone's taste and you certainly don't want some workers feeling like their money is being squandered on entertainment they never take part in.

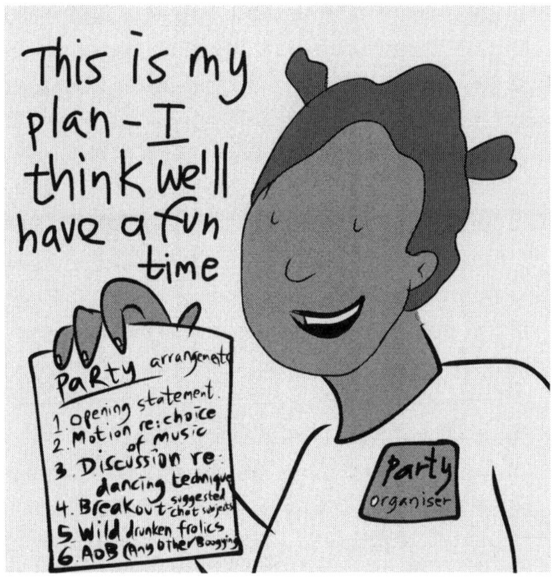

DEMOCRACY

The word democracy originates from the Greek words for 'common people' (*dēmos*) and 'rule' (*kratos*) so organising is all about increasing democracy – helping working-class people build and use power. But even though democracy is our goal, many workers' experience of unions is not one of genuinely having the power.

Even if we reject the idea that our ways of organising must foreshadow the society we want (after all, tools rarely resemble what they are used to produce), there are powerful reasons to make our organising as democratic as possible. For example:

1. Nobody knows it all, and nobody knows workers' jobs and relationships better than the workers themselves. The campaign needs everyone's knowledge, experience, eyes and ears. You need everyone's input.
2. Participation is voluntary, and people are much more willing to participate if they have a meaningful say.
3. People are much more likely to work to carry out decisions they didn't agree with if they were reached democratically. Democracy enables united action.

4. Things will go wrong and often those in the thick of it aren't the first to notice or are so involved that they can't see the wood for the trees to understand problems. Democracy helps you learn from mistakes – as long as there's a supportive culture.
5. People at the heart of organisations can leave, fall ill, be bought off, become incorporated, bureaucratised or corrupt. Democracy reduces many of these risks and helps workers to cope with such setbacks.

Real democracy means much more than just votes – it's about power. Many unions have structures that appear democratic on paper but are so labyrinthine that it's extremely hard for members to exert much influence over decisions.

Access to information is a prerequisite for workers to exercise democratic control. I discuss in Chapter 10 how employers try to tie unions up with confidentiality to create divisions between paid officers, reps and workers, and to prevent workers really controlling their own representatives. Similar problems exist inside unions – it is often hard for activists, never mind workers, to find out what is going on in our own union. So how can we exert control? A commitment to effective organising, to building working-class power, must include a commitment to democratising unions. This is discussed further in Chapter 11.

So, what would a commitment to democracy mean in practice when you are organising at work?

Nothing significant affecting union members should be agreed without them having the opportunity to understand, discuss and vote on it. All roles that involve influence over campaigning or dealing with the employer should be elected, accountable and removable in a reasonable time frame. A postal or email ballot isn't that democratic if there's no opportunity to ask questions, have a discussion or put forward alternative options. Unless there's a risk of intimidation, a show of hands is generally the most democratic method of voting at workplace level because everyone can see the result for themselves and the ability of workers to see who voted which way contributes to ongoing democratic debate between workers. A show of hands also tends to produce more decisive results one way or the other, as people are influenced by each other's votes. This is really helpful because close votes can make it hard to carry through decisions in a united way. Bear this in mind when thinking about what to propose. It can be more useful to win a vote by a comfortable margin than to win something better with too little support to be able to implement it effectively. How big a factor this is will depend on how much collective self-discipline a group of workers has.

One issue that crops up in many workplaces is whether or how to include managers in your organisation. I argued in Chapter 2 for 'wall-to-wall' organising, including everyone in the physical or virtual workplace irrespective of occupation, employer or employment status. Managers often have access to information that can help your organising. But there are obvious problems with including managers in your organisation. Will workers feel confident enough to raise issues or express their views with managers in the room? How does the union navigate conflict between members and a manager if both are members? What if managers use their knowledge or meeting skills to intimidate other members or derail discussions? If some reps are managers, might they come under pressure from above? Will managers involved in the union use knowledge gained there in their management role to frustrate union campaigns?

Before deciding how to tackle the issue, it's worth thinking about what we mean by a 'manager'. Many people have manager in their job title who aren't really managers at all. Some people who do have a supervisory role still spend most of their time doing the job themselves, rather than bossing people around, and are paid barely more than their staff. The key issue from an organising point of view is how much power over the workers someone has. At an individual level, a key boundary is the power to discipline us. At a collective level, managers can take decisions that harm us, from understaffing your team to implementing inadequate safety measures. Ideally, you want every manager in a union but organised separately from the workers they manage, so that they don't hold us back. In the coal mining industry, for example, the National Union of Mineworkers (NUM) used to organise the workers, while supervisors were in the National Association of Colliery Overmen, Deputies and Shotfirers (NACODS). Most action only involved NUM members but sometimes they were able to pull NACODS in behind them, which made action even more powerful. In some industries, both will be in the same union but have separate structures. At a minimum, try to make sure that workers can meet, discuss and decide things without managers present, and that any reps who are managers are expected to stay out of discussions and decisions where there is any potential for a perceived conflict of interest. But make sure members who are managers still have a voice, even if that is separate.

Small groups of workers can often take democratic decisions informally: on the basis of consensus, people volunteering for a task, or helping each other out when they can see someone struggling. As Jo Freeman explained in *The Tyranny of Structurelessness* (n.d. [1970]), without a structure, power relationships in a group remain informal and hidden. Democratic decision-making in any larger group requires structure, though structure doesn't guarantee democracy. This starts at the level of the (physical or virtual) workplace. Strong union organisation requires members being able to meet, discuss and decide things in their teams or departments and across wider workplaces or employers. When conflict is intense, the need to meet is greater – during strikes, we normally held a short informal meeting every day after picketing and more formal members' meetings every week or two.

If you are organising in one union in one workplace, democracy can be fairly straightforward, but workers have often needed ingenuity to create democratic structures. In multi-union workplaces it is good practice to create a 'joint shop stewards committee', with reps from all the unions.

There's a long history, particularly in engineering, of 'combine committees' (pronounced as in 'combine harvester') bringing together representatives from different workplaces in a company or group of companies. Historically, these tended to be comprised of delegates from each unionised workplace, often including more than one union. The delegates were typically elected by the reps in each workplace. Similar structures are now spreading through schools which are in Multiple Academy Trust chains. Unite uses the term 'combine' to refer to a gathering of all the reps from across a particular company or industry, which may then elect a committee. That works fine if you already have each workplace well unionised, but that often isn't the case. For example, most of the sites where I used to work didn't yet have union recognition, some had no reps, and there were lots of workers based at home.

When I knew we were heading towards our first national strike, I could see the need to set up a structure that represented every member but couldn't work out how to do it, despite asking loads of experienced activists. In the end, it was a new rep who came up with the solution. We divided the country into regions and put every member into a region based on their workplace or, if home-based or mobile, their home address. We allocated seats on the combine committee in proportion to the membership in each region. Every member was entitled to stand, whether they were a rep or not, and every member could vote to elect the combine reps for their region. Not all combine members were as effective as you'd wish in organising workplace meetings to get member input, but this structure had more democratic legitimacy than anything else we could come up with, and it enabled clear and relatively quick decisions. An additional benefit was helping members rather than paid officers remain in control of the strike. If members, elected reps or combine committee members have voted for something, it is politically much harder for an unelected paid officer to overturn it than if it's just individuals arguing with them.

Many union committees operate a system of 'cabinet responsibility' where every committee member is supposed to behave as if they agreed with all decisions – or resign. This has the superficial attraction of giving the appearance of unity. Unity in the face of the employer is an asset and everyone implementing majority decisions is vital for meaningful democracy. However, withholding information about debates and disagreements from members is unity in the face of the members, not management. It makes it harder for members to take informed decisions or hold their representatives accountable. Cabinet responsibility is a tool for top-down control, not for building workers' power. Better practices require any committee member who intends to argue against a majority decision to let the other committee members know first, which helps maintain trust, but they facilitate everyone having their say in front of the members, who take the important decisions.

People find it hard to remain open and democratic when things go wrong because we are afraid of demoralising workers. It's common to see unions dress up defeats as victories to keep spirits high. This is a mistake.

Workers usually know when there's a setback because it affects them – and management know too. Trust is incredibly important at any time in a campaign, but particularly important when things get difficult. If workers learn that you prefer to manipulate them than be straight with them, you lose that trust. Just as importantly, how can workers learn from setbacks that aren't honestly discussed?

The temptation to gloss over problems is a break from a genuine organising model in favour of a top-down model where a select few know the truth and work out strategies and plans on behalf of workers, rather than workers doing it for themselves. How can you build up workers' views of their own potential if you underestimate it yourself? One of the points in advice to rookie organisers from 1199, a US union organisation, is 'workers are made of clay, not glass' (McAlevey, 2016).

I'm not suggesting that you never need secrecy around tactics – sometimes we need to surprise or mislead management. Neither do I mean that you should take sharing bad news lightly – rather that it requires thought and planning. Democracy isn't an excuse for abdicating leadership. I once made the mistake of sharing the fact that management appeared to be preparing to victimise me at a strike meeting of union members without having prepared properly. It's unreasonable to expect members to make wise decisions about how to respond when issues are just dumped on them in this way. The strike leaders should have prepared options for how to respond, which members can consider. Our failure to do this panicked and disoriented members rather than channelling their anger in a constructive direction.

COLLECTIVE ACTION

The point of organising is to build workers' capacity to take, or credibly threaten, powerful collective action to win the outcomes we want. The process of planning and taking action is discussed in detail in Chapters 8 and 9. But it's worth highlighting here that collective action also contributes to the organising process in several important ways.

Any collective action can be used as a structure test. At the very least, you can track participation on your charts. If you mobilise people for the action through the influential workers you have identified then you are genuinely testing your structure. As noted above, actions which involve making a public commitment to the campaign firm up participants' support for it. Taking part in collective actions, particularly higher risk ones, builds and strengthens the bonds between workers, strengthening collectivity and breaking down atomisation and individualism. Doing something you are a bit afraid of together is a powerful shared experience, builds trust and makes people reluctant to let each other down.

The experience of participation in collective action can shift workers' consciousness in other ways too – partly because we are forced to think hard about power relationships and partly because action clarifies who is on our side and who is against us. Collective action has an important role in breaking down pervasive ideologies such as racism, sexism and nationalism. It undermines divisions between workers in different industries and occupations, and between those in and out of paid work. All these divisions are portrayed as more important than what we have in common. These processes are not the same in every collective action – they are strongest when large numbers of workers take high-risk action, take it for the first time, and where there are politically conscious people involved who encourage discussion.

Key points

- A leader is someone with followers.
- It's important to identify and win over the influential workers – but there is a role for everyone.
- Don't rush to try to win over the most influential workers – this is high stakes, so do your homework first.
- Mapping and charting help you avoid missing out anyone in the workplace, understand how workers interact, and track support for and participation in the campaign.
- Structure tests help you measure progress and identify your strong and weak areas. This can show if you haven't identified and won over the influential worker in an area and help you decide what to prioritise.
- Communication trees and distribution networks can help you communicate with a large group without relying on 'broadcast' messages.
- Avoid having meetings as a ritual – think about their purpose and how to make them work.
- Socialising strengthens bonds.
- Democracy is vital to strong organisation but requires more than just votes.
- Collective action is key to organising: it is how workers exert pressure and it can transform those taking part.

Discussion questions

1. Can you start mapping or charting your team?
2. Who would you talk to first, to try to gather more information and identify influential workers?
3. Think about your experiences of meetings or democracy. What made them good or bad?
4. Have you ever taken part in collective action? How did it make you feel?

7
Using your rights

As I explained in Chapter 4, the most solid basis for workers' power is collective organisation and action, rather than a reliance on 'rights'. In this book, I am using the term 'rights' to refer to rights that workers are told we have by the state or the employer. These are always inadequate, are often unenforced and can be taken away. However, rights are also a legacy of past struggles, making the terrain more favourable. Educating workers about their rights and how to enforce them can empower workers to stand up for themselves and restricts the abuse of power by managers. Because 'rights' are supposed to be universal, whether from state legislation or employer policy, workers may be able to use them before they have built much collective strength. The challenge is to use rights in ways that build collective strength rather than reinforcing the illusion that our own power is unnecessary.

In this chapter, I outline some key considerations about rights and the law, summarise some rights that often have a collective dimension and briefly discuss how they can be used. You may choose to skip some sections of this chapter and return to them as and when issues arise, but I'd urge you to read the sections on contracts of employment and discrimination, which include some fundamentals every workplace organiser should know.

RIGHTS ARE DOUBLE EDGED

The idea of 'rights' is widely used, but a lot more complicated than it first appears. The Equality and Human Rights Commission (2021) says that:

> Human rights are the basic rights and freedoms that belong to every person in the world, from birth until death … they can never be taken away, although they can sometimes be restricted – for example if a person breaks the law, or in the interests of national security.

But every right we might think of is denied to millions of people all the time, even when enshrined in legislation or employer policies. However rights are established, workers have to fight to defend and extend them. As the saying goes, the price of good terms and conditions is eternal vigilance.

When we try to assert our rights, we are leveraging victories of the past to help our campaign today. However, the laws and policies that enshrine rights are almost always written by the rich and powerful. They belong to the very states and employers that our organising challenges. Observing rights gives their rule greater legitimacy. Defining our rights helps them constrain which of our demands and actions are seen as legitimate, limiting our aims and power. As we use rights, we should aim to raise workers' awareness of their shortcomings, so that we can minimise the downsides.

CONTRACTS OF EMPLOYMENT

This is a book on organising, not an employment law handbook (the LRD produces an excellent *Law at Work* booklet every year), but anyone organising at work needs to understand some basic principles.

At the time of writing, workers (in the general sense) have a wide variety of legal statuses. The main categories are:

- *Employees*: those who work under a contract of employment (whether written down or not), for an employer.
- *Workers*: employees, plus anyone else with a contract to personally do work, as long as this isn't on a client or customer basis. A common example is workers who are offered work on a piecemeal basis and can accept or reject it each time – the employer has no obligation to offer it and the worker no obligation to accept it.
- *Self-employed*: people operating as businesses selling goods and services to their customers.

The reality is even more complex, with some workplaces including volunteers, interns, apprentices or trainees, and some employees not being employed by the company that they do work for but through an outsourcing company, agency or umbrella company.[1]

All employees are workers, but not all workers are employees. You have more rights as an employee than a worker, and more as a worker than as self-employed (see the LRD booklet for details). As a result, employers often try to treat employees as workers or workers as self-employed. This gets tested in court fairly frequently. The main tests used to determine whether or not a worker is an employee are:

- *mutuality of obligation*: a legal obligation to do some work in return for payment (usually wages)
- *personal service*: an obligation to work personally, or, in other words, no right to send someone to do your work instead of you
- *control*: the extent to which someone else decides when, where and how you do your work.

There has been a long battle against 'bogus self-employment'. For example, Uber drivers had to go to the Supreme Court[2] to show that they were not really self-employed and were entitled to the benefits of worker status, including the National Minimum Wage.

If you have an employment contract, it doesn't have to be written down. You can think of the contract as the deal between you and your employer. It usually includes far more than is written down on a piece of paper with 'contract of employment' at the top (if you are lucky enough to have one!). Employees are entitled to a written statement of employment particulars[3], setting out some of the key elements of the contract. To add to the confusion, if you *do* have a written contract, it often includes things that are not contractual, but that your employer wants you to think are.

Things can end up being part of your contract by several routes. 'Express terms' are specifically agreed, whether written down or not. And just because it's written down doesn't mean a court will accept that it accurately reflects the contractual agreement. Some of what's written down may be too vague to be an express term. 'Implied terms' have been left unsaid but are included either because it is necessary to make the contract work, are obviously part of the contract, or have become established 'custom and practice'. Arrangements don't become contractual through custom and practice just because they have applied for a long time. They have to be widely known, with an expectation that they would be legally enforced. Where there is collective bargaining between a union and the employer, agreements or parts of them can also become part of individual employment contracts, but only where this is the clear intent of both employer and union.

Contract terms can normally only be changed by agreement, but agreement doesn't have to be explicit. If the employer makes a change and you work normally under it without objection, you risk being regarded as having accepted it.

Employers can try to impose contract changes through dismissal and re-engagement, which has become known as 'fire and rehire'. They give notice to terminate the contract and offer a new one on worse terms. If 20 or more employees at one establishment (normally a workplace) would be dismissed in any period of 90 days or less, the employer must consult collectively, irrespective of whether workers are unionised. Consultation for this 'fire and rehire' follows a similar process as for redundancies, explained later in this chapter. Note that this 90-day period to *trigger* collective consultation is separate from the *minimum consultation period*, which is now shorter. In some circumstances, employees may be able to bring claims for unfair dismissal, but even if that is successful, which is rare, it doesn't prevent the change. Depending on their strength, some groups of workers refuse to sign the new contact (and risk losing their jobs), while others sign under protest while fighting the change. Signing a new contract doesn't necessarily stop you bringing a claim for unfair dismissal, as you can argue that you were mitigating your loss. Faced with such tactics, workers need good legal advice as well as a powerful campaign.

Increasing numbers of employers put clauses in contracts saying that they can make unilateral changes, but employees can still complain to a tribunal if the employer hasn't applied these 'reasonably'. The LRD explains:

> In general, where an employer relies on this kind of term to impose a unilateral change to contract terms or working conditions, any change must not exceed or fundamentally alter existing contractual obligations.

The requirement for 'reasonableness' often also applies when the employer seeks to use an existing contract clause to the detriment of an employee. It restricts managers' ability to unreasonably vary duties or require additional hours.

The point of this section is not to suggest that the law can solve workers' problems – it rarely does so, even to a limited extent. But employers often rely on workers not understanding our rights and get away with actions they have no right to. Understanding that the contract does not give the employer complete free rein to make your life a misery is often enough to achieve small wins (or at least delays). It exposes the illegitimacy of some employer actions – vital for organising.

EMPLOYER POLICIES

All but the smallest employers will have some written policies and procedures. In most cases, these don't form part of the legal contract between you and your employer, and the courts won't stop the employer changing them at will or breaking them. However, policies are still useful in several ways, so get to know them.

Most employers make at least some effort to apply their policies. Policies enable managers to treat workers more consistently, which enables them to justify their actions and their role on grounds of fairness, even if a policy is far from fair. Many managers buy into managerial ideology and genuinely try to act in a way they see as fair. Not applying policy can lead to workers raising grievances, which is time consuming and stressful for managers. Some breaches of policy can leave the employer open to legal claims. Managers may worry that not following policy will make them look bad to their own superiors or to an HR department. Have no illusions in HR though: while they can sometimes be helpful, their role is to facilitate management – they are not on the workers' side.

In some cases, merely pointing out what a policy says may be enough to win change. For example, when I first got a 'permanent' job, all of us who started together were told we couldn't have any annual leave for the first four months. I asked to see the policy, which didn't say that at all. After showing the policy to someone in the HR department and explaining it to them (several times), they eventually conceded that we were all entitled to holidays – an easy win which educated a group of new workers to question what HR told them.

It's not rare for employers to break their own policies, even after people complain. This is great ammunition for campaigning – it strengthens your case for what you want *and* it undermines the legitimacy of management decision-making.

As I explained in Chapter 3, getting to know your employer's policies can help you organise. Don't just think about their employee policies – many employers make public statements about their ethics, social responsibility, employee relations or commitment to equality. All give opportunities for workers to expose hypocrisy and demand action rather than just fine words. For example, many workers seized on their employers' responses to Black Lives Matter to demand real change.

HEALTH AND SAFETY

Health and safety issues can be great to organise around for several reasons, including:

- Many common issues can be taken up from a health and safety angle, including workload, bullying and the working environment, as well as more traditional ones such as slips, trips and falls, dangerous substances, machinery, toilets and kitchens.
- Workers have the moral high ground.
- Most employers and managers at least pay lip service to health and safety.
- Many health and safety issues are winnable even without much power.
- Workers have some legal rights even if the job isn't unionised.
- Workers' rights include consultation, which may be collective.
- Organising round safety demonstrates the potential of collective action.

Employers must, 'so far as is reasonably practicable', prevent you being hurt or made ill through work – and this includes mental health. In Chapter 9, I cover employees' rights (including walking off a job) if faced with serious and imminent danger. The TUC's WorkSmart website has a helpful section on health and safety[4], summarising key points. For more details in plain English, the LRD's annual *Health and Safety Law* booklets are hard to beat.

This book can't cover all the health and safety issues or how to tackle them, but it is worth understanding the basic structure of health and safety law. The main top-level legislation is the Health and Safety at Work Act 1974.[5] Under that sit a large number of legally binding Regulations.[6] The most important ones for most workers are Management of Health and Safety at Work, Workplace (Health, Safety and Welfare), Manual Handling, Display Screen Equipment (DSE), Control of Substances Hazardous to Health (COSHH), Health and Safety (Consultation with Employees) and Safety Representatives and Safety Committees (SRSC). Under some of these sit Approved Codes Of Practice (ACOP). These aren't legally binding in themselves, but employers must apply equally effective methods if they don't follow them. Under these sits Guidance, which employers aren't bound to follow, but if they do, they will usually be regarded as legally compliant.

State enforcement of safety legislation is almost non-existent. Depending on your work, the enforcing authority will either be the Health and Safety Executive (HSE) or your local authority.[7] A poster including details of the enforcing authority must be displayed where workers can see it, or the information must be provided to each worker. But the enforcing authorities are so under-resourced that they can't usually investigate even when something goes wrong, let alone carry out regular inspections to help keep workers safe. In reality, enforcement is down to workers ourselves – our awareness of hazards and our rights, our organisation and our action. When things do go wrong, workers may be able to bring Personal Injury claims, which can put some pressure on employers to prevent a recurrence or improve their general safety management.

In this section, I will focus on just two things – risk assessment and consultation.

Risk assessment

Every employer must carry out 'suitable and sufficient' risk assessments, act on them and update them when circumstances change. If there are five or more employees, risk assessments must be written down. The HSE has a helpful checklist[8] of what is needed for a risk assessment to be suitable and sufficient. The employer must involve the workforce, seeking our views, suggestions and comments – and communicate the relevant outcomes, such as any actions required. The employer must appoint a 'competent person' to help them comply with health and safety law:

> A competent person is someone who has sufficient training and experience or knowledge and other qualities that allow them to assist you properly. The level of competence required will depend on the complexity of the situation and the particular help you need.[9]

Risk assessments should be appropriate for the specific workers. For example, the risks of musculoskeletal damage and the effects of some chemicals can be significantly different for men and women. Some workers may have medical conditions that put them at particular risk from certain hazards. It's no good giving everyone a chair suitable for an 'average man'. Young people[10] and those new to a job are at particular risk because they will be less familiar with the job and its hazards. Workers who are mobile are still covered by safety law, including the requirement for risk assessments. They are likely to need more training to ensure they can spot hazards and take appropriate action to keep themselves and others safe.

The Covid-19 pandemic led a lot of workers in unorganised workplaces to learn about risk assessments for the first time, with many asking to see them and pointing out hazards that were overlooked or inadequately controlled. Getting workers discussing the hazards we face and what we all want the employer to do about them can be a great organising opportunity. Remember, this isn't just about physical hazards but also those which could harm mental health. The HSE 'management standards'[11] are useful for challenging employers over stress caused by work.

A key concept to grasp when discussing how to control a hazard is the hierarchy of controls.

The hierarchy is based on collective controls first and individual ones last. Eliminating the hazard is the first priority – if there is no hazard, there is no risk of harm. Only if that is not practicable should the employer consider reducing the risk of exposure to the hazard by engineering or administrative controls, and Personal Protective Equipment (PPE) is the last resort. All too often, management want to jump straight to PPE, despite this being

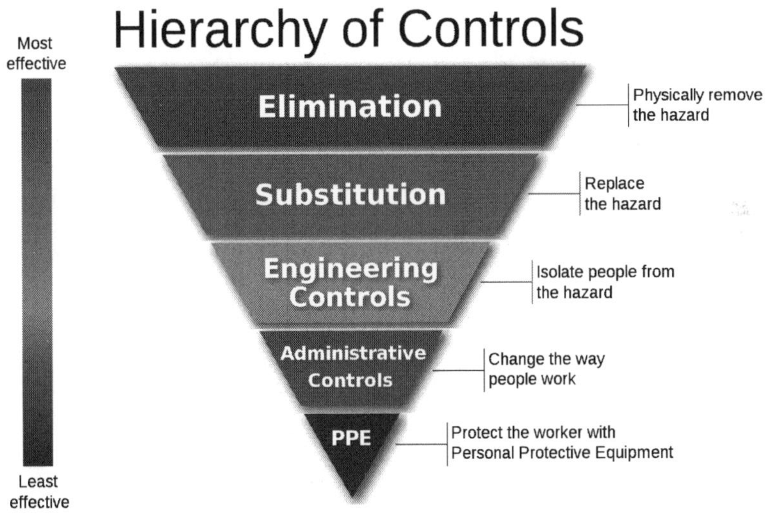

Figure 7.1 The hierarchy of controls for safety

the least effective control. Even though the employer must provide PPE free of charge, it is often ill-fitting or uncomfortable and workers may not be trained to use it properly. Then the employer blames the worker who gets hurt for not wearing the lousy PPE. PPE is sometimes essential, but it should always be a last resort when none of the other controls can adequately protect the worker.

Safety consultation

Workers' rights to be consulted over health and safety are mostly in two pieces of legislation, though there are other regulations specific to some industries. Workers with union recognition (explained later in this chapter) are covered by the Safety Representatives and Safety Committees Regulations 1977 (known as the 'brown book' or the 'safety reps' bible'). Workers without union recognition are covered by the Health and Safety (Consultation with Employees) Regulations 1996, which are similar but much weaker. Both are available in one document[12] from the HSE.

Where there is a recognised union, workers can elect safety reps and the employer must deal with them. Many employers respond to this by trying to incorporate safety reps into their own safety structures. To be clear: management are responsible for safety, including risk assessment. Safety reps have powers and functions, not responsibilities or duties. We are there to check, represent and challenge, not to do management's job for them. A union safety rep has a right to carry out their functions in work time, including having the time to get training. The functions and rights include:

- investigating potential hazards, dangerous occurrences and the causes of accidents
- investigating employee complaints about health, safety or welfare at work
- making representations to the employer and the enforcing authority
- inspecting the workplace, which can include surveys
- inspecting and taking copies of relevant documents
- receiving information and being consulted in good time before decisions.

The safety rep role gives many opportunities to find out what issues concern workers, investigate those issues and organise around them.

If you don't yet have union recognition, the weaker regulations allow the employer to choose whether to consult employees directly, via 'Representatives of Employee Safety' (RoES) elected by the workers, or a combination of both. Though consultation directly with employees is only practicable in smaller employers, many large ones try this to avoid having RoES. Organising for a large number of workers to assert their right to be individually consulted can discourage this by demonstrating to management how impractical it is. Every employee must be provided with information to enable them to participate fully and effectively in the consultation.

In a job without union recognition, getting elected as a RoES can be a big help for your organising efforts. Even the election process may enable you to make issues, or the union, visible to workers. As with union safety reps, dismissal or detriment as a result of being a RoES is unlawful, so the position can give you a bit more protection while organising. The functions of a RoES are more limited than for union safety reps – they are just about making representations to the employer and enforcing authorities, receiving information and being consulted. There are no powers to inspect or investigate. Nonetheless, you have access to a list of the employees you represent, facilities to communicate with them, and time to undertake training and perform your role.

In many workplaces without a union, the employer's safety management will fall well below the legal requirements, and wins are often possible with a bit of organising, using the law as leverage. You can also highlight how much better workers' safety rights will be once you win union recognition.

Avoid getting bogged down – there is so much to health and safety that this is an easy mistake to make. Stay focused on the issues that will really improve workers' safety and health and those that will help you organise. Another common pitfall is to slip into an advocacy approach rather than organising, as discussed in Chapter 4.

DISCRIMINATION

Discrimination is rife at work. Despite decades of anti-discrimination legislation, there is a high degree of segregation, with women and workers from ethnic minorities concentrated in certain industries, occupations and jobs that generally have lower pay and status. Disabled and trans people and those from many ethnic minorities suffer unemployment way above average.

Workers from oppressed groups suffer worse treatment by employers and higher levels of bullying, harassment and assault from managers, workmates and the public. On top of all this, women still do the bulk of unpaid caring and housework, a burden which grows every time public services are cut. Most jobs are still organised as if all workers are fit and healthy and have no responsibilities outside work, despite the fact that only a minority match this description.

In this context, any organisation at work that doesn't stand firmly against oppression and discrimination has little chance of involving all the workers and will be weaker as a result. Many workers find themselves in workgroups that are entirely or overwhelmingly comprised of people from a single gender and ethnic group. This can enable workers to mistakenly think there are no issues with racism or sexism, rather than indicating that both are major problems. It can put pressure on some activists to duck issues – pressure we need to consciously resist.

You can connect discrimination to workers' desire for fairness, dignity and respect, making it powerful to organise around. For example, the McStrike involved fast-food workplaces with high staff turnover. Many workers felt that leaving was a reasonable response to low pay but saw the importance and urgency of taking action over sexual harassment.

Some workers and activists argue that taking up issues of discrimination and inequality is divisive, and that the union should stick to issues that unite all the workers. In practice, this means only taking up the issues of concern to those who don't face discrimination, so those who do will never fully trust the union to be on their side. It's worth reminding people that unions always take up issues that only affect some workers. The old slogan 'An injury to one is an injury to all. A victory for one is a victory for all' didn't come from nowhere. It's a recognition that we only build real power and a better life if we all look out for each other. Solidarity means backing each other up even on issues that don't directly affect us.

If taking a principled stand on equality is important for the union, it is doubly important for you as an activist. Unless people can see that you consistently challenge bigotry and discrimination, will people on the receiving end feel confident to bring issues to you?

If you are in a job where those experiencing discrimination are a minority, you will have to think hard about how to get the majority on board with opposing it. In some situations, individuals are willing to be open with workmates about how issues affect them, which can help. Don't just think about the material impact, but also how discrimination or harassment makes people feel. In many cases, the changes needed to tackle discrimination would be welcomed by everyone. Who wants a secretive and arbitrary pay system? Who wants long working hours with no flexibility? Who wants recruitment, promotion or redundancy selection processes that depend on the whim of the manager? Who wants an inaccessible working environment? Who wants their workmates to be unable to do their job safely because information hasn't been provided in a form they understand? As Chapter 5 explained, fairness and respect are powerful concepts to motivate workers.

It can be hardest to tackle discriminatory behaviour at work when it comes from a member. It's a mistake to duck it. A common mistake when tackling prejudiced members is to rely on the law or employer policy, trying to persuade members to change their behaviour to avoid 'getting in trouble' or seeing disciplinary action by management as the only option. At best, this restrains the member's behaviour without changing their mind. At worst, it can make oppressive behaviour seem like an act of rebellion and you like a management spokesperson. Much better for workers and the union to deal with issues ourselves – if we can. I gave the example in Chapter 5 of dealing with BNP supporters in a workplace by educating and empowering workers to challenge them. Ideally, you want to persuade the member to change their behaviour by highlighting the harm it does to other workers and how that undermines the unity required to win on issues they care about.

In recent years, employers have increasingly sought to side-line struggles for equality and against discrimination by promoting a 'Diversity and Inclusion' (D&I) agenda. This rests on claims that greater diversity and inclusion is good for business because it enables employers to draw on a wider talent pool and because happier workers are often more productive. While this is preferable to employers openly defending discrimination, it is a fundamentally flawed approach. While there is some evidence to support this 'business case' in relation to some types of workers in some contexts, it certainly doesn't apply to everyone – particularly at the bottom end of the labour market where workers who face discrimination are concentrated. The experience of many women and migrant workers, for example, can be that employers are keen to 'include' them – only to pay and treat them appallingly.

D&I is perfectly compatible with gross levels of inequality, as long as different groups are equally represented at the top. The result is nearly always a focus on helping a tiny minority of women or people from ethnic minorities to break through the glass ceiling into senior roles, while the majority are left stuck on the floor clearing up shards of glass.

When employers pursue a top-down D&I agenda, it can produce an unhelpful reaction and make some workers see transgressing its 'political correctness' as a form of rebellion against authority. This makes it even more important that unions pursue their own equality agendas, rather than leave the field to employers or be co-opted into their D&I initiatives. Unions should aim to reduce inequality, not just give everyone an equal chance to be at the bottom of a very tall pile.

The main piece of equality legislation is the Equality Act 2010.[13] This defines nine 'protected characteristics': age, disability, gender reassignment, marriage and civil partnership, pregnancy and maternity, race, religion or belief, sex, and sexual orientation. The legal framework is similar for most of the protected characteristics, banning direct discrimination (where A treats B less favourably 'because of' a protected characteristic) and indirect discrimination (where a 'provision, criterion or practice' (or PCP) puts some people with a protected characteristic at a substantial disadvantage). The EHRC has produced a document[14] explaining some of the terms in the Act. A PCP is some sort of formal or informal 'rule'; it doesn't include all one-off unfair acts[15], and employers can defend a PCP as a 'proportionate means of achieving a legitimate aim'. The Act also bans harassment related to protected characteristics, which is defined as conduct with the purpose or effect of violating someone's dignity or creating an intimidating, hostile, degrading, humiliating or offensive environment for them. Unwanted conduct of a sexual nature, or relating to gender reassignment or sex, is explicitly included. It is unlawful to discriminate against or harass someone because they are perceived to have a protected characteristic or because they are associated with someone who has a protected characteristic. As with most employment law, it is unlawful to victimise someone for taking action using the Act.

There is an important additional element to the Equality Act in relation to disabled people – the duty to make 'reasonable adjustments'. The definition of a disability is much wider than many people realise – it covers everyone with a physical or mental impairment that has a 'substantial and long-term adverse effect' on their ability to carry out normal day-to-day activities. The 'effect' is considered without any benefit from measures such as drugs or prosthetic limbs (but not ordinary glasses or contact lenses). In most cases, 'long-term' means a year, and 'day-to-day activities' does not just mean those related to work. Reasonable adjustments don't just mean physical equipment, but could mean changes to any 'provision, criterion or practice' – for example, the operation of trigger levels in a sickness policy, the allocation of work or changes to working hours. It's important to ask for the necessary adjustments, making clear that you are doing so under the disability provisions of the Equality Act, to prevent the employer claiming they were unaware of your needs.

An important issue to be aware of in relation to disability discrimination is the difference between the 'medical model' of disability and the 'social model'[16] that campaigners want. The social model means that someone is disabled by the way society is organised rather than by their impairment or difference. It encourages a focus on removing the barriers to disabled people fully participating in society, irrespective of whether there is a medical 'solution' to the impairment.

Almost every process that happens at work will be influenced by widespread prejudices and structural discrimination. The fact that some forms of unfairness are covered by legislation is a powerful weapon to expose and challenge more general unfairness too. For example, while no redundancy process can be 'fair', reflecting as it does the power of management over workers, it's highly likely that a redundancy process will disproportionately impact on groups with protected characteristics. Unions frequently tell reps to check for discrimination in redundancy selection, but rarely explain how to do it. I had to get together with a professional statistician to produce our own guide to checking for discrimination in selection.[17]

The Equality Act includes a Public Sector Equality Duty (PSED)[18] requiring public authorities (which includes some private organisations providing public services) exercising their functions to have due regard to eliminating unlawful discrimination, advancing equality of opportunity and fostering good relations between people who share a protected characteristic and those who don't. This is an unusual piece of the legislation in that it focuses on outcomes rather than process, and it requires positive action, not merely the absence of discrimination. Employers often try to demonstrate compliance with the PSED by producing Equality Impact Assessments (EIA). These aren't explicitly required and don't necessarily show compliance, particularly if it's a tick-box exercise. A threat to publicise the lack of an EIA, let alone legal action over a failure in the PSED, can put a lot of pressure on some employers and help win concessions.[19] All these processes can be valuable for campaigning.

REDUNDANCY AND TUPE

Some things that employers do can trigger collective rights, not just individual ones – and these are organising opportunities. Two (sadly) common situations that trigger a right to collective consultation are some redundancies and most situations where a group of workers is transferred from one employer to another. The latter is known as a TUPE transfer (pronounced more like chew-pea than toupee), from the Transfer of Undertakings (Protection of Employment) Regulations.

As with the other parts of this chapter, I won't cover all the details about redundancies and transfers but will focus on the organising opportunities they present. The LRD produces two booklets – *Redundancy Law: A Guide for Union Reps* and *TUPE: A Union Rep's Guide to Using the Law* – which provide lots of useful information.

The right to collective consultation over redundancies kicks in when an employer proposes to dismiss 20 or more employees from one 'establishment' (usually a workplace) in any period of 90 days or less.[20] The requirement is only triggered if the dismissal is for any reason or reasons not related to the individual (like conduct and capability). This includes where employers want to force through worse terms and conditions through fire and rehire. If the employer proposes to dismiss 20–99 workers within any period of 90 days or less, the consultation must start at least 30 days before any dismissals. If there are 100 or more dismissals, it must start at least 45 days before. This time period was cut from 90 days by the Tory/Lib Dem coalition government in 2013. This did not change the 90-day period for triggering the requirement for collective consultation. The fact that the 90-day consultation period still applies in Northern Ireland can be helpful where an employer is making job cuts across the UK. The short timescale is a big problem, not least because the anti-union laws make it almost impossible to ballot and take lawful industrial action (see Chapter 9) before the dismissals. Remember that these time periods are minimums – you can campaign and bargain for more.

TUPE, which is intended to preserve employees' continuity of employment, doesn't apply in every transfer. For example, it doesn't apply if one company simply buys another. It nearly always applies when outsourced services move from one supplier to another at the end of a contract, or when one business sells part of itself to another. Workers generally have no choice about transferring where TUPE applies, other than simply resigning. There are some cases[21] when a transfer would cause substantial detriment (e.g. unsuitable location) and employees have successfully objected to the transfer and claimed unfair dismissal.

There is no minimum number of employees to trigger collective consultation over TUPE. Unlike redundancy, there is no minimum timescale for TUPE consultation, but it must start 'in good time' before the transfer. If workers have a recognised union, collective consultation for redundancy or TUPE must be through the union. When there is no union recognition, the employer must arrange elections for employee representatives for the consultation. In some circumstances, this could be through an existing standing body of reps, but usually they are elected to deal with a particular collective consultation.

The employer must provide information to the representatives and time and facilities for the consultation. If there is a failure to consult in line with the legislation, the rep can bring a tribunal claim for compensation (up to 90 days' pay) on behalf of the workers they represent. If you are standing for election as a consultation rep, this is an incredibly powerful argument for workers to elect a union member as their rep. Would a non-member really have the knowledge and legal representation to bring such a claim? If there are no consultation reps, workers themselves may be able to bring a claim for failure to consult.

Any election is itself an organising opportunity. If it is contested, you may be able to get a short election statement circulated to workers with the voting form or do other campaigning. If elected, you acquire new rights which can help you organise. You are entitled to carry out your consultation rep duties, including training, in paid work time. Push to get your training independently, ideally via a union – training arranged by the employer is hardly going to equip you to challenge them or hold them to account. If you are using the redundancy or TUPE as an organising opportunity, the union might agree to open up the training to consultation reps who aren't members yet. That's a great opportunity to show people the expertise, experience and networks of support available through a union.

As a consultation rep, you are entitled to communicate with the workers you represent, to keep them updated and get their views – another organising opportunity. Can you establish channels that will remain after the consultation is over, like groups on messaging apps? Can you use the consultation process to get people involved, build collectivity and encourage collective action? But be careful – organising collective action is not part of the official consultation rep role.

If some affected workers have union recognition and others don't, the union will have to decide whether it wants to be consulted separately by the employer or to do it together with the reps elected by workers without recognition, who may be non-members, hostile or even management. There are pros and cons. Joint consultation can help you build organisation in areas without recognition, but weak reps can undermine the union's efforts. Many employers love consulting a disunited group of reps so they can pick and choose the views that are useful to them.

In a redundancy situation, don't restrict your organising to those most likely to lose their jobs. As well as helping those workers, you want to leave stronger organisation behind afterwards, whatever the outcome. It can be useful to set a deadline for people to join the union if they want individual help. For example, if the employer is going to select who is made redundant, you could say that people will only get individual help if they join before selection. Most of those who join will learn the benefit of taking part and remain members. Bear in mind that workers left behind often suffer increased workload after redundancy. When unions accept voluntary redundancies, those leaving may be happy, but those left covering their work rarely are.

If there are lots of workers facing redundancy or TUPE, there is a risk that reps become overwhelmed by supporting individuals in innumerable one-to-one meetings with management. In my old workplace, the reps wrote checklists of standard points and questions to raise in one-to-ones, which workers could adapt to suit their own situation. We asked for volunteers from beyond the reps, so that members could accompany each other to one-to-ones when there weren't enough reps, and ran mini-training sessions to give the volunteers confidence. Of course, members still expect trained reps or paid officers when it comes to formal appeals, but managing the casework workload is vital if reps are going to have capacity to do campaigning and organising.

Don't lose sight of the fact that employers have their own goals in a collective consultation. In many cases, they don't believe workers have anything useful to say, and just want to get through the process in a way that takes as little effort as possible, minimises the risk of litigation and maximises management control. It's a huge boost for management if they can get reps to 'agree' things – whether that is a whole redundancy programme, selection criteria or detrimental TUPE measures. Management are required by law to consult 'with a view to reaching agreement', but there is rarely much benefit to workers from reps agreeing to anything that might harm a worker. How can you campaign against something you agreed? Agreeing selection criteria up front hampers you in helping a worker challenge their selection. Workers taking the employer to tribunal after losing their job are not helped if the union agreed the redundancy programme.

Redundancy consultation is meant to be about avoiding the dismissals, reducing the number of dismissals and 'mitigating the consequences' of the dismissals, which means reducing their impact on workers. However, many employers much prefer to discuss selection criteria for choosing who loses their job, which helps reduce their litigation risk, rather than getting into discussions where workers might save jobs by challenging their business plan or demand they spend money on retraining or redundancy pay. Similarly, many employers love to bog down TUPE consultations by discussing trivia.

For workers, the key items in most TUPE consultations are:

- which people are in scope to transfer
- the future viability of the new employer
- the impact on those who don't transfer
- whether the transferred group remain intact after transfer or merge into an existing organisation structure
- pensions
- location
- collective agreements
- mapping onto the new employer's job/grade structure.

In both redundancy and TUPE consultations, you need to ensure you are talking about what matters to workers and not let the employer set the agenda. In a TUPE, it can help to contact the union in the new employer, if there is one. They may be able to give you information about how things really work and suggest questions to raise.

Employers sometimes try to strengthen their control and fragment workers' response by breaking up a consultation into multiple groups which focus on particular teams or occupations. While having subgroups to look at detail can be helpful, structuring the whole consultation this way is usually a disaster. Management will have all the information centralised, while workers only get to see fragments of the picture. Measures that work best if applied to workers in several of the groups become harder to win. Managers can selectively make concessions where and when it suits them, rather than for the whole workforce.

Another common trick during consultation is for managers to try to impose unreasonable confidentiality requirements, so that reps can't communicate properly with the workers we represent. The law allows for some information to be shared with reps in confidence – for example, if revealing it would threaten national security or do serious harm to the organisation, but this doesn't include harm caused by workers reacting angrily to the truth. It can also be sensible for reps to agree to be told information shortly before it is announced generally, so they can prepare. But beyond that, keep things as open as possible. One approach is to be clear up front with the employer that you will only be bound by confidentiality when you've agreed to it in advance.

Organising around redundancy and TUPE can seem a bit dispiriting, in the sense that there's a significant risk that many of the workers you organise end up outside the employer you are organising in. But if you get it right, you'll have built organisation amongst those left behind, and TUPE can spread the beginnings of union organisation to the new employer. Redundant workers may stay in a union for their next job.

If you've been outsourced, you can build most power by trying to build union organisation both across your employer, who may be providing outsourced services to many clients, and linking into your own client organisation. This also helps protect you against future changes of employer or to the boundaries of what is outsourced.

WHISTLEBLOWING

Whistleblowing means revealing a hidden truth about your employer's operation. If you are victimised for revealing wrongdoing in the public interest, there is some legal remedy (compensation) under the Employment Rights Act 1996.[22] Immorality isn't covered, only certain types of wrongdoing disclosed to certain organisations. The legislation is designed to encourage disclosures to the employer and discourage going to the press. Employers often have whistleblowing policies that try to get you to report the wrongdoing to them, but this often results in no effective action. There are many pitfalls with whistleblowing, so you should always seek advice – the charity protect-advice.org.uk runs a helpline.

From an organising point of view, it's possible that whistleblowing could add to pressure on an employer, but the confidential nature of the process and your lack of control over the timescale make it hard to use. It's more likely that you can organise outside the legal framework. For example, unions have set up hotlines for workers to report issues with a particular employer, then used what they learned anonymously. On a smaller scale, workers can feed information to *trusted* contacts outside the employer to pass on to the media or use in campaigning. This isn't risk free though – if the employer finds out who has blown the whistle, they may victimise the worker, who would then lack recourse under the legislation.

UNION RECOGNITION

An early milestone for any campaign is forcing a decision-maker to react or respond in some way. Arnie Graf (2020) calls this recognition – their recognition that they have to deal with you. 'Union recognition' has a more specific legal meaning – the employer recognising that a union (or several unions) represents a group of workers. It triggers legal rights[23] including:

- the right to reasonable paid time off for union 'duties', primarily for union reps
- the right of union members to reasonable unpaid time off for union 'activities'
- rights for safety reps, including through safety committees
- the right to reasonable time off for union learning representatives (who deal with staff training and education)
- the right to be consulted through the union over collective redundancies and TUPE transfers, as discussed above
- the right to information for collective bargaining.

It is a common misconception that you need union recognition before taking industrial action – this is completely untrue. Indeed, industrial action or the threat of it has historically been a common way of winning or enforcing union recognition. The right to time off to accompany a workmate in a grievance or disciplinary hearing, covered in Chapter 4, doesn't depend on union recognition either.

Once you are bargaining with the employer, you can make collective agreements providing rights above the statutory minimum. These can affect many aspects of employment, including those elsewhere in this chapter. Remember that your statutory rights provide a floor (at best). You are aiming to establish better rights through bargaining and to keep building up from there.

Union recognition can be achieved using a statutory procedure or, when the employer agrees, on a 'voluntary' basis. A voluntary agreement could be the result of a lot of pressure, or the employer knowing that workers would be able to successfully use the statutory procedure. Some employers make voluntary agreements with ineffective unions to try to prevent workers winning recognition for their preferred union, or in the hope that recognising a union before it has much support will mean it disappoints workers and remains weak.

A voluntary agreement can include anything – some are very good indeed. Others are far worse than what workers would achieve through the statutory process. Some don't even include collective bargaining, usually seen as the essence of union recognition. Some effectively give the employer a veto over union communications or activity or have 'no strike' dispute resolution procedures.

A key concept in union recognition is the 'bargaining unit'. This is the defined group of workers that the employer recognises the union as representing – typically some combination of locations, jobs or grades.

It is usual, but not essential, to have a written union recognition agreement. These typically set out the bargaining unit, topics for bargaining, arrangements for negotiations, time off for reps, etc.

The statutory route to union recognition[24], in place since 1999, was introduced by New Labour. It includes lots of hurdles that employers wanted, so the coverage of union recognition hasn't grown significantly. The legislation only covers employers with 20 or more workers, not including agency workers.

The first issue to be aware of with the statutory process is the definition of the bargaining unit. If the union and employer don't agree, the union can decide the boundaries of the bargaining unit it applies for. The employer can challenge the bargaining unit and propose their own. The Central Arbitration Committee (CAC)[25], which operates the statutory recognition process, decides whether the union's proposed bargaining unit is appropriate[26], and can impose an alternative. This could include groups of workers who aren't organised or exclude key groups of members. This can make it harder to achieve the support to win union recognition or the power for workers in the bargaining unit to win meaningful change. Early in an organising campaign it is worth thinking about groups the employer might try to add to your preferred bargaining unit – and organise them too.

There is lots more to the complex statutory recognition process (the LRD's annual *Law at Work* booklet includes details), but, in general, you want well over 50 per cent of the workers in your chosen bargaining unit to be union members before you start the process, so you maintain a majority even if the employer uses dirty tricks like hiring new staff into the bargaining unit, reorganising or getting rid of union members. If the CAC orders a ballot (ideally you want enough support to avoid one) there are some rules against unfair practices.[27] Any ballot is only part of a long process. If your application for union recognition fails, you can't bring another one for three years.

If the CAC awards union recognition, the union then has to try to negotiate a collective bargaining procedure. If agreement isn't reached with the employer, the CAC imposes recognition with very limited bargaining rights only covering pay (not including pensions), hours and holidays. Though the law can force an employer to negotiate, they can't force the employer to negotiate meaningfully. Unless workers build real power, collective bargaining may deliver little or nothing.

Workers must build power: union recognition can only help consolidate and institutionalise it.

FACILITY TIME

'Facility time' is the jargon for the time within working hours that reps (and occasionally union members) get from the employer to deal with union business when we have won union recognition. In many jobs, winning facility time is a huge boost to union organisation – particularly if reps would have little opportunity to speak to most other workers while doing their jobs. It can help widen participation – while some find it easy to do union work outside working hours, that's less realistic for people, usually women, with a lot of caring responsibilities.

Arrangements for facility time vary wildly. In some workplaces too few reps are allowed time, or the time is so restricted that reps can barely cover casework, let alone campaigning and organising. The right to reasonable facility time is in legislation (see note 23) and if an employer refuses a reasonable request, you can complain to an Employment Tribunal (ET). Your rights are explained in the *Acas Code of Practice on Time off for Union Duties and Activities*.[28] Facility time shouldn't be 'time off' - it's time to do important work. You should treat legal rights as a minimum, not a maximum, and push for the facilities workers need to organise effectively. In some jobs, being allowed to do union tasks in work time doesn't stop the work piling up for when you get back. It is vital to negotiate a reduction in workload or targets to make being a rep bearable, and to ensure that the reduced workload doesn't mean getting all the worst jobs or allowing your skills to get out of date.

The law only provides paid facility time for certain roles and tasks, which are known as 'union duties'. Other union tasks are known as 'union activities', for which the law only provides unpaid facility time. For example, many unions encourage members to elect equality reps and environmental or green reps, but neither role is currently recognised in law so isn't automatically entitled to paid facility time. If you can't force your employer to recognise these roles, you may need to 'double up' the roles with ones that are recognised by having equality reps also being workplace reps and environmental reps being safety reps – but not taking on the full normal responsibilities of their second role. They can then gain access to facility time using their recognised roles to deal with many (but not all) equality or environmental issues. If you have environmental reps, try to ensure they focus on the big issues such as pushing the employer to decarbonise its operation while protecting workers, rather than getting sucked into employer greenwash or trivia.

Facility time isn't without its dangers. At the extreme, there are workplaces where some reps treat facility time as 'time off' work that they'd rather avoid and who cling on to union positions as a cushy option. Even when this isn't the case, management may portray it that way to turn workers against the union. This is another reason why reps, while maintaining the privacy of members we are helping, need to communicate with workers and report on what we do.

There are particular risks if reps have lots of facility time, such as the majority or even all of their working week. The longer a rep is in this position, the greater the dangers. Firstly, if you are in that position (I was for a number of years), you have less first-hand knowledge of the issues on the job. You are more reliant on other people telling you and it's harder to spot what's important or organising opportunities. As a rep, you mainly hear when things go wrong, and it can be hard to maintain a balanced view of how other workers see things. Secondly, it can become hard to hand over your role to other people when you should. Your job skills may be rusty, making it hard to return to normal work. A knowledge and experience gap grows between you and other activists who spend less time on union work. Increased dependence on you combines with your reduced job abilities to increase the risk to you and your union or your employer victimising you. Thirdly, and perhaps most importantly, the rules on facility time push you to spend a lot of it dealing with management (or perhaps with paid officers) rather than your workmates. This can distort your perspective and in the worst cases reps can tend to see members as a nuisance and to value a good relationship with management above getting the best outcome for workers. These tendencies are even more prevalent for paid officers, which I discuss in Chapter 11. When reps spend a lot of time attending union conferences and committees not related to their employer, there's a tendency to build close relationships with paid officers and pick up some of their perspectives and weaknesses. I served for ten years on the national executives of Amicus and then Unite, and though it was useful, I was aware that the longer I was involved at that level, the more unhealthy pressure I was under. Ten years was quite enough.

Some activists take this critique even further and are more generally hostile to facility time. This is partly based on the experience of the 1970s. The retreat of a strong trade union movement began under the Labour governments of 1974–79 before Thatcher. Though 1979 marked the high-point of union membership in the UK (13 million), the solidarity that had enabled impressive victories in the early 1970s had been broken by union cooperation with Labour incomes policies which suppressed real wages. Workers paid a heavy price for unions' lack of independence from Labour in office. This coincided with big changes in the role of reps following the 1968 report of the Royal Commission on Trade Unions and Employers' Associations, known as the Donovan report. The report sought to rein in workers' militancy by giving the reps who led it training and better facilities and by encouraging the growth of full-time reps. In other words, it wanted improved facility time as a way to bureaucratise reps, disconnect them from workers and make them less militant. There is considerable debate about whether, and to what extent, this worked, and what part it played in the downturn of working-class power.

Activists need to be aware of the dangers of bureaucratisation but should look at their concrete situation. In 2018 and 2019, I interviewed reps and workers from several companies and examined their agreements. Rather than better facility time being linked to a partnership approach and less militancy, I found the reverse. The employers tried to minimise facility time, and where they had succeeded activists were overwhelmed by reactive individual and collective representation, leaving little time for proactive organising and campaigning. The lack of capacity caused by inadequate facility time was a barrier to organising and militancy.

Some practical guidelines are:

- Fight for enough facility time so that reps can do a good job without excessive impact on their home lives.
- Share out facility time – better three people with a day each than one person with three days a week.
- Ensure reps are spending time talking with workers, organising and campaigning, not too much time in meetings with management or in the wider union structures.
- Beware of keeping people in positions with lots of contact with management or paid officers for too long.
- Reps should report back to workers on what they are doing.

EMPLOYEE FORUMS AND WORKS COUNCILS

Employee forums are common, including in workplaces with no union organisation, but workers aren't always aware of them. Many employers set up staff forums or councils as a way of gaining workers' buy-in to their plans, channelling discontent in a harmless direction, and making independent workers' organisation seem superfluous. We shouldn't make the mistake of confusing 'voice' (having a channel to put forward views) with the power to get what we want. UK-wide 'Information and Consultation of Employees' (ICE) bodies and European Works Councils (EWCs) can serve these functions too, but also provide workers with collective statutory rights that can't be obtained through other routes. None of them get set up automatically; they require an initiative from workers or the employer. ICE bodies and EWCs are fairly common in large private sector companies. In this section, I outline the different types of structures and some of their organising opportunities and pitfalls before discussing strategies for dealing with them.

Information and Consultation of Employees

Though they originated from a European Directive, the Information and Consultation of Employees Regulations 2004[29] are still in force, applying to undertakings (usually an employer) with 50 or more employees in the UK. There is a detailed guide from the LRD.[30] The Central Arbitration Committee (CAC), the same body that deals with union recognition claims, deals with complaints about ICE bodies[31] and EWCs. As usual, I won't attempt to provide a full guide, but will draw out some of the organising issues.

The process of setting up an ICE body can be initiated by the employer, employee representatives or at least two per cent of employees (subject to a lower limit of 15 and an upper limit of 2500). In response to a 'data request' the employer must specify the number of employees in sufficient detail to show whether the undertaking is covered by the regulations, which can be useful information if pushing for union recognition. A 'pre-existing' ICE agreement from before the process was triggered must be in writing, cover all the employees, have been approved by the employees, set out how the employer is to give information to the employees or their representatives and seek their views on such information. If there was a valid pre-existing agreement, a request for a new ICE body has to be supported by at least 40 per cent of employees – a much higher hurdle – so beware of allowing one to be established. A pre-existing agreement could cover multiple undertakings, have different arrangements in different parts of an undertaking or even multiple agreements each covering part of the undertaking.

If the requirement for an ICE body is successfully triggered, there will be elections for reps to negotiate an ICE agreement. The election is an

opportunity to raise the profile of the union and its activists, for the elected reps to network and gain skills, and to communicate with employees. It's possible for the reps to negotiate an agreement that is worse than the default 'standard provisions', giving away the rights of the employees they represent. The standard provisions include a list of areas over which the employer must inform and consult employees through the ICE body. These include items that are not automatically included in union recognition and require earlier information and consultation on some that are. However, an employer cannot (though they often try!) discharge their obligations to deal with a recognised union by dealing with an ICE body. ICE agreements vary wildly in quality. Once ICE arrangements have been finalised, either by negotiation or using the standard provisions, there should be elections to the new body.

European Works Councils

European Works Councils (EWCs) are similar in many ways to ICE bodies but deal with matters affecting employees in more than one of the countries they cover.

EWCs originate from European Union (EU) legislation[32] which is transposed into national legislation in each country, with some national versions being significantly better than the UK one.[33] The UK's exit from the EU has caused confusion about the rights of workers in the UK in relation to EWCs. On the one hand, the legislation remains on the UK statute book. However, the scope of the EU legislation is countries in the European Economic Area (EEA), which comprises the EU plus Iceland, Liechtenstein and Norway. In other words, the EU legislation says UK workers are not included, and the UK legislation says we are. Many employers have been trying to kick UK worker representatives off EWCs and unions have been resisting this. For existing EWCs, the situation may vary depending on which country it is based in or even on the wording of the agreement. This is a rapidly developing situation, so it is worth seeking the latest advice from your union if there is an existing EWC or you are considering setting one up.

To be eligible for an EWC, a company (or group of companies) must have at least 1000 employees in the countries covered by the legislation and at least 150 in each of at least two. An EWC is created through a similar process as a national ICE body, starting with a request from employees or the employer. Reps are elected to a Special Negotiating Body (SNB) which tries to agree arrangements for the EWC. If that fails, default 'subsidiary' arrangements apply. Reps are then elected to the EWC itself. You can find out more in *European Works Councils: An LRD Guide.*

The fact that an EWC covers a group of companies rather than a single undertaking, as an ICE body does, can be a help if the employer fragments itself. Another important difference is the right to use experts, often paid officers, to advise the EWC. Workers have used this to hire consultants to crawl over company books and come up with alternatives to harmful proposals. In large companies, many of the most important decisions may be taken at a level above the legal entity that actually employs the workers in the UK, so access to information and consultation at a European level can be a help.

From an organising point of view, EWCs tend to be even more remote from the workers than ICE bodies, and this can be exacerbated if reporting back is poor. However, opportunities to build direct connections and relationships with employee representatives in other countries are rare. Such connections make it harder for the employer to feed different bullshit to workers in each country. They can help workers organise international solidarity. In some cases, EWCs help workers in the UK benefit from better legal rights or stronger unionisation in other countries.

Informal forums

Many employers set up informal employee forums which have no legal basis at all. Some managers see them as a way to gather workers' ideas and feedback to help them run the organisation more effectively. But they are often a tool for preventing workers organising independently and building power. They can funnel grievances into a powerless structure, divert vocal workers from organising and help the employer argue that a union is unnecessary. These informal forums vary dramatically. Some are regarded as a joke by workers and management alike. In other cases, management work hard to give them credibility as a non-union channel for workers' views.

Strategies

Despite the important differences you've seen between ICE bodies, EWCs and informal forums, there is a lot of commonality in the issues they pose for workers trying to organise.

Britain has no real tradition of non-union employee representation. The idea of works councils has been imported via the EU from countries such as Germany, where they date back to the 1920s. It is closely tied up with a partnership model that seeks to incorporate workers and their representatives into management decision-making. In some countries, certain decisions require works council approval, and there are even worker representatives on company boards. While this can seem attractive to unions in Britain struggling to get a seat at the table, it means a loss of independence. It's difficult to fight hard for workers' interests if our representatives share responsibility for decisions about how we are treated.

Many employers in Britain, including companies like Amazon, use forums of some sort as part of their union avoidance strategy. Employers often try to tie up worker representatives with confidentiality restrictions to stop them sharing information or getting informed feedback from constituents. This also obstructs the use of positions on forums to help organise. Activists elected to forums can easily find their time and energy soaked up there rather than building power. When unions are relatively strong, there is a risk that dealing with issues via a forum including reps who are non-members or even managers can dilute union influence.

These problems with forums have led some unions to oppose involvement with them outright, or to try to get ICE rights incorporated into union agreements so an ICE body isn't needed. However, not only do EWCs and ICE bodies provide additional legal rights, they also offer significant organising opportunities. The process of elections can raise the profile of unions and activists. For activists without union recognition, they can be a route to get some training and facility time, as well as access to senior management. Being on a forum can help you to communicate with workers and network with other reps.

In my opinion, there isn't one right answer – you have to assess the possibilities and dangers in your own situation. The most important thing is for pro-union workers to have a clear collective strategy for a forum, rather than tailing management's agenda. You could decide to side-line a forum and make it irrelevant. You could decide to take it over. Or something in between. But you should never allow a forum to be, or appear to be, a substitute for independent union organisation.

For example, my former employer had an ICE body and an EWC. There was a significant minority of union members in the company, but most

workers didn't yet have union recognition. We coordinated members to stand for the ICE body. Most referred to the union in their election address, raising its profile and enabling workers to contact them about it irrespective of whether they were elected. Having members on the ICE body helped us build a national network of union activists and reps that connected areas with recognition and those without. We gained information via the ICE body which helped us organise and communicated with employees about issues the union was campaigning on. Reps made visible to employees the difference in treatment between workers with union recognition and those without. Overall, it helped us extend union organisation from our stronger areas. It wasn't without difficulties though. In particular, some members on the ICE body put nearly all their energies into it and neglected building independent organisation. Our EWC enabled us to build links with trade unionists in other countries and give solidarity during disputes.

Key points

- Rights are double edged. They result from past victories but are defined by those in power in ways that legitimise their authority.
- Law in Britain mainly comes from primary legislation, secondary legislation, case law and law from the EU that is now part of UK domestic legislation.
- Employees have more rights than other workers, who have more rights than the self-employed.
- Get to know your contracts of employment and employer policies, but don't assume everything in them is valid.
- Many health and safety issues are great to organise around. If you don't have union recognition yet, can you get elected as a Representative of Employee Safety?
- Discrimination is rife. You need to understand and oppose it, winning workers to supporting each other. Be wary of employer Diversity & Inclusion initiatives.
- Redundancy and TUPE are organising opportunities, but make sure you don't just organise those about to leave.
- Union recognition is an important step where the employer agrees to deal with workers collectively through their union. It gives some extra rights, but without building power it delivers little.
- Facility time helps build union capacity and participation, but there are dangers if some people use a lot of it.
- Employee forums and works councils can be used to side-line unions, but you can use them to organise too – if you have a clear strategy.

Discussion questions

1. What do you need to find out about contracts and policies where you work?
2. What is your employer doing about discrimination and is it addressing the big issues?
3. What formal or informal consultation arrangements are there? How should you relate to them?

8
Planning action

This chapter will cover how to work out how hard it will be to win a concession, the different types of potential power that workers can draw on, how to analyse our own power and that of our enemies, how to plan to win a campaign and how to plan individual actions.

Just as you haven't lost until you give up, you haven't won until the relevant decision-maker concedes what you want. This happens when they decide that doing what you want serves their interests better than opposing you. In general, workers don't have much we can trade with our bosses in exchange for what we want, so winning depends on being able to credibly threaten disruption that would cost them more than what we want and ensuring they don't have other more attractive alternatives.

DISRUPTION COSTS AND CONCESSION COSTS

It's worth unpicking the phrase 'credibly threatened disruption costs'. Each word matters. A threat that the decision-maker doesn't believe you can or would deliver has no impact. You often have to demonstrate your capacity and willingness to impose costs on them. It is threatened costs that influence decision-makers, not costs already imposed, because they still bear past costs even if they concede. The disruption can be to anything that is important to the decision-maker, not just your employer's finances. They might be on the board of another company or want a knighthood. Costs don't just mean money. They could relate to a decision-maker's reputation or their control in the workplace. For example, in one local dispute, strikers visited un-unionised sites of the same company to help workers get organised in a union. From the employer's point of view, having their other sites unionised was a cost, so this helped us win even though the strike ended without workers at those sites joining it. Remember that while pressure unrelated to your employer may give the decision-maker a *reason* to concede, they usually still need a *justification* which they see as legitimate and can use with others.

The decision-maker will balance credibly threatened disruption costs against the cost of conceding what you want. Just as disruption costs aren't just money, neither is the concession cost. The decision-maker may be ideologically opposed to what you want. They may see conceding as a loss of control or power. They may worry about setting a precedent or harming their reputation or career.

At the start of a campaign, identify the decision-maker(s) and assess the concession costs as best you can, though you may revise this as you learn more. Key decision-makers may be beyond your employer, for example, if you need action from your employer's source of funding, or if your employer is going bust and you need to get it taken into public ownership.

In Chapter 2, I discussed a definition of power: 'the ability to achieve the outcomes you want'. So, your power reflects your ability to credibly threaten disruption costs.

DIFFERENT TYPES OF POWER

Different groups of workers have different types of potential power, and it is useful to help workers think about theirs and the implications for how they might win their demands. There are many ways of thinking about types of power. A good starting point is the categories Beverly Silver used in *Forces of Labor* (2003). She contrasts nineteenth-century textile workers with twentieth-century automotive workers – both of whom built powerful unions, but in very different ways.

Structural power

Some groups of workers have potential power because of where they are located in the production process or wider society. I previously discussed oil refinery workers who had the power to shut off fuel supplies to a large part of the country. Dockers and other workers in logistics hubs have the potential to cause massive disruption to trade. Some workers in the electricity supply industry, telecoms or IT have the power to shut down whole swathes of the economy. Perhaps less obviously, action by workers in schools and childcare can cause huge disruption across the economy as parents can't attend their own workplaces. The Covid-19 pandemic taught a lot of people about which workers really are essential to keep society and the economy functioning.

The idea of structural power can also apply to particular groups of workers within a workplace. Some manufacturing processes use a production line where the work moves from one group of workers to the next. Any group of workers along the line has the potential to stop the whole line. Planes can't take off or land at an airport without its fire service – a relatively small group of workers. The huge Nissan car plant in Sunderland was nearly brought to a halt when half a dozen IT workers threatened to strike.

One factor to consider is whether work is organised in parallel or sequentially. Sequential work doesn't just happen on a production line. On construction sites, work has to be carried out in the right order and particular trades are needed, along with the right supplies, at a particular time. Much office work is now organised into sequential workflows. Sequential work, if workers can't easily be swapped around, gives groups of workers much greater structural power. 'Just-in-Time' and 'Lean' production and distribution systems have tended to increase the structural power of many workers at the same time as putting them under more pressure. In contrast, if work is organised in parallel, such as when supermarket checkout staff operate tills independently from each other, action by a few workers doesn't stop everything.

Employers are often acutely aware of which workers have structural power. One common response is to separate them from other workers and treat them much better – separating grievances from power and hoping to prevent solidarity. Another is to try to reduce workers' structural power by changing technology or work processes.

Employers or the state may invest in breaking union organisation amongst groups with lots of structural power – it is dangerous to over-rely on them and neglect organising workers with less structural power. For example, one airport's management decided to break the power of their firefighters, without whom no planes could take off or land. They built a second fire station at the airport and recruited workers willing to scab (break a strike by working through it). They kept the two groups separate for a while, building up animosity, before mixing up the workers. When conflict broke out between the workers, management used it as an excuse to sack unionised firefighters. Unions at the airport had relied too heavily on the structural power of the firefighters and neglected organising the far larger numbers of workers in other roles, who were then unable to defend the firefighters. Even workers with the most structural power need solidarity from others when the stakes are high, particularly if state violence is deployed against them.

Market power

The most obvious aspect of market power is how hard workers are to replace. Not only does this affect workers' fear of dismissal, it also affects employers' ability to find people to cover our work if we take industrial action. It is also connected with whether workers believe they could readily get another job. Some workers are hard to replace but have skills and knowledge that are specific to that employer and which aren't easily transferrable. Market power helps workers feel less precarious.

A strike is a race. Can workers prove that we can sufficiently disrupt the employer's operation before the employer can seriously disrupt our social reproduction (our ability to sustain ourselves)? Another aspect of market power reflects how dependent workers are on their job. If workers have savings, an allotment, a community hall where food can be organised collectively, access to adequate state benefits or the ability to pick up casual work, we have more market power because we are better placed to outlast the employer.

Many workplaces include workers with widely varying market power. It helps to organise all of them. For example, in my old workplace there were some very hard-to-replace workers doing technical design and development work, and other workers in call centres who were easier to replace. The development work often had a timescale of weeks, months or years, while calls had to be answered in seconds. Taking action together was powerful. The involvement of the harder-to-replace workers made sacking strikers highly unlikely. Action by the call centre workers had a more immediate effect on the employer.

Associational power

Associational power comes from organising collectively – whether that is through a union, single-issue campaign, community group, rank-and-file network or political party. It allows pressure to be brought to bear on a decision-maker by many people or organisations acting together. Even unorganised workers have some associational power – social networks and connections. No workers can exercise collective power without organisation. To win, you may need more associational power if you don't have much structural or market power, or if, as Katy Fox-Hodess and Camilo Santibáñez Rebolledo's (2020) work suggests, you have so much structural power that the state or employer makes defeating you a strategic priority.

When textile workers in England organised in the nineteenth century, their work was largely done in parallel, with multiple machines in multiple mills performing the same tasks fairly interchangeably. To win, they had to build powerful unions that could strike across a whole region. In contrast, as the automotive industry grew, the sequential production line process meant sit-down strikes by small groups of workers could bring huge factories to a halt. Car workers needed less associational power than textile workers because they had more structural power.

Until the late nineteenth century, unions had often only organised workers with niche craft skills, aiming to control entry into an occupation and knowing that unity between workers with those skills could have a big impact. This pattern was shattered with New Unionism in the 1880s when women match workers, dockers and gas workers organised in general unions. Whereas craft workers' market power meant they only had to organise with certain workers who might replace them, these easier-to-replace workers had to organise everyone in their area and build much more associational power. Despite having strong structural power, dockers needed quite a bit of associational power to overcome their lack of market power.

In 2021, there was a lot of discussion[1] about the lessons from the failure of an attempt to unionise Amazon in Bessemer, Alabama. Amazon knows how vulnerable its big logistics hubs are to disruption, so it arranges its business to be resilient to one being shut down, with goods going via multiple routes and hubs. For Amazon workers to develop real power they would need to organise beyond just one workplace. Given the size of these workplaces and the volume of goods coming in and out, building associational power with community supporters who could blockade exits could also be very powerful. I'm not saying this to argue how to win at Amazon, but to illustrate why workers need to consider how their employer and their work is organised in order to plan how to win.

Another example would be attempts to unionise McDonald's. The decision-maker you need to target would be different depending what issue you are fighting over, and whether you work for a directly-owned store or a franchise. If you work for a single-store franchise, you might be able to make some gains just by striking at that store. But McDonald's as a whole suffers little impact (beyond brand damage, which can be significant) from the closure of one store, and the impact on wider society is limited if other fast-food outlets nearby remain open. Even at a single-store franchise, what you can win would be limited unless you challenged the relationship between the franchise and the corporation.

We should consider other aspects of associational power, not just union organisation. Many employers are susceptible to pressure due to their relationships with the state at national or local level – as customers, legislators, regulators, financiers, etc. Workers' associational power through political organisation adds to their power mix. For example, Manchester saw the longest bus strike in British history in 2021[2] and the fact that the Greater Manchester mayor planned to re-regulate bus services through franchising represented both an opportunity and a threat for the employer.

Some models of power treat 'moral' power – the pressure on an employer from being seen to be in the wrong – as a separate category. Moral power relies on ideological power, which I will cover later, but I think it is most useful to think about it as another variant of associational power because it is collective organisation and struggle that determines what is considered moral or immoral. A successful campaign can turn a particular type of employer behaviour into a public relations disaster. There are many examples of unions trying to do this, whether against not paying interns, zero-hours contracts, poverty pay, bogus self-employment or fire and rehire. Such campaigning doesn't just put pressure on an employer, it increases workers' sense of the legitimacy of our struggle and helps us win allies. All parties to industrial relations engage in what Richard Walton and Robert McKersie (1965) called 'attitudinal structuring' – trying to shape the ideological terrain on which battles will be fought – shaping what is seen as legitimate or immoral. For workers, this can only be effectively done collectively, as an element of, and an expression of, associational power. Activists often complain about the difficulties caused by the hostile or uninterested media. But while media outlets shape public opinion, they also have to reflect it or risk losing their connection with their audience. When workers have strong associational power, the media has to reflect our agenda more, or lose influence. I discuss the media more in Chapter 9.

It is increasingly common for unions to try to deploy moral power in disputes by targeting a brand associated with the mistreatment of workers. Some of the micro-unions working with low-paid outsourced workers rely heavily on this approach, knowing that big concessions to low-paid workers such as cleaners or security guards can represent a trivial cost to a wealthy client organisation. Unite's 'leverage' strategy often associates individuals and organisations with bad behaviour to try to force them to act. I will return to the question of leverage later in this chapter.

The need for associational power is one reason why, while your power is based on organising with your workmates, it is wise to make build relationships with other workplaces, unions, movements, community groups and activist networks.

Institutional power

One type of power that doesn't fit easily into Silver's model is institutional power, for example, legal enforcement. This isn't unproblematic, as discussed in Chapter 7, but the use or threat of the law features somewhere in many conflicts.

Workers can also use other institutions to apply pressure to an employer. Many employers need accreditation, sign up to ethical codes of conduct, are part of trade associations with particular standards, or compete for business awards. There could be particular educational establishments from which they tend to recruit workers.

Ideological power

People's decisions on how to behave are based on our experiences, but these are mediated through our ideas about how the world works, including understandings of the power relationships in society. The dominant ideology justifies, legitimises and reinforces the power of managers, the wealthy, the police, the courts, the government and all those who dominate society. This means that management don't need to rely on direct coercion all the time. They can often rely on workers' consent. The dominant ideology doesn't just come from education, the media or corporate training sessions; it is also generated by workers as we try to justify our own compliance with managerial rule.

Pro-management ideology doesn't completely dominate – or there would be no resistance. The Italian Marxist Antonio Gramsci used the term 'contradictory consciousness' to describe how workers' 'common sense' comprises both ideas derived from the ruling ideology and alternative ideas (Brook, 2013). For example, many workers in the early 1980s thought unions were too strong at the same time as having the 'good sense' to realise that their own union was too weak. Many accept management's 'right to manage' in general, but object to particular instructions. As discussed in Chapter 5, workers are ingenious at turning elements of managerial ideology to their advantage, and they also create elements of a view of the world opposed to the dominant ideology (Armstrong, Goodman and Hyman, 1981).

In Chapter 2, I discussed how ideas are vital for converting potential power to actual power. Jane Holgate (2021) treats ideological power as a separate category. This is a useful approach because different groups of workers have different ideological resources at different times. If a group has little awareness of the working-class movement and its struggles, they will find it much harder to apply their own potential power and win. This is one reason why what Holgate calls 'political education', which need not look at all like formal education, is an important part of organising. In *Revolutionary Rehearsals in the Neoliberal Age* (Barker, Dale and Davidson, 2021), Gareth Dale gives a powerful example, contrasting Poland with other countries in Central and Eastern Europe. There were several post-war waves of unrest across the region, but in Poland workers played a much bigger role than elsewhere from the 1970s. One factor in this was that

> networks of militants in Poland succeeded in keeping alive collective memories of resistance. The familiarity of sections of the workforce with the industrial-action repertoire and with trade-union norms and values were important factors that contributed to the success of strike action in the 1970s and 1980–81.
>
> (Barker, Dale and Davidson, 2021, p. 76)

By building our networks, making sure that workers are discussing struggles past and present, and debating the lessons of them, we can increase the ideological power of workers and make resistance more successful.

UNDERSTANDING OUR POWER AND THEIRS

It's valuable to get workers collectively discussing what types of potential power they have, and what would be required to use them. It raises workers' confidence to fight and helps develop a plan to win. It demonstrates the importance of unity and solidarity.

One technique for understanding our power and that of our enemies is Power Structure Analysis (PSA), which comes in many varieties. Probably the most common is a professional researcher or experienced organiser sitting at a desk with a computer and a phone, identifying individuals and organisations and their relationships. This is (much) better than nothing but has some serious limitations. It relies on information that is in the public domain or held by a few key people. It struggles to identify connections involving 'ordinary' people or to tap into our knowledge. And the process doesn't do much to educate workers about our power. McAlevey advocates supplementing research with a more participatory process where workers complete a survey (or give you the answers to fill it in for them) about all our own connections. An example is in Figure 8.1.

All kinds of useful connections and patterns may emerge from the answers, and getting workers together to discuss the results can prompt more information and ideas.

Another simple exercise you can use for PSA is to put workers involved in the campaign into small groups and give them a sheet of flipchart paper, some sticky notes and pens. You ask them to write the names of individuals and organisations on the sticky notes and position them on the paper. Workers' power isn't something that stands on its own, it is always in relation to the power of others, such as their employer or the state. The most sympathetic organisations to your cause go on the left, the most hostile on the right. The most influential or powerful go at the top, the least at the bottom. You could think of the most powerful as those who actually take the decision, then those who actively participate in the decision-making process, then those who influence the process, those who can get decision-makers' attention but have little influence, right down to those whom the decision-makers wouldn't even be aware of. As workers compare their charts, they are discussing and learning about who has what power. It often becomes apparent that the 'obvious' potential allies might be very sympathetic but have little power to improve things. You can drill down into the

Growing stronger to win more

Name.. Date...

Employer.................................... Workplace...............................

Shift... Department...........................

Private email............................... Mobile phone.........................

Do you consent for your data to be processed by the union? YES / NO

What are the most important changes you want to see in your **workplace**?

If you were elected in charge of **your town/city** tomorrow, what would be the three things at the top of your agenda?

Is there anything you volunteer for outside work? (**be specific**)

Are there any groups, clubs or organisations **you or a member of your family** are involved in? (**be specific**). For example:

- Sport group?
- Charity?
- Church or other religious congregation?
- Neighbourhood or community group or centre?
- Migrant, language or nationality-based group?
- Campaign group or political party?
- Regular pub?
- Music or other performance group?
- Educational group?
- Other?

Which **family members live locally**? What do they do? Which union are they in, if any?

Do you have **any other connections** to anyone who has some kind of profile, power or influence? E.g. MPs or other elected officials, celebrities, media people, religious figures. (**be specific**)

Figure 8.1 Survey form for Power Structure Analysis

types of power for each sticky note. Bear in mind that these are *not* the same types of power discussed above for workers. Relevant power for allies and enemies could include ability to mobilise people to take action, ability to turn out voters, influence over media and public opinion, expertise, money, and relationships. As a group you can discuss not only what you could do to move the people or organisations leftwards on your chart, making them more supportive, but also how you could increase the power of those who are supportive and marginalise those most hostile.

Remember that the current attitude of an individual or organisation can be changed but changing their underlying interests, if it is possible at all, generally requires you to change their circumstances in a much more fundamental way. As Arnie Graf (2020) points out, interests aren't just material, they also include needs for recognition, meaning and respect.

You can approach a strategic PSA using eight steps:

1. Sketch the competing agendas – yours and those causing the problems.
2. Define the systemic problems or conditions negatively impacting on your side.
3. Identify the decision-makers over the problems.
4. Outline the major relevant issue or policy battles going on.
5. Identify your major organised opponents.
6. Identify the major organised forces whose position is unclear.
7. Identify the major organised potential allies.
8. Identify relevant unorganised forces.

The scale of this task is clearly different if you are organising on multiple issues across a major city or planning to win one battle in one workplace.

PLAN TO WIN

Early in almost every campaign, you need a credible plan to win. This doesn't mean that you need to have the details fully worked out for every eventuality, but you should have identified the decision-makers over your issues, assessed the costs to them of conceding and know how you could credibly threaten a disruption cost that is considerably higher – to allow for your estimates being inaccurate.

Remember that concession costs and disruption costs both include elements which aren't financial. Some smaller fights can be won without threatening the employer with financial costs. For example, managers value their control, so action which threatens that may get results. Someone once told me a story about a protest by prisoners which illustrates this well. As they were returning to cells, each in turn whispered to the same guard 'the prison only runs with the cooperation of the prisoners'. It's easy to imagine how powerful this action would be – it conveys the fact that the prisoners are organised and tells the guard that they are losing control. Workers in a university library won by all refusing to speak to one senior manager, even in meetings – using their associational power to make a credible threat to managerial control. You need to understand the self-interest of the decision-makers and how you could damage it.

Without a plan to win, you risk leading people into a defeat which may harm them, you and the organisation you are trying to build. Without a plan to win that you can explain clearly, you will find it hard to involve people. Workers aren't stupid – they are prepared to take some risk if they believe they have a realistic chance of winning something important to them, but they generally won't if the goals are smaller than the risks or if they don't believe the plan can work.

Campaigning without a credible plan to win means going into battle preferring to lose than not fight. There aren't many situations where workers feel so strongly that they want to do this, or where it would be right to do so. It's the industrial equivalent of a suicide mission. On the other hand, if you lose a battle despite having a plan to win, you may still build power in the process. A plan helps prevent people being disoriented and demoralised by setbacks and helps workers learn from them.

In each battle, you need to polarise people about the issue and pin the blame on the individuals responsible (Graf, 2020). You'll then need to be able to lower the temperature as they make concessions, unless you are immediately pushing for more. In most of our lives, we want relationships where we are liked. Relationships with opponents are different – they are 'public relationships' where it's far more important to be respected than to be liked.

When making your plan, remember that decision-makers make concessions based on anticipated future disruption costs, not disruption already suffered that they can't avoid by conceding. This is why most organisers avoid 'firing all their bullets at once', preferring to escalate disruption over time, so that early action demonstrates the capacity to inflict future disruption. It's important not to misunderstand this though. An immediate, indefinite, continuous strike (see Chapter 9) where workers stay out until they win is often highly effective if you can pull it off. In many industries, the disruption escalates even if the action doesn't – an organisation may run down stocks, lose customers or exhaust the capacity of management to work long hours to cover strikers' work. One exception to the general rule of escalation is if you are going for a quick win against an unprepared target. Many employers who have never previously experienced collective action by workers may not believe workers will really do it. Calling lots of action quickly can force them to concede by denying them time for preparations a more experienced employer would already have made.

When planning escalation, remember that the employer won't be passive. The longer you keep doing the same thing, the more the employer can take countermeasures. For example, during a strike, an employer may subcontract work to other companies, transfer work to other locations or train up other staff to cover strikers' duties. It's wise to think in advance about what you would do to pressure the decision-makers if striking alone wasn't enough.

Escalation doesn't always mean doing more of the same – there are many ways to apply pressure – even an indefinite, continuous strike can be escalated. Action can be spread to different groups of workers and different locations. While the organising methods of Saul Alinsky have been widely criticised[3], he was spot on when he argued in *Rules for Radicals* (1972) 'wherever possible go outside of the experience of the enemy' and 'a good tactic is one that your people enjoy'.

Leverage

The term leverage has been popularised by Unite, but it is nothing new. Just as a lever enables you to apply greater force to an object by using a pivot point, a leverage campaign seeks to apply greater pressure to a decision-maker by doing so indirectly. For example, if your employer has an important customer who might switch supplier, pressure on that customer might force your employer to concede quickly. Actions which might not be powerful enough on their own to force your employer to concede might be enough to force other individuals or organisations to act – for example, by contacting your employer to ask what is going on, or making a public statement about your issue.

Secondary targets for a leverage campaign could include customers, suppliers, partners, communities, investors, other companies in a group, industry associations, regulatory authorities, the media, politicians, councils, devolved governments[4], competitors and the individuals associated with them. Some examples may illustrate the point. During a dispute with Mayr-Melnhof Packaging (MMP) over the sacking of its Bootle workforce, Unite found out that the boss in Austria was active in his local church and leafleted the congregation to tell them about his behaviour. During a dispute with Go North West buses in Manchester, Unite contacted Swedish unions because the Go Ahead group was bidding for a huge contract in Sweden, where the company's conduct would have been unlawful. Unions organising cleaners often go after the wealthy companies owning or using the buildings rather than the workers' own employer. Gaining support and solidarity from workers elsewhere in the supply chain (customers, suppliers and distribution) has always been a staple tactic for strikers. The pressure isn't always financial. We once arranged for strikers to demonstrate opposite a marquee where our boss was due to speak at a Tory Party conference fringe meeting. The company caved in the night before. This illustrates another point about leverage – for some of your actions, you want the employer to know in advance what is coming their way, so they can avoid the threatened disruption cost by conceding first.

While big leverage campaigns need lots of expertise and resources from beyond the workers involved, it's perfectly possible for workers to use elements of this approach ourselves. In a strike by UNISON care workers in Birmingham, the workers themselves leafleted the wards of council cabinet members. I worked for a company that supplied many high street stores. It was relatively easy for workers to identify the customers and turn up with flags, leaflets and a public address system to make our presence known. If you're hitting a secondary target, be clear what you are asking them to do, and what it will take for you to stop targeting them. Are you asking them to issue a public statement? To contact your employer with a particular message? To cease trading with your employer? It can help to prepare letters to give to the people at the target location on the day and to send to management at the top of their organisation.

Leverage campaigns vary enormously, even if you get support for one from your union, and the differences matter. Some 'corporate campaigns' put the employer at the centre and follow all their connections to find potential targets. Though this is a useful way to think about your target, such campaigns often miss opportunities. At the other extreme, a campaign can put workers at the centre and map out all the connections workers have to individuals and organisations which might be able to apply pressure. The sort of Power Structure Analysis (PSA) discussed earlier in this chapter is at the heart of such an approach. Many people look back fondly at the support that some large workplaces, at the heart of their local community, used to be able to draw on, when most people lived near their work. But the flipside of workers commuting from bigger areas these days is that they will have more varied connections rather than shared ones.

A danger with leverage is that it can be seen as a substitute for workers' own collective action. Workers may see it as an alternative, so they don't need to organise or fight themselves. Or, if leverage helps them win, they can lose the sense that it was their own victory. Workers owning and feeling proud of their successes is vital for building confidence and combativity. It's vital to ensure that leverage actions are not taken by paid union staff alone, leaving workers themselves and their supporters passive. Workers need to retain control of both the strategy and the implementation, and ensure that their collective action remains central. Another problem is that unlike workers' solidarity action, most leverage depends on portraying an employer as unusually unethical. This can't be done for every fight – not just because some issues are harder to portray in moral terms, but also because we can't portray every employer as especially bad – it can only work against one or two at a time.

Plan each action

Once you have your overall plan to win, you need to plan individual actions. Actions without a purpose are just letting off steam. It is helpful to think of three objectives for each action:

1. *A campaign objective*: winning something that moves you towards your overall goal. For example, this could be getting a secondary target to make a helpful statement or getting your primary target to recognise the campaign by reacting.
2. *A mobilisation objective*: e.g. how many people take part or getting particular allies to join in.
3. *An organising objective*: how the action will improve the workers' power, for example, by being used as a structure test, checking that you have correctly identified leaders, improving your organisation or educating people.

You often want your action to give your target a dilemma – a choice between giving you a win or appearing to overreact and undermining their legitimacy and control.

Being clear what you are trying to achieve from an action not only helps you plan it better, it helps you assess how it went. Arnie Graf (2020) argues strongly that you should get people together immediately after an action to collectively evaluate how it went. This maximises collective learning from the action and, particularly if things didn't go well, provides mutual support.

The ACORN community union has some great guidance for action that involves confrontation. It was written for meeting a landlord but can be adapted to other situations such as a 'march on the boss' – a collective action workers can often stage without leaving work. Acting in a collective and disciplined way displays organisation and power – adding to the impact of the action. Be clear in advance what your demands are, including deadlines, and have a written copy you can hand over. Agree in advance how you will deal with different responses from the manager and run through the confrontation beforehand. Arrive and leave together. Keep control of the situation: don't get into a debate or get side-tracked – say and do what you've planned, get a reaction, and leave on your own terms. That gives you time to consider their reaction and your next steps together. It's useful to have clear roles when heading into a confrontation. These, adapted from ACORN's approach, aren't quite the same as for a negotiation, which I cover in Chapter 10:

- *Opener/closer*: introduces the group to the target and explains why you are there. Decides when to end the confrontation. Everyone needs to agree to respect their decision – disarray in the presence of the target undermines the message. They need to be observant and have calm judgement.
- *Demander*: explains the group's demands and offers a written copy.
- *Testimonials*: people who explain how the issues affect them personally. This adds emotional pressure, gives them back some power and provides material for publicity.
- *Checker*: firmly (but not aggressively) stops the target interrupting or controlling the conversation, using phrases like 'let them finish' and 'listen to them'.

- *Recorder(s)*: one or more people responsible for recording what happens by taking notes, recording audio, photos or video, depending on the situation. The record is used to review how the action went, and for publicity. A clear record can help protect you against false allegations of violence and deter violence against you.[5] Recorders need to position themselves to capture key moments, such as the target's reaction and response to the demands, and avoid getting embroiled in events.
- *Police liaison*: engages with any security guards or police. It's often helpful to try to move these discussions a short distance away to avoid disrupting the action or distracting people, but stay in sight for safety. The liaison should be calm and reasonable and clear about the options you've discussed together in advance for dealing with them. Your action will often be over before the liaison has explained why everyone is there and what's happening.

There's a 'battle for interpretation' after each conflict ends. People's understanding of what happened and why will shape what happens next. That's why, when workers win a concession, employers often try to claim that they had always planned it, or that it was due to changed circumstances, rather than resulting from workers' action. But this isn't just about employer spin. Negotiators may fall into the trap of believing it was their skill that achieved the result. Workers may come up with weird and wonderful explanations for an outcome. The more you can reinforce the crucial role of workers' own collective action, the better placed you'll be for the next battle.

The interpretation is even more important when things go badly. It's all too easy for workers to turn on each other, for activists to blame the workers, or for people to conclude that the battle could never have been won. Put some effort into working out how the result could have been better – what would workers have had to do differently? – and popularise it as widely as possible. This might be as simple as the need for more organising. In other cases, it might be about building a better solidarity network, planning the campaign better or avoiding a blunder. Quite often, problems arise from the relationship between the workers and their reps on the one hand, and the wider union structures on the other – issues I discuss in Chapter 11. Sometimes there is an element of bad luck. Whatever the lessons, fight for an interpretation that helps workers be stronger and more successful next time.

Key points

- Workers win by being able to credibly threaten a greater disruption cost for the decision-maker(s) than the cost of the concession we want. These costs are not just financial.
- Different workers have different mixtures of potential power: structural power, market power, associational power, institutional power and ideological power.
- We can map out the power of potential allies and opponents, and our connections to them, using Power Structure Analysis.
- Make a credible plan to win for every campaign. This should include proving the credibility of your threatened disruption cost, possibly by escalation.
- Leverage means applying pressure on a decision-maker via a secondary target.
- Plan each action to have a campaign objective, a mobilisation objective and an organising objective.
- Have clear roles in any confrontation.
- Fight the battle for interpretation after every conflict.

Discussion questions

1. What mixtures of potential power do different workers have where you work?
2. Thinking of a change you would like to see: how much disruption cost would you need to credibly threaten to win it?
3. Thinking of a collective action you might take (e.g. a letter to the boss which workers sign): what would be the campaign, mobilisation and organising objectives?

9
Industrial and direct action

Having looked in the previous chapter at how we plan effective action, we now look at industrial and direct action in more detail. I'll start by briefly discussing the repertoire of collective action, look at the industrial action process in detail and consider types of industrial and direct action. The chapter then moves on to practicalities of strikes, money, participation and democracy; building solidarity; handling the media; and winning and settling a dispute.

Workers have a huge range of collective actions at our disposal. It's not just that strikes come in many flavours. There is industrial action short of a strike (often abbreviated to ASOS). Workplace occupations can take the form of sit-down strikes or work-ins. There is every sort of direct action available to any other group of people. Robert Tressell's classic book *The Ragged Trousered Philanthropists* (2003 [1914]) described workers' acts of sabotage. Airline workers have refused to smile. French workers invented the term 'le bossnapping' for an occupation where managers were held hostage. Petitions and the 'march on the boss' are widely used as structure tests. IT workers have shut themselves in server rooms and threatened to unplug equipment. US teachers popularised 'wear red' days.

A great activity with any group of workers is to come up with as many ideas for collective action as possible[1], then rank them in order of how risky they would be for participants. This can help you plan a campaign of escalating action. The riskier the action you plan to take, and the more it could lead to individuals being singled out, the stronger you need to be to protect each other from employer pressure or reprisals.

THE INDUSTRIAL ACTION PROCESS

Industrial action (strikes and ASOS) is a key weapon in the hands of workers, so it's worth looking in detail at how to take it. In Britain, the law makes lawful industrial action very hard, and in some cases impossible. So before

diving into the process for lawful industrial action, it's worth considering the alternative.

British law provides no positive 'right to strike'. Instead, it provides limited 'immunities' to protect unions from being sued for organising a lawful strike, and compensation for workers who suffer retribution from their employer for taking part in one. Contrary to popular myth, striking outside the legal framework is not illegal (banned by law), it is merely unlawful (there is no law permitting it).[2] There are risks involved in unlawful industrial action:

- If the union fails to 'repudiate' the action and work to end it, it is open to being sued for damages. More importantly, as you will see later, an employer can seek a court injunction against the union telling it what to do, and failures to comply expose it to unlimited fines and sequestration (confiscation) of its assets for contempt of court.
- Workers who take part in unlawful industrial action have no legal recourse if the employer responds with dismissal or other disciplinary sanctions. We are wholly reliant on the power of our action and sticking together to protect each other.

While some unions, such as Unite and CWU, have become skilful at avoiding repudiating members' actions, there are no recent examples of unions backing ongoing unlawful action in the face of an injunction. As a result, such action tends to be organised by rank-and-file workers themselves. Sometimes reps leave meetings while votes are taken in order to reduce the risk of them being singled out. In other cases, a secret signal for a walkout has been pre-agreed. But the main ingredient of successful unlawful strike action is a collective determination to stay out until everyone goes back together.

At team level, it's often possible for action to be organised informally without formal 'union' involvement, let alone ballots. The union's paid officers have plausible deniability and in many cases it won't even occur to managers that this might be industrial action. Individual managers are often reluctant to escalate things if higher management or HR would discover that they've lost control of their team. For example, workers not doing certain tasks or working slow can be highly effective. Workers discussing issues in work time or going to discuss them with a manager can also hold up the job without walking out. Construction workers 'cabin up' – refusing to leave the canteen or changing room until their demands are met. Some workers stage 'sick ins', where lots of workers go off sick at the same time. While this does risk disciplinary action, it's hard for the employer to prove which individuals weren't genuinely ill.

During the Covid-19 pandemic, lots of workers learned for the first time about the possibility of walking off the job under health and safety legislation. Under section 44 of the Employment Rights Act 1996, it is unlawful for an employer to inflict 'detriment' on an employee for refusing to work in circumstances that we 'reasonably believe' cause serious and imminent danger.[3] It's not industrial action, so there's no requirement to ballot. It's not relevant legally whether the employer shares your reasonable belief. A big weakness in this right is that it can only be exercised individually. If the union organises for people to collectively walk off the job, that would be regarded as unlawful industrial action. The National Education Union (NEU) put huge energy into educating members about their rights and why they should reasonably believe there was serious and imminent danger from the coronavirus, leading to many schools being shut and thousands of lives saved. It's far more common for such action to happen at workplace level. For example, I led walkouts on two occasions when workers were exposed to fumes and the employer was unable or unwilling to tell us what the chemicals were, let alone provide risk assessments for them. In reality, your main protection is the number of people participating and the strength of your organisation, not the law, but safety law can help legitimise action.

The process for lawful industrial action is designed to prevent action and to make what still takes place as ineffective as possible. The process is bureaucratic and complex, giving employers' lawyers plenty of opportunity to seek injunctions. To secure an injunction to prevent a strike, the employer doesn't have to prove their case, or even that they are likely to win. They only have to demonstrate that there is a serious question to be tried. In some cases, injunctions are granted without the union being allowed to present a defence!

Giving notice for a lawful strike requires the union to provide information to help the employer organise scabbing. It delays action, often giving employers time to implement changes and create a fait accompli. However, following the legal framework can help convince workers to take action, not just by reducing the fear of negative consequences and bringing benefits of official union support, but also because the law confers legitimacy on lawful strikes. Nonetheless, always remember that you have a choice between lawful and unlawful strike action, and there are pros and cons to both.

It's worth finding out as much as you can about the process – both in law and in your own union. Many unions have their own procedures to follow before they will initiate a ballot – you want to know all the requirements and hurdles before you hit them. Because strikes aren't that common, many paid officers have limited experience and give wrong or unhelpful advice. The LRD has a useful booklet *Taking Industrial Action: A Legal Guide*, there's a government *Code of Practice*[4], and many unions have their own guides too. Here, I'll just try to give a short summary of the current legal process for lawful industrial action. *Always check the latest rules.*

First, you need a 'trade dispute' with your own employer. This is narrowly defined to restrict the issues you can take lawful action over and to prevent solidarity action and political strikes. But, as a guide to striking for climate (workers-can-win.info/climate-strike) shows, with a bit of imagination you can find a trade dispute linked to most issues. You must attempt to resolve the trade dispute with the employer before taking industrial action. At a minimum, this usually entails the union putting the issues in writing, seeking a meeting with management to discuss them and engaging meaningfully if talks do take place. This doesn't have to take ages.

You have to work out who will be included in the ballot. This can only be workers for the employer with the trade dispute, though there are some circumstances where a single ballot can cover several associated employers who are party to the same trade dispute.[5] You must include all union members who will be called on to take part in the action and exclude anyone expected to be off work throughout the period when action could take place (e.g. long-term sick, maternity leave). Ballots are often carried out separately for each workplace, but multiple workplaces can be balloted together if there is at least one member in each workplace directly affected by the trade dispute, or if you ballot all members employed by the employer, or all members in a particular category (e.g. job type) employed by the employer.

Since the Trade Union Act 2016 made it harder to win industrial action ballots by imposing turnout thresholds, there has been a lot of debate about the merits of 'aggregated' or 'disaggregated' ballots. An aggregated ballot is a single ballot covering multiple workplaces or associated employers, producing a single ballot result. A disaggregated ballot has separate results for each workplace or employer. Some unions favour aggregated ballots because a high turnout and 'yes' vote in better organised workplaces can offset weaknesses elsewhere, and if the result is positive, all the workers can take action together. But an aggregated ballot means putting all your eggs in one basket – risking weaker workplaces pulling down the overall result and preventing any action at all. Many unions favour disaggregated ballots because they ensure at least some workplaces can take action, and others that missed the thresholds can be re-balloted later with greater focus. A disaggregated ballot can help motivate activists in each workplace to run an effective campaign, knowing they are responsible for their own result.

Before you can ballot, you need to check that membership details are correct and up to date – even small errors can give employers the excuse to seek injunctions against action. Try to keep membership records accurate all the time so that you are 'strike ready', but you'll still need to check them for a ballot. You can treat the process of cleansing membership records as a dry run for getting the vote out in the ballot – using email and texts to get most people to confirm or correct their details, then individually following up those who don't respond. We used the 'mail merge' tool in Microsoft Word to generate emails and letters to send to members showing the information we held. Not only was confirming or correcting it easier and less error prone than asking people for fresh information each time, but people are more

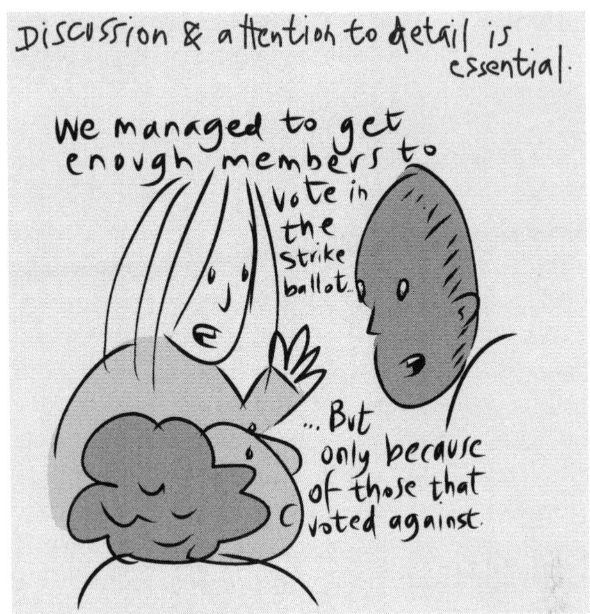

likely to respond if you send them wrong information about themselves. You can use a bulk text message service to contact everyone and verify you have their correct mobile number, just following up verbally with those who don't reply. Having personal emails and mobile numbers will be a big help when you need to get out the vote. You need to keep membership lists up to date throughout the dispute as they are needed every time notice of action is served.

You need to decide what forms of action you want to ballot for. This could be strike action, ASOS or both, and I'll discuss the pros and cons shortly. If it's both, you must include separate questions. If you plan to take ASOS, you need to decide what types of action, as this will be included on the ballot paper. It can be surprising what courts regard as strike action that most people would see as ASOS. Bear in mind that even if you only want to take ASOS, the employer might try to deduct 100 per cent of earnings for 'partial performance', leading members to want to strike instead. In general, it's safest to include both questions and get a 'yes' vote to both.

The union will issue a notice of ballot to the employer at least seven days before it opens. This also has to be shared with members. Other than where members pay their union subs by deduction from salary (known as 'check off' or 'DOCAS' – Deduction Of Contributions At Source), the union has to provide a breakdown of the numbers of members to be balloted by workplace and category (usually job). The union must provide a summary of the trade dispute, a sample ballot paper and an indication of the period(s) when industrial action of each type is expected to take place.

The ballot will be fully postal and include a scary legal statement about industrial action breaking your contract (that's the point!). You can include a leaflet with the ballot paper – this is the single most important bit of campaign material, so make it good! Your audience is members who may not vote or may vote 'no', and you need to motivate them to vote right away. Chapter 5 included tips on written communication.

As soon as the result comes in, it must be notified to the employer and members promptly if any action might result. The Trade Union Act 2016 introduced new hurdles. Not only do you need a majority of those who vote to vote 'yes' to the question, you also need to exceed ballot turnout thresholds. In all cases, at least 50 per cent of those entitled to vote must have done so. For 'important public services', at least 40 per cent of those entitled to vote must also vote 'yes'.

If action is to go ahead, the union must serve a 'notice of action' at least 14 days in advance, again including lots of detail which employers can use to plan scabbing or seek injunctions. These notices reflect the latest membership changes, including new joiners. Further notices of action must be issued for additional or different action, but action can be cancelled without any notice requirements. Though managers often try to pressure workers into doing so, there's no requirement for a worker to individually inform their manager in advance of whether they plan to strike or not. Why tell them? Managers use such information to refine their strike-breaking plans. Anyone in scope of the ballot (e.g. locations, bargaining units, grades) can take part in lawful action under the ballot, whether they are members of the union or not.

Though the ballot result is valid (meaning that action can be lawfully taken under it) for six months from the date the ballot closed, the strongest legal 'protection' (rights to compensation) for strikers only lasts for twelve weeks from when action started. As a result, it's common practice in a long dispute to run a new ballot before the twelve weeks expire. Because of the lengthy process, you'll need to allow at least three weeks plus the ballot period if you want to avoid gaps between the twelve-week periods when workers feel safest. Some unions (e.g. Unite) require a re-ballot to be on a new trade dispute, as they fear that a court might decide that the twelve-week period doesn't restart if it's substantially the same dispute. If you are taking this approach, make sure you've got a trade dispute ready in time. This can often be achieved by simply highlighting different aspects of the same real-life situation and careful choice of wording.

You can see from this summary that the process for lawful industrial action is slow and bureaucratic. If you go down this route, make sure you get the result you need – not just a 'yes' vote but a high turnout too. Many unions encourage the use of consultative ballots to check the support is there before going to a statutory ballot. If you run a consultative ballot in a way where you can tell which area a vote came from (even if it is anonymous) you can use it as a limited structure test. Posters, flyers, emails or texts counting down the days till the ballot opens can ensure people are expecting the ballot papers when they arrive. Many unions encourage you to contact every member one-to-one before and during the ballot process. In some cases, a group of people use tools to contact members as a phone bank or text bank. Getting members to photograph themselves posting off their ballot and post the photos on social media can help create a buzz. The CWU postal union uses gate meetings with members holding up posters for collective photos. An 'I voted' sticker can play a similar role. You could ask members to sign a 'pledge' to vote 'yes'. You should always ask members to tell you when they've posted off their vote. We used to use emails and text messages to ask people to do this, so we could quickly tick off a large minority who voted right away and concentrate our 'get the vote out' reminders and conversations on those who hadn't yet confirmed they had voted.

Having looked at the tortuous process of taking lawful industrial action and the relative pros and cons of unlawful action, we'll discuss different types of action you might take.

TYPES OF ACTION

A strike is a temporary stoppage of work by a group of workers to express a grievance or enforce a demand. When an employer refuses to allow employees to work unless they accept management's demands, this is known as a lockout. As Richard Hyman (1989) pointed out, strikes and lockouts can sometimes be hard to distinguish. In either situation, workers and management are both willing for workers to work – under their own preferred terms. Explicit lockouts have been rare in Britain for some time, with 'fire and rehire' being a preferred tactic for employers because they can seek to enforce terms without losing production.

You have seen that lawful industrial action can include action short of a strike (ASOS), and how actions that common sense would see as short of strike may be regarded as strikes by the courts. ASOS can take many forms. Common ones include overtime bans, work to rule or contract, go slows, or refusal to perform certain tasks. Before Just-in-Time production was common, workers often used overtime bans to deplete stocks before starting a strike. They can still be used to make a strike threat more powerful by starting to delay work with a deadline. ASOS appeals to many workers because it appears a way of pressuring the employer without losing so much pay. Employers can make a deduction from pay for 'partial performance', but more aggressive employers refuse to accept partial performance and deduct 100 per cent of pay. This is an argument against balloting for ASOS alone. If you have a mandate to strike as well, the employer may be more reluctant to make big deductions for fear that members will decide they might as well strike.

It's generally a mistake to see ASOS as an easy option. It's easier for management to put individual workers under pressure when we are in work than when we strike. Many forms of ASOS rely on individual workers refusing particular instructions, whereas striking is a more collective experience. It may seem counterintuitive, but you generally need stronger organisation to make ASOS a success than you do for a strike. Forms of ASOS that actually improve workers' lives (such as refusing to work away from home) or refusing onerous and boring tasks (such as completing timesheets or other paperwork) can be easier to implement. A great example of ASOS is transport workers refusing to accept fares, which seems sure to win public support. But this is much harder on London Underground than on buses, because even if passengers enter where ticket gates are held open, you can't be certain a manager or scab isn't operating gates where they will get off. Passengers aren't too happy if they have to pay a fine instead of a fare – illustrating how pulling off ASOS successfully can require tighter organisation than a strike.

Large groups of workers taking sustained action is expensive. No union can afford meaningful strike pay for a large proportion of members striking for long. Even Unite, which boasts a strike fund of over £40m, would burn through that in little over a week if 100,000 members received Unite's standard strike pay, which is currently £70 per day. Big, long strikes can happen. The miners' strike of 1984–85 lasted a year and involved well over 100,000 strikers. Sustaining that meant miners going into debt and selling possessions, as well as the working-class movement fundraising. Sadly, unlike in the 1970s, that solidarity did not extend to industrial action from other industries, which could have led to victory, nor to support from the leadership of the Labour Party. The whole movement paid the price for defeat. The cost of big strikes has always pushed some in the movement to favour 'selective action', where only some groups of workers strike, and sometimes the rest contribute financially through a regular levy to support them. The difficulty of successfully balloting large groups since the Trade Union Act 2016 has added to the attraction of selective action.

Selective action can be spectacularly successful. One of the best examples was the engineering unions' push for a shorter working week in the late 1980s, the 'Drive for 35'. Workers across engineering paid a levy to provide full pay for selected workplaces to take indefinite strike action, moving on to new workplaces as each settled. Though the settlements fell far short of achieving a 35-hour week, they did win a widespread reduction in working hours. My own employer reduced our working week by 30 minutes without loss of pay, and we weren't even covered by the dispute!

Historically, employers respond to selective action across an industry in two ways, both of which rely on employer associations with significant coverage and meaningful discipline. Firstly, employers not targeted may contribute financially to support those who are hit by strikes – the employers' equivalent of the workers' levy. Secondly, employers may lock out non-striking workers, refusing to allow workers not striking to work until the dispute is settled, imposing greater costs on the union. The lockout is also a key tool when selective action is taken within one company. Now, thanks to years of union ineffectiveness, employer associations are very weak in Britain's private sector. This would suggest a vulnerability to industry-wide selective action.

Selective action has drawbacks, particularly at workplace level. Workers' power is based on solidarity. At our most powerful, 'never cross a picket line' was treated as the eleventh commandment by millions of workers. Telling non-striking workers to cross picket lines undermines that. More generally, selective action prevents workers experiencing mass collective action and gaining such a sense of their own power.

If unions rely heavily on selective action, employers will find ways to counter it, whether through the creation of employer associations or by tackling the power of the groups of workers relied on to strike. Groups with lots of structural power can see it reduced due to technological changes. The employer may try to buy those groups off or divide them from the rest of the workforce. Their work can be moved to a different location in Britain or internationally – away from other workers. They may hire workers specifically to scab on key groups, as you saw in the airport example in Chapter 8. Workers have sometimes countered this using 'chequerboard strikes' during which everyone strikes, but at different times. This can wreak havoc in some work processes – but it often prompts a lockout.

Employers and the government know that solidarity is our biggest weapon. Not for nothing is 'one out – all out' a well-known slogan. That's why the Thatcher government made 'secondary' action – action over a dispute that isn't with your own employer – unlawful. If solidarity is to go beyond messages and money, it often has to circumvent or defy the law.

The 2021 Manchester bus strike, which defeated fire and rehire, involved drivers at one bus depot. The other depots in Greater Manchester were operated by competitors. Go North West attempted to break the strike by subcontracting services to other bus and coach companies. Supporters blockaded the depots that were being used to provide scab services[6] when, because of the anti-union legislation, strikers didn't feel able to. Even where workers don't feel confident to defy the anti-union legislation, workers taking action elsewhere can help a strike win. Drivers at Go Ahead depots elsewhere in the country could have taken lawful strike action over their own issues, knowing their employer was already stretched financially and managerially by the Manchester strike, giving both strikes a better chance of success. The union tried to get the Greater Manchester mayor, Andy Burnham, to ban companies that used fire and rehire from being awarded contracts when implementing his plan for bus franchising. Drivers at competitors' depots in Greater Manchester could have struck lawfully over their own issues, which would have put more pressure on Burnham. Go Ahead was already using the available scab subcontractors, making more strikes harder to break. More striking depots would have magnified pressure on the mayor to intervene. Even if the law deterred Unite from leafleting other depots to argue for workers to take action over their own issues, supporters could have done so. When the state tries to restrict our ability to take effective action, we need to be creative when we don't feel ready to defy these unjust laws.

If you are going to strike and you've decided who will be striking, you need to decide the pattern of strike days. In most cases, the most powerful action is a continuous, indefinite strike – which means staying out on strike until you win. Confusingly, this is often called an 'all out' strike, in the sense of 'going all out to win' rather than 'all out together'. Continuous strikes avoid management pressure on workers between discontinuous (on/off) strikes. They are particularly useful if workers would face a backlog of work each time they were back on the job. They are often easier to organise because a routine of picketing and other activities can be established. Continuous strikes avoid feelings of unfairness between workers whose normal work patterns may be affected differently by strike days. It's much easier to build support for a continuous strike – other workers see that this is a serious fight and are more likely to help, whether that's chipping in to a strike fund or more practical solidarity. Supporters who want to visit the picket know they can do so any day, rather than needing to keep track of strike days.

Discontinuous strike action, which ranges from short single strikes to complex patterns of strike periods, has its attractions. Workers, particularly in unions that don't offer much strike pay, may feel that they can't afford the loss of earnings of a continuous strike. This is sometimes misplaced – disputes with widely spaced strike days can drag on and need more strike days to resolve. In some industries, discontinuous action can cause more disruption per strike day. For example, some food or chemical production processes have to be shut down days before a strike and take several days to ramp up again afterwards. In some industries, a strike can leave vehicles or equipment in the wrong places, continuing disruption after the strike is over. It can be harder or more expensive for an employer to arrange cover for discontinuous strikes. Ultimately this could lead to an employer deciding to lock out the strikers until there's a settlement, to make strike-breaking more practicable. ASOS can supplement discontinuous strike action by preventing the employer clearing a backlog of work.

'Demonstration strikes' are another form of industrial action. Rather than attempting to force the employer to concede, they merely express discontent and demonstrate that the workers have the capacity to strike if we choose to. There was a period when one-day strikes were the norm, particularly in the public sector. They often served little purpose beyond letting off steam, but sometimes established the credibility of a threat or provided negotiators with an additional bargaining chip for a compromise. They are very different to strikes as part of a serious plan to win.

Industrial action is a powerful form of direct action, but the latter term is more often used for other forms of protest which deploy our own power rather than merely appealing to those in power. Just as the anti-union laws try to make strikes difficult and ineffective rather than banning them outright, they permit some picketing, but try to limit pickets to peacefully persuading workers not to cross a picket line at their own workplace. Sometimes peaceful persuasion is enough, but when all the might of the employer, the landlord, the bank and the media are trying to break your strike, more militant direct action is often needed to win. Legal restrictions on strikes and picketing have pushed some unions to explore other forms of direct action. In 2016, the Unite policy conference agreed a motion[7] committing the union to provide direct action training for activists and consider its use in disputes and campaigns.

Mass pickets may try to physically block workplace entrances or other strategically important locations.[8] Such action has been rare in Britain in recent years, but there are exceptions, such as the rank-and-file construction workers who have repeatedly blockaded or occupied major sites. The rarity of mass picketing isn't just because of the fear of police or court action, it also reflects a lack of confidence that workers will stick together enough to protect each other from employer reprisals. While effective mass picketing has always relied on support from the wider community, the dependence is increased when workers don't feel confident enough to mount an effective picket against their own employer. The community blockades during the 2021 Manchester bus strike didn't involve mass numbers but used a 'slow walking' tactic copied from anti-fracking protesters.[9] This was enough to stop services for an hour or two each time, but isn't sustainable without a much stronger movement or the strikers themselves taking part.

The tactic of workers occupying their workplace has a long history. An occupation prevents the employer bringing scabs in and ties up capital – the building and any equipment or stocks in it. Workers can be safer from violence when barricaded inside a workplace because any attack would risk damaging the employer's property. Work-ins are a variant of an occupation in which workers run the workplace without management. While not having the same economic impact as a strike, it challenges management control and, if linked to a wider movement, can create a political crisis to force government intervention, as during the successful work-in at Upper Clyde Shipbuilders (UCS) in 1972.

At the same time as curtailing lawful strike action, successive governments have attacked the right to protest, including the Public Order Act 1986, the Criminal Justice and Public Order Act 1994, the Criminal Justice and Police Act 2001 and the Serious Organised Crime and Police Act 2005. Anti-terror legislation has been used against peaceful protesters for everything from wearing a t-shirt[10] to protesting outside a power station.[11] As I write this in 2022, the Police, Crime, Sentencing and Courts Bill is being pushed through parliament.

Part of how repressive legislation works is by making people uncertain about what we can safely do, so that we restrict ourselves to less risky and less effective forms of action. We can't afford to police ourselves like this.

History tells us that when we comply with restrictions on our freedom, they are successively tightened, but when we make unjust laws unenforceable, they are scrapped. This isn't just about historic events like mass protests and strikes defeating the Industrial Relations Act 1971 and freeing the 'Pentonville Five' dockers jailed for picketing.[12] The police and courts don't enforce the law consistently; they judge what they can get away with. The bigger and broader the support for action, the less likely it will face repression – so solidarity is key.

STRIKES, MONEY, PARTICIPATION AND DEMOCRACY

If you've got a credible plan to win and workers have decided to strike, there's still lots to think about and do – how you sustain yourselves financially, keep participation and morale high, organise yourselves and take decisions.

Some unions, but not all, offer strike pay as a membership benefit, and this is tax free. This is easier for a general union like Unite, which is unlikely to have a big proportion of members striking at once, than for unions concentrated in one industry or occupation. In 2021, Unite increased its strike pay to £70 per day, payable from the first strike day. Find out early on what the rules, criteria and processes are for any strike pay in your union. You'll need one or two activists staying on top of this, making sure the union knows who to pay and resolving any problems. If members don't get paid on time it can cause chaos with their personal finances and undermine confidence in the union.

Whether or not your union offers strike pay, I strongly recommend creating your own strike fund in advance of any strike. This will enable you to cover costs associated with a strike immediately, provide extra money to top up strike pay where needed, and make it harder for paid officers to use their control of official strike pay to pressure members into accepting a deal they don't like.

In some cases, you may be able to create a strike fund officially through the union. In Unite, for example, a branch can vote to create its own fund and charge members an additional amount, collected with the standard union subscription fees. This won't work for every job though – your union may not offer this facility or the branch structure may not fit closely enough with your workplaces and employers. If you have to create your own fund, start well in advance – bank bureaucracy and money-laundering legislation make opening bank accounts slow and cumbersome. In some unions, paid officers may oppose you setting up your own strike fund. Workers sometimes get round this by setting one up separately from any official union structure. Whatever you do, ensure the money is properly accounted for. There's a useful online guide to setting up a strike fund.[13]

If you add money to your strike fund regularly, it can build up to a useful amount. There are many ways to do this. If you have access to any money via the union, for example, through a branch, you could propose regular contributions. You could ask members to set up standing orders, though getting good uptake is hard. Some workplaces run a regular lottery, football card or fundraising social events. Once your strike starts, don't be shy about fundraising. This isn't charity: people are contributing because they want you to win, and they know your outcome will strengthen or weaken their own position. I cover building solidarity later in this chapter.

Put in place a process where strikers can decide on any exemptions from the action. In many industries, it's not safe for every worker to strike. You might need workers to keep an eye on dangerous industrial materials and processes or ensure the safety of patients and service users. We created a form which workers themselves or their managers could complete to apply for exemptions. When reps granted exemptions, we expected workers to contribute to the strike fund to support striking colleagues. Decisions aren't always straightforward. In many caring jobs, staffing is below safe levels even without a strike! But, in any job, there will be activities that can be stopped and you want to force the employer to spend extra money coping with the strike – making use of managers or drawing in workers from elsewhere. Health workers – including junior doctors, nurses, specialists, porters, security guards and cleaners – have taken effective strike action. Part of the impact is creating a political crisis – health workers striking is newsworthy and they can get huge public support. One nurse who was part of a strike in the 1980s told me that their collections easily raised more than their lost wages. When mental health nurses in Manchester went on indefinite strike in 2007, they acknowledged that some harm to service users was unavoidable, despite their best efforts, but not striking would have meant a worse service forever and far greater harm.

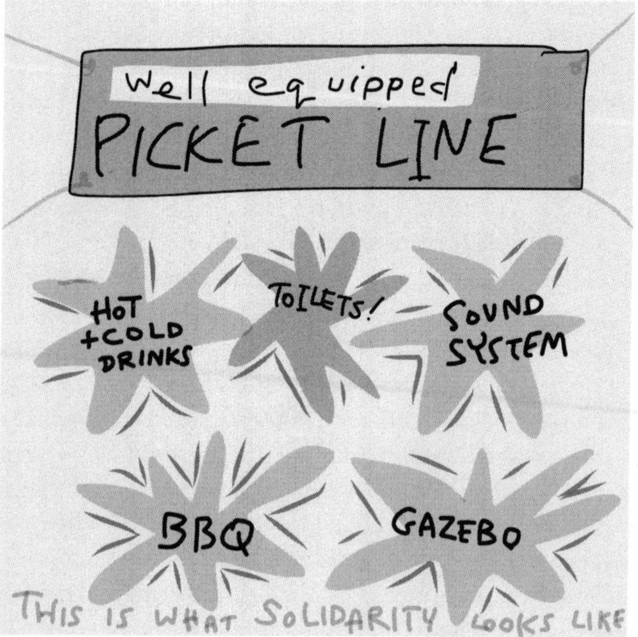

If you have funds, it's easier to make your picket line visible, lively and fun. Go big from the start – a well-equipped picket line boosts morale and sends a message to management that you are ready to be out for as long as it takes. As well as flags, banners, hi viz jackets, whistles, air horns and leaflets, think about shelter, food, drink, heat, a sound system and toilets.

The 2021 Manchester bus strikers hired a van so that they could easily bring and take away their gear each day and get bulk supplies from shops. They also rented some land near the picket to use as a base – initially part of a school field, later an industrial yard which included a small building. They hired portable toilets. Some strikers took responsibility for catering. They had electric hot-water urns powered by a portable generator and a gas barbecue for cooking on. Big marquees and gazebos provided shelter for gear and people. Workers from a successful strike at Rolls Royce Barnoldswick donated an oil drum with a solidarity message cut into it for use as a brazier. A large portable PA system provided music and amplification for meetings.

The core activity for strikers is picketing, which can mean anything from small groups trying to peacefully persuade workers not to cross to mass physical blockades. The government has published a *Code of Practice on Picketing*[14] but this isn't legally binding, only taken into account if things end up in court. Through much of the 1980s, the police behaved as if only six people were allowed to picket an entrance, but this was never in the legislation, only the *Code of Practice*. You have to judge your specific situation, but I've fended off complaints about too many people by pointing out that picketing was peaceful irrespective of numbers. The Code points out that it is a criminal offence to 'use threatening, abusive or insulting words or behaviour' and employers often use this to pressure people not to refer to strike-breakers as scabs. After a number of arrests during the 1984–85 miners' strike, pickets divided themselves into two groups, one of which would shout 'sca' and the other 'ab'.[15] One positive point in the legislation is that pickets can lawfully ask workers who are not directly involved in the strike not to cross the picket line – for example, agency workers, subcontractors or drivers making deliveries. However, the ballot doesn't give those workers rights to compensation if their employer gets nasty when they refuse to cross, so strikers need to be ready to defend them. It's not unusual, even if a picket is peaceful, for workers to say that they don't feel safe crossing a picket line and relying on their rights under safety law (discussed above) to reduce the risk of sanctions.

It's important to get as many of the workers involved as possible. This isn't just because high participation enables more activity and so more pressure on the employer. Workers learn from taking part in struggle. Though few think of it this way beforehand, active participation in a strike is often a positive experience. There's a sense of liberation in defying the boss. You get to talk to workmates in ways you can't in work. You experience for yourself the solidarity from other workers. There's an intense shared experience, fighting for what you believe in, that creates a strong feeling of collectivity and camaraderie. These quotes from different drivers involved in the 2021 Manchester bus strike[16] illustrate the point:

> 'The experience has been great. We were close in the depot before this strike, but now after 80 days … we're even closer. We're definitely a family.'
>
> 'I've absolutely loved being on strike. I know you're not supposed to say that. We've got each other's backs and I've absolutely enjoyed every minute of getting to know my colleagues and actually making friends.'
>
> 'It's the best experience of my life … it was so much fun.'
>
> 'It's been overwhelming. It's been so nice to see. I didn't think there were so many good people around, but there is.'

Those who mope at home miss all this. They aren't seeing what's happening for themselves or discussing the dispute with other strikers. They are more susceptible to rumours and management misinformation and are the most likely to wobble in their resolve. It's common practice to require members to take part in strike-day activities such as pickets in order to receive strike pay. Getting members involved in building solidarity can be a transformative experience.

Consider what other activities can be organised on strike days. Announcing 'solidarity days' can provide a focus for supporters to visit the picket and give strikers a boost. Can you involve strikers in solidarity meetings and rallies – in person or online? These can help involve strikers' families, who have a stake in the strike but often miss out on direct involvement. Can you get groups out leafleting the public or other workplaces? Why not take advantage of the time to organise education and training for strikers? This could range from learning their rights at work and organising skills to discussions about labour movement history or politics – it all helps make the workforce stronger, ready for when you go back. In 2012, teachers in Chicago divided their collective agreement into sections, with groups of workers taking responsibility for each. They studied the text, worked out what they liked and didn't like, and what they wanted changing. When new proposals came through, each group was ready to study 'their' section, explain what the proposals meant and feed back into the negotiations. A bit of playfulness helps maintain morale too – people on picket lines have taken part in pancake races, formed conga lines, played bagpipes or worn fancy dress.

Even if members are highly involved, it's still possible for unhelpful rumours to circulate. People tend to form particular social groups, there may be groups with shared languages and workers won't always raise things with reps, who they know are busy. It's good practice to meet every day on or after the picket (with toilets and hot drinks!), to ensure everyone knows about any new developments and can raise ideas, questions or concerns. Bear in mind that when a worker has a bit of a wobble, the issue they raise may not be the main one. For example, people may raise concerns about money when the central issue is a loss of confidence in the plan to win – any financial sacrifice can seem too much if you don't think you can win.

Whatever arrangements you make for meetings, not everyone will be there. Many strikers use social media such as Twitter to rapidly share information, and messenger apps such as WhatsApp for rapid internal communication.

However many reps and activists you had before the strike, it is unlikely to be enough for everything that you'd ideally do. Creating a strike committee that any striker can join, either by volunteering or being elected, can be a real help. Strikes draw in new union members and new activists, so keep the door open and get them as involved as they want.

Before moving on to building solidarity, I want to return to the question of democracy, which I discussed in Chapter 6. Workers are most likely to sustain participation if we take important decisions collectively after we've all had our say. Democracy is a vital safeguard against those leading a dispute misjudging members' mood and making serious mistakes. When workers are taking action, participation goes through the roof and much richer forms of democracy become possible.

Putting a restricted range of options to a vote without discussion, or without members having the information to reach an informed view, is not democracy. Depending on the scale of your dispute, you need different layers of involvement. I would often talk informally with the most active reps about what to do, then take our thoughts to a reps' meeting which might agree, change the proposals or occasionally disagree completely. Taking proposals to the strike committee before going to a full members' meeting was useful. We could improve them with a wider range of perspectives from active members beyond the formal union structures. If we could reach a good level of consensus at a strike committee, we could be very confident in taking the proposals to a full members' meeting – not only because we'd got lots of input already, but also because lots of active members understood the thinking behind them and would back them up. This layered approach to decision-making delivered a good combination of deep discussion that can only happen in smaller groups and the active endorsement of the majority for the final decision.

Chapter 6 covered some of the difficulties of organising democratically across multiple workplaces and the tools to overcome them. If you're heading into a multi-site strike you need to give some thought to democratic structures. Some decisions will be too urgent to enable a full consultation with members, so these structures need legitimacy in the eyes of members.

Your union may have permanent elected structures that fit who is involved in a dispute well enough to be used to take decisions during it. However, if few were involved in their election or lots of new people have joined or got involved since, they may lack legitimacy with members. The University and College Union (UCU) has a facility for branch delegate meetings[17] during disputes. The idea is that each branch in the dispute has its own meeting, then delegates from all those branches meet together and vote on next steps. However, delegates' votes are just advisory. Actual decisions are taken by permanent committees in UCU's formal structure.

Secrecy is the enemy of democracy. Nobody can make informed decisions without good information. Employers love to tie unions up in knots during negotiations, demanding that discussions are confidential until the end. Let's be clear – this is utterly unreasonable. Whenever they want, the employer's negotiating team go back to stakeholders in their organisation for opinions, information or even decisions on particular points. Because employers are hierarchical, they can do this without going public. If workers can't provide opinions, information and decisions then our negotiators are at a massive disadvantage. Allowing the employer to control how and when the union consults its members is a massive concession which paves the way for an unnecessarily bad deal. Management often use secrecy to try to create divisions between workers, reps and paid officers. In Chapter 10, I discuss radical responses to this known as open bargaining and big bargaining.

BUILDING SOLIDARITY

Building solidarity is nearly always essential for any successful dispute. It can play two distinct roles – adding pressure towards a victory and sustaining the action. The process of building solidarity also educates workers elsewhere who aren't directly involved in the dispute and creates and strengthens their networks. Most of the time, most workers aren't engaged in intense struggle, so giving solidarity helps workers keep available the possibilities and lessons of a wide repertoire of struggle. This means that when we do take action, we start with more knowledge and understanding. Solidarity strengthens the giver as well as the receiver – solidarity is not charity.

Some solidarity has a direct impact on your dispute by putting pressure on a campaign target in various ways. Sometimes supporters can take action – from talking to the media to blockades and occupations – that strikers see as too risky because of potential employer reprisals. A public statement from an individual or organisation with power over your employer may have an impact a celebrity endorsement never would. Just as some workers are more influential than others, so are some supporters. Some faith leaders are generally sympathetic to progressive causes, but these are rarely the ones with the biggest congregations or the most influence over politicians. As discussed in Chapter 8, we need to work out who has influence and how to win them over.

Support from the wider workers' movement and the community can be politically crucial in enabling strikers to sustain action. Strikers need to feel that what we are doing is right. Solidarity bolsters that conviction and undermines the attempts of employers, politicians or the media to portray strikers as selfishly acting against the public interest. As well as boosting morale, solidarity helps sustain a strike financially and practically.

It's helpful to draft a short appeal for support that explains what the dispute is about in a punchy way, offers a range of ways people can help, and provides links for more information and for contacting the strikers. You can use the appeal for support online or on leaflets and you can update it during the dispute. Think about how you can get it circulated widely using your union structures, trades councils, individual contacts and other organisations (see Chapter 3). You can add details of your strike to strikemap.co.uk and publicise news coverage of it via labourstart.org. If you haven't already, bag suitable social media accounts and spaces and set up a simple website or blog to share information and dispute updates.

As you receive messages of support, share them online and print them out to bring them to the picket line for everyone to see. Use the messages to build a mailing list and keep people informed about developments and any further action people can take to support you.

You quickly need to identify a bank account you can use for your strike fund, as discussed above. Make it as easy as possible for people to contribute. Many union branches still make payments using cheques, so be sure to include payee details and a postal address, as well as the information for people paying with online banking. Options to contribute using PayPal or a crowdfunding platform can encourage individual donations.

A great way to raise money for disputes is for workers in other workplaces to take round a collection. You can make this easy by producing a collection sheet to use alongside the appeal for support. Taking a collection round at work is a great way to make more people aware of a dispute and to take inspiration and lessons from it – it strengthens organisation wherever it is done. Always start by writing in your own donation and making it as big as you can afford, then go to one or two people you think will be supportive and generous. This helps show others that this is something important and raises expectations.

You can get word out about your dispute by offering speakers at other organisations' meetings and events. As well as union events, many campaign organisations would be delighted to hear from a striker. Look out for protests, demonstrations and marches happening locally. If the strikers support the cause, bring your placards, flags, banners and leaflets and join in, as well as seeing if one of you can speak.

Public speaking is something most people find terrifying. Remember that people primarily want to hear you because of what you are doing, not because you are some expert or great orator. Talking about why you are on strike, how you feel about the situation and how people can help you win nearly always goes down well. It's a mistake to leave this to a few key activists who will be overrun with other tasks. Every striker knows why they are on strike and how they feel about it. The details of how people can help are in your appeal for support. Speaking about a strike you are involved in can be a life-changing experience for workers, experiencing solidarity first hand and doing something they never imagined themselves doing. It's good to pair up more and less experienced people, so the more experienced one does the talking the first time, then they swap, and then the newly experienced worker gets paired with someone new.

If you are looking for someone to speak to a particular group or at a protest over a specific issue, try to find someone with a genuine interest in that cause if you can. This makes it much easier to build lasting relationships with groups you are in solidarity with. The relationships many unions build with other groups are often ineffective. Too often they are transactional – we'll support X if you help us with Y. Too often relationships are only at an organisational level – with affiliations, donations and alliances, or between the leaders of the respective groups. These approaches form relationships that are shallow, not involving many workers, and which tend to fade away once the immediate need is over. In contrast, a 'whole worker organising' approach recognises that workers have all kinds of issues and connections stretching way beyond the job. Harnessing those creates strong and lasting connections between your organisation at work and other groups.

The tradition of 'delegation work' needs reviving. This involves strikers sending delegations to visit other workplaces and union branches to let them know about a dispute and ask for support. I've often taken workers from strikes in my area or elsewhere in the country round local workplaces. If you send delegations elsewhere in the country, you need a local activist willing to act as host, to arrange people the strikers can stay with and to take you round local workplaces. They may know whom to ask for at some workplaces or you may be able to find out from union websites or directories. If necessary, you can just show up at a workplace's reception desk and ask to speak to the union rep without even knowing a name. Sometimes you will draw a blank or only be able to leave leaflets at reception for them (always take envelopes with you!), but often you will have a good conversation. If you or your host know someone already then you can arrange a good time to call and maybe speak at a meeting. If you have a delegation visiting another town or city, local activists may be able to arrange a solidarity public meeting in the evening so that you can reach even more people while you are there. I remember one lunchtime solidarity meeting involving dockers, teachers and IT workers, who were all surprised to discover just how much they had in common.

Partly because delegation work is so rare these days, the reps you visit are usually intrigued and keen to help. During the university strikes in early 2020, I took strikers round local workplaces.[18] The strikers had never heard of doing this, let alone done it before. The academics found support from bus garages and fire stations, food and electronics factories, and learned that workers in all of them faced similar pressures. Delegation work gets a broader and stronger response than just sending out emails or relying on social media. It builds class solidarity across industries and occupations, and it creates networks that can last beyond any individual strike.

Because activities like public speaking or delegation work are way outside most people's comfort zone, there can be pressure to leave them to the main activists. This is a missed opportunity for workers to experience solidarity for themselves. When workers arrived back at our picket lines with stories of leaving meetings or workplaces with hundreds of pounds in donations, the impact was more than the money and much greater than if the 'usual suspects' had told these tales. One way to prevent people leaving it all to you is to arrange several activities at the same time. During one strike, we had seven teams out doing delegation work across the country at once.

THE MEDIA

The experience of a dispute usually teaches workers how hostile most of the media is. The main form this takes is lack of interest – the media is generally more interested in celebrity antics than a struggle affecting the lives of working-class people. When they do cover disputes, their coverage is usually inaccurate and unsympathetic. This is for several reasons. The media is overwhelmingly owned and controlled by the rich and powerful[19], who aren't enthusiastic about the rest of us getting uppity. Much of the media relies for income on corporate advertisers who aren't keen on pro-worker coverage. The media reflects (and reinforces) dominant ideas in society, which include a steaming pile of managerial ideology – that managers have a right to manage, that employers' financial success is more important than workers' ability to pay the bills, that workers only strike because 'union bosses' tell us to, and so on. Many media outlets now employ few journalists, so most have little time away from their desks, forcing them to rely on sources seen as authoritative, like corporations or politicians, rather than mere workers. Decades of decline in union power has had its impact on the media too – gone are the days when newspapers employed specialist correspondents with a good grasp of industrial relations – so any coverage we get tends to be superficial and error prone. But despite all this, the media isn't consistently hostile. Those who control the media need to reflect 'public opinion' in order to shape it. Many media workers don't share their management's agendas. There are decent journalists, and some good reporting gets through the editorial filter even in generally anti-union outlets.

The default tool in many organisations for engaging the media is the press release.[20] At the heart of a press release is a piece of text written so that a journalist can copy and paste it – so don't write from your point of view, write as if you were the journalist. You can include quotes from participants and provide photos or a link to where they can be downloaded. Include clear contact information and other details, such as where and when there will be a photo opportunity, or where to get pictures. Specify an 'embargo' date and time (which can be 'immediate') before which you don't want them to run the story. Make sure you include contact details for someone who will be available to deal with any queries. It's good practice to start press releases with one or two sentences that summarise the story and hook people in, then gradually go into more detail if people read on. Most unions will have departments used to writing press releases and dealing with the media, and some of them offer training if you might be interviewed on radio or television.

The reality is that emailing press releases to news desks gets very little response. It's much more effective to contact specific journalists, so spend some time looking for any who have written on related topics. A phone call to follow up from a press release hugely increases the chances of it being used. If you can get local or trade press to cover something, you have a much better chance of the bigger outlets picking up the story. It seems the definition of 'newsworthy' is something that's already in the news.

It can be easier to get coverage by strikers calling phone-in programmes or writing letters to papers. Don't neglect independent and left-wing media outlets. While they won't generate much pressure on your employer, they can be useful in getting the word out to potential supporters.

The growth of social media has made it a lot easier to publicise a dispute in the movement. Try to enlist supportive people and organisations with big social media followings and look out for social media spaces where trade unionists and other relevant groups hang out. Using social media to put pressure on the employer is more difficult – if only a few people get involved it is relatively easy for the employer to block anyone posting critical comments. To build a social media following, set up accounts in good time and post regularly. There are various tools to schedule posts across multiple social media platforms – it's far less onerous to spend a few hours scheduling most of your posts for the next few weeks rather than having to do it every day.

There are various guides for activists on using the media. For example, George Monbiot's *An Activist's Guide to Exploiting the Media* (2001), which is useful but rather dated now, the *Press Officer Handbook* from the New Economy Organisers' Network (NEON) (Butcher and Edwards, 2019), and tips from the Electronic Frontier Foundation.[21]

WINNING AND SETTLING DISPUTES

You win a dispute when you can credibly threaten a big enough disruption cost to force the decision-maker(s) to change their approach and to make your preferred outcome the most attractive option for them. Can you escalate the credibly threatened disruption cost far enough before the employer exhausts workers' ability to sustain themselves and their families?

Major conflict happens when the balance of power has to be tested in practice because the two sides have different estimates of it. So you need to show more militancy and power than the employer expected. The sooner you can demonstrate this, the sooner you establish the credibility of your threatened disruption cost.

The longer a dispute continues, the more an employer can do to mitigate its impact. For example, they might transfer work between sites, hire scabs or subcontract work. Try to anticipate what the employer might do and be ready to escalate action so that pressure grows over time rather than diminishing due to their countermeasures.

At some point during your dispute, at least some workers are likely to have a bit of a wobble, losing confidence in the plan to win or your collective ability to deliver it. My first piece of advice is 'don't panic'. It's inevitable that some workers will feel like giving up before others. Take the time to understand what's really behind the wobble, which may not be the first thing they raise. Think seriously about any real problems in the dispute they are reflecting. Reassure wobblers that everyone is aware of the problems and discuss how to overcome them. Do you need escalation to rebuild confidence in the plan to win? Point out some of the strengths of the campaign – people having a wobble often take a very one-sided view. Weaknesses on our own side are usually more visible to us than weaknesses on the other side, but those will exist too. No employer is going to say 'if you just last one more week we'll give in'. They pretend to be immovable – until they move. That's why the labour movement in North America uses the slogan 'one day longer' – you only have to last one day longer than the boss to win. Above all, emphasise to any wobblers the importance of any change in approach being decided collectively rather than allowing the employer to pick off individuals. In the words of the film *Gladiator*, 'whatever comes out of these gates, we have a better chance of survival if we work together ... if we stay together, we survive'.

Disputes eventually end – a strike is, after all, a temporary stoppage of work. The settlement is always a compromise. I don't mean that the deal is always somewhere between the strikers' demands and the employer's initial offer. That isn't the case – some strikes win outright. But any strike settlement involves going back to work and, as explained in Chapter 2, exploitation and oppressive inequality are inherent to the capitalist employment relationship. And no settlement is permanent – employers and workers will be back to change the terms of any deal as work or the balance of power evolves. The most lasting impact of any dispute is the change in the confidence, organisation, understanding and combativity of the workers involved – this legacy will impact on future struggles long after details of the settlement are forgotten. Remembering all this helps keep your feelings about the actual content of the settlement in proportion.

It's better to settle with a good win under your belt and build on that success than to push on for more than the balance of forces can achieve.

And if the dispute isn't going well, there's no shame in agreeing concessions after you've fought to resist them. It is better to retreat in good order, so that workers are ready to fight again if they need to, than to press on to a terrible defeat. For the avoidance of doubt, I'm not urging caution – you are unlikely to win anything worthwhile without taking some risk, and you need to hold your nerve if things get difficult. But the true balance of forces becomes clearer once a battle is under way and you need to keep reassessing it and adjusting both your plan to win and your goals for the settlement accordingly.

There is a point just before a strike starts when settlements are common. This is because the employer can see your preparations establishing the credibility of your threatened disruption cost. All the disruption cost is still in the future – none has been 'used up'. Once a strike gets going, the likelihood of a settlement falls sharply. Both sides will be annoyed by the actions of the other and will be focused on organising their side of the fight. As time goes on, the costs mount up on both sides and weariness can set in. Your job is to ensure that happens to the employer faster than it happens to you. At the same time, the true balance of forces becomes more apparent, helping both sides understand what settlement is achievable.

An astonishing number of paid officers seem to think that as soon as there is an offer, or even talks, action should be suspended. Let's be clear – this isn't wisdom, this is internalising habits generated by weakness. The strongest thing to do is to keep the pressure up until members have voted to accept a deal, including a negotiated return to work. Of course, you may not always be in a position to do the strongest thing, or you may have other reasons for wanting to suspend action before a deal is done. But be clear that suspending action increases the risk of the employer delaying things or moving the goalposts at the last minute. While you are taking action, the pressure is on them to remove any obstacles to a settlement.

Employers, sometimes with the help of paid officers, often try to rush workers into deciding on an offer. In the worst cases, members are asked to vote on an offer that hasn't even been written down. Most workers aren't used to reading legalistic documents, some may not be great readers, and English won't be everyone's first language. The best practice is to ensure all members have access to both the full text of any proposal and a summary or explanation of it. When we received an offer that replaced or amended an existing agreement, we would also prepare a version that showed tracked changes from the previous one. Once members have the offer, they should have the opportunity to ask questions and discuss it collectively before voting on it. For example, in their 2012 strike, the Chicago Teachers Union gave strikers several days on the picket lines to discuss the offer before voting.

Even if the employer hasn't attempted to pick on any of the strikers, you should still ensure that any settlement includes clauses protecting workers as they return to work. If the return is at short notice, there should be leeway for any worker who doesn't get the message in time that the strike is over. There should be a clear commitment to no detriment or recriminations for any actions taken by workers as part of the dispute and associated campaigning. If, as is all too common, bosses have brought disciplinary charges during the strike, get them dropped as part of the settlement.

Industrial and direct action may seem remote prospects when you first start organising, but we mustn't shy away from the fact that without building workers' capacity to take powerful disruptive action, we can't build the power we need to improve our lives. Far from being a 'last resort', strikes are central to any realistic strategy for change.

Key points

- There is a huge range of industrial and direct action. Consider the pros and cons before choosing.
- There are some risks to workers and their unions if you take unlawful industrial action. The main protection is the numbers taking part. Some work stoppages might not be seen as strikes.
- The process for lawful industrial action is long and complex and is only available for certain issues.
- Solidarity is crucial for spreading action and gaining practical, financial and moral support. It strengthens the giver as well as the receiver.
- Set up your own strike fund in advance of a potential strike.
- If striking, go big from the start – look like you are there to stay and get everyone involved.
- Make use of the media and don't just rely on press releases.
- Keep the pressure up until members have accepted a settlement and make sure it protects them from retribution.

Discussion questions

1. What types and patterns of action would be effective at your work?
2. What can you do to build solidarity from your workmates for workers in struggles beyond your workplace?

10
Management mischief

The previous two chapters were all about collective action, particularly industrial action. The final three chapters of this book are about some of the complexities you'll face as you organise. In this chapter, I'll look at some of the tactics management use to get their way – how they try to intensify work and keep control, and how they try to derail, divide or attack the union.

INTENSIFYING WORK AND KEEPING CONTROL

In Chapter 2, I discussed how an employment contract can't specify how hard you have to work, so employers manage workers to get us to work as hard as possible. This isn't just a matter of your boss being on your case if you're slacking a bit – many employers spend a small fortune on schemes to indoctrinate us with their ideology and on repeatedly reorganising our work.

The list of management initiatives is long. It includes performance management, absence management, suggestion schemes, continuous improvement, Lean, Six Sigma, Kaizen, Agile, Kanban, performance-related pay, bonuses and incentives, employee share schemes, team working, Corporate Social Responsibility, customer care, quality, staff forums, buzz sessions, briefings, reorganisations, restructuring, rationalisation – and there always seems to be a new fad.

Broadly speaking, these initiatives can have an impact on workers in three ways: ideology, work intensification and disruption. Let's consider each in turn before looking at how we can respond to them.

Ideology

Many management initiatives try to get workers or their representatives to see things from management's point of view rather than their own – prioritising financial success, 'efficiency' and 'customer service' irrespective of

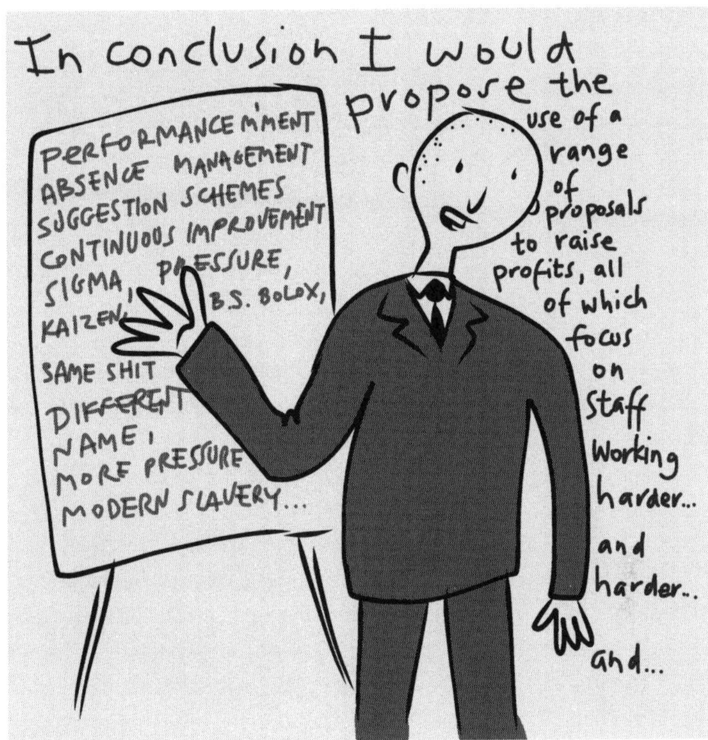

whether these are achieved at our expense. For example, staff forums and bonus schemes are often used to generate interest in and commitment to the employer's financial performance. Schemes may promote the idea that any problems are caused by poor communication or bad individuals undermining shared interests. This obscures the conflicts of interest on any job, including those between workers and management.

My own research suggests that though many workers accept a vision of how things *should* work that corresponds to managerial ideology – shared interests, partnership, managers being best placed to decide things, etc. – they are nearly always acutely aware of the gulf between that vision and reality. But even if all the bullshit doesn't stop workers resisting, it can still help create an atmosphere where workers feel less confident to articulate views that clash with it. This can contribute to 'pluralistic ignorance', where workers don't realise that others share their views, as well as promoting individualism.

Workers, especially those with more experience, often respond to management initiatives with cynicism. This can have contradictory effects on your organising. On the one hand, cynical workers may resist by minimising their participation. On the other, displays of cynicism can assist compliance through 'emotional distancing', enabling workers to comply despite hating what they are doing. Cynicism can also divert dissent away from effective channels into futile posturing.

Work intensification

Lean management is the first example I'll explore of a management initiative that aims to intensify work or make workers more productive. Lean claims to reduce waste, which appears laudable. But the waste being eliminated is often any slack in your day. Management need fewer of us if we're working harder. Some production lines using Lean manufacturing operate a traffic light system where if there's a hold-up on your job, your light goes amber, and if it lasts more than a certain time, it goes red and the whole line stops. It is sold as a way to eliminate hold-ups and make everyone's job easier. People imagine that the aim must be to keep all the lights on green. But management really aim to have all the lights flickering between green and amber, so every worker is just on the edge of being unable to cope with the work-rate. An equivalent in customer support call centres is to make each group of agents cover several systems, customers with different patterns of demand or time zones, so that instead of having natural peaks and troughs during the week, all the agents are fully busy the whole time – and fewer are needed overall.

Performance management is widely used to intensify work and encourage unpaid overtime. Objectives are set higher than can be achieved in standard working hours at a reasonable pace. They may be linked to performance-related pay, work allocation, promotion or disciplinary action under capability procedures. Targets that can't realistically be achieved in normal working hours are discriminatory against those with caring responsibilities, usually women.

When managers have any discretion over work allocation this can be used as both carrot and stick to extract more work. Those not seen as performing so well may be given work that is boring, unpleasant or offers little opportunity to develop new skills. They may be first to face redundancy if the volume of work falls.

When a worker leaves, many employers don't immediately replace them and don't fill vacancies until the remaining workers can't cope. Understaffing is especially pernicious when workload is shared by a team because workers can end up policing each other's effort or resenting colleagues who don't overwork quite as much. Vacancies pile stress onto the remaining workers, particularly in jobs such as health or care work where not keeping up has human consequences. But in reality there are often only two ways to get enough staff to do the job properly – to fail to cover for the vacancy or to take collective action.

Disruption

Whether or not your work is unionised, managers and workers always reach some sort of understanding of how much effort is expected. This is a part of the employment 'deal' that can't be written down. Almost without exception, managers know that they have more control over you if they occasionally cut you some slack, which acts as leverage over workers because we fear losing it.

Many management techniques disrupt established work practices, throwing the deal up in the air. Even if there's nothing in the initiative that directly intensifies work, managers often take advantage of the situation to rewrite the unwritten deal at workers' expense.

Responses

There are several things that workers can do to limit the harm caused by management initiatives. The most basic is to discuss any new initiatives collectively, to try to understand what they mean, how they might work to your disadvantage, how to counter that and whether they offer any opportunities. This process helps counter all three impacts of initiatives – ideology, work intensification and disruption. Take the time to discuss established management techniques with new workers – they shouldn't have to learn all the lessons the hard way. But think hard how to do it – if you tell them what to think rather than helping them think it through, you can end up coming across a bit paranoid. For example, I once got people discussing performance management, Lean and stress by sending round a video[1] of a talk about them by Professor Phil Taylor which had the added appeal of including cat videos.

A very effective response is to maximise workers' control over work allocation and staffing levels, and to minimise the scope for management discretion. This is hard to achieve, but every step in this direction reduces the workload pressure and makes it harder for management to make you compete against or blame each other. All too often, bargaining is so centralised that it can't grapple with these issues, which are often most visible at team or department level. It's another reason you need to build power in every team rather than relying too heavily on formal and centralised processes.

DERAILING THE UNION

When workers organise, management often try to portray conflict as due to bad people or poor communication, rather than being the inevitable consequence of the unequal employment relationship. The union is often portrayed as a malign external influence (outside agitators!), or a third-party barrier to communication between managers and workers.

Chapter 5 discussed how to avoid reinforcing the image of the union as a third party. If you've built your organisation on the basis of workers' own collective action, rather than a service or advocacy model, then attempts to bad-mouth union organisation shouldn't get much traction.

Management love to promote a 'we're all in it together' mindset. One reason is that it helps them present the potential impact of worker organisation on the employer's financial success as a threat to jobs. In reality, many organisations get rich while cutting jobs. When unions buy into these ideas, they adopt a partnership approach and the union is often co-opted by management. A union is little use to workers if it promotes a management agenda rather than our own. It's fine to look for wins that cost the employer little or even benefit them ('integrative' bargaining), but if that is the main focus then we can't maximise our share of what we produce ('distributive' bargaining) (Brown, 2010).

A common management tactic is to foster a sense of futility amongst workers – the belief that nothing we do will make any difference. Futility, alongside fear, is one of the biggest obstacles to organising. Timewasting is a valuable management tool. Reps might be busy in lots of talks with management or tied up in a legal process, while all workers see is a lack of progress on their issues. It helps to avoid over-reliance on formal procedures and keep workers' own collective action central instead. Keeping workers informed is vital. If you've got an issue that will take ages to win, consider taking up some smaller issues in parallel so workers know they are still making progress and winning.

A useful bit of industrial relations jargon is the 'level' of bargaining. This is about whether deals are done at the level of the workgroup, department, workplace, employer or industrial sector, for example. Employers manipulate the bargaining level to their advantage, so we need to think about the pros and cons of different levels.

If bargaining is at a very local level, outcomes are highly dependent on organisation in each area. Low level bargaining encourages workers to build organisation and power in every workgroup. It's easy for workers to retain control over negotiations. Bargaining can deal with issues of immediate concern to each group of workers. However, groups with less power may get left behind. It's relatively easy for management to divide workers, and if we aren't united, we may struggle to win bigger concessions that need higher management approval. In general, the side that is advancing is helped by bargaining being at a low level. If workers are making gains, groups can try to 'leapfrog' each other, each using what another group won as their starting point. If the employer is on the offensive, they can pick off weaker areas first, then take on stronger groups who are left defending terms that others have already lost and who may therefore struggle to win solidarity.

Centralised, high-level bargaining tends to be conducted by paid officers, or by senior reps with lots of facility time. It's often harder for workers to keep control of negotiations. It's easy to bargain centrally over 'market relations' (pay, hours, etc.) but harder to deal with 'managerial relations' (how people are managed, work allocation, etc.). Organisation at lower levels can wither if it has little role in bargaining or decision-making. Centralised bargaining can protect weaker groups of workers but may limit what stronger groups can achieve. It can help unionise new areas. For example, a partly unionised company may introduce bargaining at company level to limit the power of unionised sites, but this creates an opportunity to unionise the remaining workplaces.

Bargaining at industry level requires strong employer associations. As discussed in Chapter 9, if they are weak or there isn't sectoral bargaining, unions can use selective action to pick off employers one at a time and gradually win improvements across a sector.

Employers usually have a lot of control over the bargaining level and change it in response to threats and opportunities. As well as trying to influence it, we need to mitigate its weaknesses and take advantage of the opportunities it presents.

DIVIDING THE UNION

Employers often undermine workers' collective strength by dividing us: 'horizontally' by dividing workers from each other or 'vertically' by dividing workers from their reps or paid officers.

Some of the potential lines of division are around oppression. If white, male or able-bodied workers cling to preferential access to pay rises or jobs and don't support their colleagues to fight racism, sexism, ableism and other forms of oppression then the whole workforce is weakened. You can't remove these divisions by ignoring them.

There are other lines of division that are often taken for granted – between occupations and teams. It is management who create demarcations between groups of workers and limit communication and cooperation between them, to maintain their power and control. They often require workers to go up through the management chain and back down again when dealing with other departments. This, combined with broken work processes and under-resourcing, generates tension between groups of workers. For example, in a call centre that spanned two locations, workers in each site looked down on the other, convinced they didn't work as hard and made more mistakes, causing extra work to put things right. In an IT company, it's common for the system designers to blame sales people for selling things that can't be delivered, for support staff to blame system designers for making designs that can't be implemented or supported properly, and sales to blame the designers and support staff for letting costs rise so that it's hard to make sales. When it's pointed out, and when workers talk across departmental lines, they realise that these problems and the lack of communication between teams are actually caused by management.

It doesn't help that many workplaces have multiple unions. This is less common in manufacturing than it used to be, thanks to union mergers replacing 'craft' unions for specific occupations with general ones, but it remains rife elsewhere, such as in health and education. Having multiple unions isn't necessarily a big barrier to unity, as long as workers organise across union boundaries at workplace level. Historically, in manufacturing this has often been through Joint Shop Stewards Committees. Failing to build effective workplace-level organisation that includes all workers reduces our strength and usually leaves some workers very vulnerable. Workers like cleaners, security and maintenance are too often outsourced, badly treated and ignored by other sections of the workforce – and their unions. Trying to maximise strength by including all the workers has implications for the way issues are framed. It's easy to slip into making the case for better treatment based on characteristics not shared by all the workers – from loyal service (devaluing new workers) to occupational skills, knowledge and qualifications. To include everyone, your arguments have to be based on shared working-class interests rather than narrow occupational ones. For example, it is easier for teachers to build unity with other school staff if a campaign emphasises delivering quality education for all than if it is based on teachers' specialist training and qualifications.

Once reps or paid officers start talking to the employer, another opportunity for management to encourage division appears. Typically, most workers don't know everything going on in negotiations. What they hear is conflicting accounts from the two sides. It's easy for managers to sow doubts and present the union as a third party. When workers hear conflicting claims, they often assume that the truth lies somewhere in between, and get frustrated with both parties for not producing the outcome they want. Some managers go further and make entirely false claims about what's said in talks. How can you counter all this?

If you're meeting management, don't do it alone. Have at least one colleague with you, even if they only act as a witness or note-taker. In negotiations, aim higher than that – prepare a team where you each have specific roles, just as you do for confrontational actions, as described in Chapter 8. You might have someone who opens the meeting and introduces other speakers, someone to do most of the talking, other people who explain particular points (maybe with personal examples of the impact of issues), someone who takes notes, someone who watches body language and someone who keeps track of time and brings the discussion back to your agenda, stopping the other side if they talk over or interrupt anyone on your team. The team acting collectively and with self-discipline demonstrates organisation and power to management.

Never rely on notes taken by management or HR. Some managers are so prone to misrepresenting talks that the union side insists both teams sign notes each day before they leave negotiations. There are cases when even that hasn't stopped a manager who signed the notes one day denying what happened the next. But at least the notes give you evidence to show any doubters. Dealing with management misinformation mustn't obscure your main messages. Focus on what workers want and the plan to get it – even if you make detailed rebuttals available for anyone who wants them.

If reps should avoid meeting management alone, this goes double for paid officers. Most workers won't know the paid officers personally but are aware that they won't be directly affected by the outcome of talks. Allowing paid officers to negotiate with management without reps present is a recipe for disaster. Not only is it harder for them to spot bullshit because they nearly always lack the detailed knowledge of the situation at work, but even if they do a perfect job, management can create suspicion amongst workers. I talked in Chapter 9 about how employers use confidentiality to prevent workers knowing what's going on and to weaken our side. Secrecy undermines trust in the union team.

The most radical responses are known as 'open bargaining' or 'big bargaining'. Open bargaining means any worker can hear what's going on in the negotiations. When the huge Solidarność (Solidarity) union was challenging the dictatorship in Poland in the early 1980s, talks at the giant Gdansk shipyard were broadcast over the tannoy system for all the workers to hear. Their boos and cheers could be heard in the meeting room and undoubtedly concentrated minds on both sides. Jane McAlevey advocates any worker being able to attend talks and combines it with 'big bargaining' – having lots of workers in the room (McAlevey and Lawlor, 2021). She expects every member to attend at least once.

The process of building a big bargaining team can be used as part of the organising process. Workers in an area don't elect a member of the bargaining team until a majority have signed up to the campaign. At this point, workers are encouraged to take a group photo with a sign saying they are ready for bargaining which they share on social media. This creates momentum and encourages weaker areas to get organised so they too have a voice in the talks.

Figure 10.1 Chicago Teachers Union bargaining team preparing, 2016. Photo: @CTULocal1 on Twitter. Note: distortion from the original panoramic photo.

An obvious objection to big or open bargaining is 'our boss would never agree to that'. But if you haven't got the power to make your boss negotiate in the format you want, you haven't got the power to win major demands. In that case, why not focus on building power rather than bargaining prematurely?

People also worry about how to prevent workers messing up the talks. McAlevey operates some basic rules which workers have to agree to before they can be in the room with management:

1. Poker face at all times.
2. No one except our negotiator speaks unless planned.
3. Send notes to the negotiator any time if you want to talk, let her know something, or request a 'caucus' (a break without management).
4. No mobile phones, photos or recording.

Big bargaining takes even more preparation than small bargaining, to make sure everyone agrees what will happen and understands why. This has a huge benefit in educating workers. You can encourage a hostile worker to ask their manager for what they want. Then when their boss refuses, get the worker to put forward that demand in the negotiations. This dispels any confusion: it is management blocking their demands and the union supporting them.

Big, open bargaining can also help counter divisions in the workforce. McAlevey describes planning negotiations for a hospital and discussing with the workers that management would probably make an offer that benefited nurses (who have bargaining power in the USA) but left other workers with little. Sure enough, this happened. When it was nurses who stood up and objected to the proposal, management knew their attempt to divide the workers had failed.

Of course, you may not always be strong enough to implement big and open bargaining, or you may not yet have overcome objections from your own side. Sometimes reps and paid officers cherish the power that comes from being able to choose how to report back from talks. But you can still aim to move as far as possible towards big and open bargaining.

ATTACKING THE UNION

When an employer feels threatened by workers organising, they may go on the offensive, which can take many forms.

Management often try to give you dilemmas, hoping you will make bad or hasty choices. For example, if they bypass the union to ballot workers themselves – how do you respond? What if none of the options they present are what you want? No book can tell you how to respond to every situation – you need a network of people on and beyond your job with whom you can talk things through. Remember that sometimes doing nothing, at least

STAFF
REDUCTION
"We're offering you a choice..."

for a while, can be the best option in response to a provocation. Just as your actions try to force a reaction from management, they try to force one from you, so think before deciding whether and how to respond. When you do respond, it's often better to 'get ahead of the curve' by responding strongly rather than half-heartedly.

If you think management are getting aggressive, it sometimes helps to appear stronger than you are. Animals that feel threatened fluff up to appear bigger than they are – you can do the same. In one poorly unionised department, workers were having a problem with a bullying manager. Though most weren't (yet) in the union, they agreed it would send a powerful message if they covered their work area with union 'tat'. They plastered their desks with union mouse mats, wore ID cards on union lanyards, and even attached union branded 'rear view mirrors' to computer screens. When the manager walked in, he was shocked and asked one of the workers 'is this because of me?' The display of unity gave the worker the confidence to say 'yes', much to his workmates' amusement. The manager was much less confident to bully staff after that.

Employers in Britain don't use full-on 'union-busting' tactics as much as in the USA, but they are used. If you suspect your employer is using a union-busting consultant, do your homework on what they are likely to do. Martin Jay Levitt and Terry Conrow's *Confessions of a Union Buster* (1993) is a highly regarded exposé of the 'union avoidance' industry. Union-busters try to portray the union as a third party that's interested in you paying subs rather than improving your life. They often dredge up scare stories about links between union leaders and left-wing politics and suggest that unionisation threatens job security. They will mirror your organising efforts by mobilising first-line supervisors to identify influential workers and try to turn them against unionisation. They will encourage workers to front the campaign against unionisation. This helps them portray the debate as between workers rather than an employer trying to crush workers. And they will use the employer's wealth and power to try to force workers to attend indoctrination meetings where they are exposed to slick propaganda.

The description of union-busting reinforces the importance of your organising focusing on the workers, rather than on the union as a third party (see Chapter 5), right from the start. But don't be defensive when the mud starts flying. We shouldn't be embarrassed about union subs. The employer will hire lawyers, public relations experts and maybe union avoidance consultants. Workers have to pool our resources to be able to fight for our rights. Neither should we be ashamed about unions' links with left-wing politics. Being a leftie isn't a condition of union membership – we aim to organise almost every worker and a sizeable minority of union members vote Tory. But people on the left are more likely to support union values such as collectivity, economic democracy and opposition to inequality. The political views of prominent individuals aren't relevant to whether a worker should support unionisation, because the key decisions will be taken by them and their workmates. Hopefully you will have already countered many of the employer's tricks through inoculation (see Chapter 5). Remember that if workers are afraid, anger and humour are useful, but humour must be used with care.

Key points

- Management use lots of initiatives to intensify work and maintain control. They work by promoting ideology, intensifying work directly or disrupting existing working arrangements to enable work intensification.
- Discuss initiatives when new ones arise and with new workers.
- Maximise workers' control over work allocation and staffing levels. Minimise management discretion.
- Keep workers informed about their issues and ensure progress is visible.
- Look out for management manipulating the bargaining level.
- Counter division between workers, whether based on discrimination, occupations, teams or multiple unions.
- Never let reps or paid officials deal with management alone and resist confidentiality restrictions on reporting to workers.
- Open bargaining and big bargaining help keep people united and empowered. If you aren't strong enough to do them fully, how close can you get?
- Don't be defensive if management attack the union.

Discussion questions

1. What management initiatives are used at your work, and what impact do they have?
2. What divisions exist between workers and how might you counter them?

11
Dealing with your union

I start this chapter by discussing how the union beyond your workmates can help and how to access that support. I then explore the implications of the fact that a union is an institution with its own dynamics, even though members are the heart of a union. Unfortunately, trying to deal with the wider union can sometimes seem as challenging as dealing with your employer. It can feel doubly frustrating if you're having trouble with people you'd hope would be on your side.

USING THE UNION BEYOND YOUR WORK

Union structures vary widely, so get to know yours. Typically, there will be a paid officer responsible for covering your work and it's worth finding out who that is and where they are based, and trying to establish a working relationship. They are often gatekeepers to other resources such as support from a union's legal, research or media departments.

Membership records are a key resource. A union can't give these out to just anyone because they are members' sensitive personal data. But if you are an elected rep or branch officer you should be able to get access to the details of the members you cover. It's important to keep these up to date and accurate so you can communicate with members and in case you need to ballot for industrial action. If you haven't yet been elected as a rep or branch officer, you'll need to find someone who does have access to the membership records and get them to send information out to members – for example, to call a members' meeting. If nobody helpful can access membership information, don't let that stop you. Firstly, organising is about involving workers in collective action, irrespective of their union membership status. Secondly, if you need to, you can get a reasonable indication of whether a worker is a member by asking them directly, unless it's when they want to access union support.

Most unions have some sort of branch structure, which may be based on your workplace, employer, industry, occupation, geographical area or some combination of these. Depending on the union and the size of the branch, it may be run by members elected on a voluntary basis or may have paid officers either allocated from above or elected by branch members to run it. Branches normally have at least some meetings open to all members, but in some cases you have to get yourself elected to a position or onto a branch committee to play much of a part. In some unions, branches have access to a proportion of members' subscriptions. For example, Unite branches get 7.5 per cent and UNISON branches, which are rarely small and often employ staff, get 23 per cent. Find out how members can access financial resources – where are they held and how are they controlled.

Many unions have specific communications such as email lists for particular groups of members, sometimes including newsletters on particular issues such as bargaining, health and safety or equality. Try to find out what there is and get yourself included.

Some unions (e.g. UNISON) are open about what branches exist and how to contact them. There may be a branch directory or a list on the union website. In others, such as Unite, information about branches is a secret guarded by the bureaucracy. However, Unite reps can access a 'Work, Voice, Pay' database of thousands of workplaces where there are members. This includes useful information such as union recognition status, pay deals and which paid officer deals with the workplace. Find out what information and resources are available in your union.

Details of other branches and workplaces are important to build your networks for advice, support and solidarity. If you have a dispute, don't be shy about asking for solidarity in your own union and beyond (see Chapter 9). Many branches sit on lots of cash and are happy to support workers fighting back. As well as the official structures, there are many other networks, as discussed in Chapter 3.

If you get the opportunity to go to a union conference, take it. The opportunities to meet other activists, build your network and pick people's brains are at least as important as the formal business.

Most workers see the paid officers as powerful people with a legitimate role. So when a paid officer says something, it often carries more weight than if you say the same thing. This means it can help your campaign if an officer is willing to make helpful arguments. Employers generally pay more attention to paid officers than to reps, so their intervention can be very useful. For example, if you find yourself being picked on by management, consider asking the paid officer to write to the management asking them to back off and saying that the union will back you up forcefully if that doesn't happen.

THE UNION ISN'T JUST THE MEMBERS

Accessing support from the wider union is important, but it isn't always easy. Unions are inherently contradictory. They are organisations of resistance to employers but we also use unions to agree the terms of our exploitation with management. The balance between resisting and accommodating to employers varies. It is affected by factors including employer attitudes and the prevalence of bargaining relative to organising, as well as the union's politics, culture, rules and policies.

Those most involved in bargaining with employers are typically most accommodating to them. To negotiate effectively, you must put yourself in the head of your counterpart and learn to see things from the employer's perspective as well as that of workers. The stress and workload of the bargaining process puts negotiators under extra pressure to reach a settlement. Negotiators want good ongoing relationships with their counterparts and may be tempted to make concessions on substantive issues to protect them. The contradictory nature of unions affects everyone, but it affects those directly involved in bargaining most. Officers paid by the union to negotiate face even greater pressures to accommodate than reps involved in bargaining.

Historically, when workers started taking collective action and met opposition, they found that they needed strike funds and organisation extending beyond a single workplace. Workers need permanent organisation which, if it reaches any scale, requires its own rules, resources and staff. So while the statement 'the union is the members' is a good assertion of members' centrality, it isn't the whole picture – unions are institutions in their own right.

In nearly all unions, paid officers play a big role. In Chapter 1, I explained how jargon varies between unions, but I'm using 'paid officer' to designate those who bargain with employers and are employed by the union. Unlike reps, paid officers are not directly affected by the outcome of negotiations and they are far less exposed to pressure from, and accountability to, members. Though paid officers are the union's workers, when it comes to the relationships in the industries they cover, they are neither workers nor bosses – their role is to mediate between them.

All of us who get heavily involved in a union can begin to see defending and building it as an end in itself, whereas most workers see the union as a means to an end – good job security, pay, dignity at work and so on. Instead of seeing high membership as a way to strengthen campaigns, campaigns may be seen as a way to increase membership. The more that people prioritise the union as an institution over the needs of members, the more risk-averse they are likely to become in struggles. If someone is employed by the union, their livelihood depends on the union's financial health much more directly than it depends on good bargaining outcomes. As the American sociologist Charles Wright Mills (1948: 8–9) put it:

> [E]ven as the labor leader rebels, he holds back rebellion. He organizes discontent and then he sits on it, exploiting it to maintain a continuous organization; the labor leader is a manager of discontent.

Their caution is magnified by the fact that judging workers' mood is much harder for paid officers than it is for reps who are in amongst the workers themselves. Many paid officers, particularly higher up, have close relationships with the Labour Party. This often puts pressure on them not to rock the boat, particularly when Labour is in office nationally or locally – they can act as a transmission belt for government (or would-be government) agendas to workers more than the other way round. These structural factors are more fundamental in the behaviour of paid officers than the fact that their pay is sometimes closer to that of the managers they bargain with than to that of the members they represent. It's not mainly about corruption or cowardice. Even in societies where being a paid officer puts your life at risk, workers complain that they are too timid and quick to compromise. Resistance means extra work for paid officers, creating pressure for a quick resolution rather than the best one.

There are crude caricatures of this analysis. I'm not arguing that paid officers are all lazy and always sell us out, or that workers are all champing at the bit for action, if only bureaucrats would stop holding us back. Many paid officers were once activists themselves. Most of the time, most paid officers are more radical than most union members, let alone the working class as a whole. Because paid officers deal with industrial and political issues all the time, their ideas are much more developed and less fluid than those of members, who have rarely given as much thought to them. Workers' ideas often change rapidly when they are involved in struggle, usually becoming much more radical, particularly on issues connected with their fight. The result is that when members are in struggle, they often find that paid officers they saw as radical suddenly seem very conservative. Unless your union deals overwhelmingly with one employer or industry, it's unlikely that all the members will be involved in action at once. Paid officers continually balance between conflicting pressures from an active minority and the passive majority.

In periods when struggles get really big, they threaten the employment relationship central to capitalism. This threatens the social role of paid officers who mediate the terms of that relationship. In such situations, paid officers collectively capitulate rather than risk victory. A particularly sharp example comes from a conversation between the radical miners' leader Bob Smillie and the prime minister Lloyd George in 1919, reported in Aneurin Bevan's book *In Place of Fear* (1952). Lloyd George told a trade union delegation that the government was at their mercy and they must either take on the functions of the state or withdraw. Smillie commented 'From that moment on, we were beaten and we knew we were.' Struggle rarely reaches such heights – in the meantime, paid officers are more like unreliable allies.

Many of these pressures apply to reps to a lesser extent, but they apply even more the higher up the union structure you go. Senior paid officers

often spend more time with employers, politicians and state functionaries than they do with members. It's easy for them to get frustrated at members' lack of understanding of the big issues they grapple with. One way this can be manifested is paid officers being reluctant to put pressure on Labour politicians. It was union leaders who set up the Labour Party to represent them in parliament. Since then, paid officers and MPs have operated a mutually convenient division of labour. Paid officers can duck responsibility for serious campaigning over issues deemed 'political', redirecting energies away from workers' own power at work and harmlessly into the Labour Party. MPs can duck responsibility for supporting workers industrial struggles, saying they don't interfere in union business. This division between economics and politics suits paid officers and MPs well, but makes it harder for workers to win what we need.

Since the 1980s, anti-union legislation has exploited the institutional aspect of unions. Instead of threatening strike activists with jail, as in the 1970s, sanctions are applied to the union's funds and the state relies on paid officers to police their own members and persuade us to comply with the law.

There is a big range of behaviour from paid officers, but these are some of the common problems:

- prioritising bargaining over organising
- prioritising recruitment over outcomes for members
- avoiding things that cause them work
- acting as gatekeepers to information, resources and support which workers need
- caution if conflict could risk union funds or organisation
- holding back on actions which might upset politicians they see as sympathetic
- limiting member involvement during negotiations
- over-valuing relationships with management
- reaching understandings with management without members' consent
- prioritising any settlement over its impact on members.

The differences between members and paid officers mean that unions aren't just tools for workers to fight employers and government, they are also sites of struggle. Workers must fight to make their union their servant, not their master. I want to look briefly at the main responses workers have tried over the years, apart from what is perhaps the most common – giving up in frustration and disillusion.

Blame paid officers

Short of giving up, blaming paid officers is the least helpful response, even when it is at least partially justified. Being right doesn't build anything or overcome the problem. Worse still, you simply appear anti-union to most workers.

It's simply not true that 'paid officers always sell you out'. The contradictory nature of the union bureaucracy means their behaviour varies considerably. The problems listed above are common tendencies, but they are neither consistent nor universal. Even timid paid officers can sometimes be provoked into backing action. The 'Drive for 35' campaign for a shorter working week in engineering, discussed in Chapter 9, was one of the most effective strike campaigns since the defeat of the miners in 1985 – and it was led by a right-winger, Bill (later Lord) Jordan.

Ignore or bypass paid officers

Some people react to bad experiences with paid officers by excluding them from involvement as far as possible. This has obvious benefits – it builds workers' collective self-reliance and means focusing on building workers' own power. However, it denies you access to resources from the wider union because paid officers often act as gatekeepers. It prevents workers seeing the problems with paid officers themselves, leaving them uneducated and unprepared for occasions when paid officers do get involved. Far more workers will respond to a call for action from a general secretary than from a local rep. This means that bypassing paid officers often makes it harder to involve as many people in the struggle, which is the foundation of collective learning and power.

There are, however, times when excluding a paid officer makes perfect sense, such as if they talk to management behind your back.

Replace paid officers

Some paid officers are clearly better than others, so it's natural to want the best ones you can get. While it's a good idea to replace bad paid officers, this can't fully address the problem. The reasons paid officers make unreliable allies are structural rather than personal, so good paid officers tend to deteriorate the longer they do the job or the higher they rise, and even the best ones may let you down at crucial moments.

Union hopping

Sometimes workers get so frustrated with their union's bureaucracy that they individually or collectively switch unions. There are occasions when workers are left little choice, having exhausted attempts to overcome or bypass barriers to effective organising. But more often workers engage in union hopping *instead of* making their own attempts to organise. Workers may have accepted the dominant view of the relationship between a member and their union as being that of consumer and service provider. If workers don't understand the structural division between rank-and-file workers and the union bureaucracy, they may wrongly attribute problems to individuals or union policies.

When people hop unions, they rarely take most of their workmates with them, so switching often makes it harder to achieve united action or challenge the bureaucracy. If the most radical people hop unions, most members are left at the mercy of the existing bureaucracy with even less opposition than before.

Red unions

The creation of new and explicitly radical or 'red' unions can raise some of the same problems as union hopping.

After the Electrical, Electronic, Telecommunications and Plumbing Union (EETPU) had organised scabbing on print workers at Rupert Murdoch's new Wapping plant, it was expelled from the Trades Union Congress (TUC) for signing single union 'sweetheart' deals that excluded other unions. In 1988, around 5000 of the EETPU's best members left to form the Electrical and Plumbing Industries Union (EPIU), leaving the vast majority of members behind with only a tiny number of radical trade unionists challenging the leadership. The EPIU later joined the Transport and General Workers Union (TGWU), which is now part of Unite – as are the former EETPU and the printers.

Following the death of 167 workers in the Piper Alpha disaster in 1988, North Sea workers set up the Offshore Industry Liaison Committee (OILC) – a rank-and-file group which included members of various unions. OILC later established itself as an independent union in its own right and then became a branch of the Rail, Maritime and Transport (RMT) union. Having begun by bringing together workers from multiple unions, OILC ended up as part of one of them.

More recently, a group of low-paid Latin American workers in London joined the TGWU, but frustrations over conservatism and bureaucracy led them to break away, join the Industrial Workers of the World (IWW) and then split to form the IWGB. They were joined by a group of low-paid, mainly migrant workers for the University of London who felt UNISON wasn't giving them the support they needed.

There are now several independent micro-unions including United Voices of the World (UVW), the Cleaners and Allied Independent Workers Union (CAIWU) and the App Drivers and Couriers Union (ADCU). Though people often group these unions together, there are significant differences. Some rely heavily on strikes, others more on litigation. Some are more dependent on external funding than others. Not all are equally democratic, and some have a larger bureaucracy than others. I can't do justice to their contribution here, but they are doing important work and have achieved some remarkable successes. They can generally be nimbler and more responsive, and it's easier for groups of members to shape their internal culture to meet their needs. They mainly organise workers who are often neglected by more established unions. Neither are they simply red unions – they are more complex, including groups who were never part of a traditional union or in areas where TUC unions have little presence. But some also draw in individuals attracted by their radicalism but lacking collective organisation in their jobs.

If we want a powerful workers movement, we must ultimately win over the majority of workers, not separate a radical minority from them. As well as achieving important wins now, red unions can be valuable grounds for experimentation with new approaches. But, as with the new unions of the 1880s, the big gains usually happen when those new approaches are implemented in the big unions too. It remains the case that there are more low-paid and migrant workers organised in the large, mainstream unions than the new small ones.

Whatever the strengths of red unions for workers responding tactically to specific situations, a key question is whether they will reproduce the traditional problems if they are successful and grow large. If, as I'm arguing, the problems of bureaucracy arise from the nature of trade unionism, even if some unions make them much worse than necessary, then red unions can't be a general solution.

Improve the rules

The fact that paid officers are subject to pressures from employers and the state is central to the problem of the bureaucracy. So it makes sense for workers to try to counter that with our own pressure. This can be done in two ways – increasing workers' self-reliance and power, and changing the union's rules to shift the balance of power between workers and paid officers.

There are many rules and practices that can make paid officers and senior lay members less distant and unaccountable, for example:

- strong democratic structures of lay members that take key decisions
- resources being controlled by lay structures, not paid officers
- making paid officers clearly accountable to specific lay structures
- lay member involvement in negotiations
- members voting on all agreements
- open and big bargaining (see Chapter 10)
- publishing all agreements
- election rather than appointment of paid officers
- making paid officers subject to re-election
- paid officers on wages comparable to those they represent, rather than those they bargain with
- limits to the terms of office of the most senior paid officers, like general secretaries
- a right for members to attend any union meeting as an observer
- lay members, rather than paid officers, being delegates to other organisations
- recording who voted which way in meeting minutes.

Democratising a union in this way can help, but it can't completely remove the problem of the bureaucracy.

A rank-and-file approach

I'd advocate integrating elements from several of the responses above into a rank-and-file approach. The classic statement of this approach came from the Clyde Workers' Committee (CWC) in 1915:

> We will support the officials [paid officers] just so long as they rightly represent the workers, but we will act independently immediately they [sic] misrepresent them. Being composed of Delegates from every shop, and untrammelled by obsolete rule or law, we claim to represent the true feeling of the workers. We can act immediately according to the merits of the case and the desire of the rank and file.
>
> (Gallacher, 1915)

The CWC didn't automatically oppose the paid officers, they supported and worked with them where they were doing the right thing. The words 'just so long as' are sometimes misinterpreted though. It isn't advocating supporting each paid officer until they do something wrong and then opposing them. It's about working 'with and against' them (often at the same time on different points), cooperating where possible, but not being tied to them. This approach maximises workers' participation in collective action, which builds power.

The rank-and-file approach recognises that workers' power in relation to the bureaucracy is an echo of our power in relation to the employers. When workers are weak, we are more dependent on the union bureaucracy for support and assistance. Building workers' collective power and self-activity is central to reducing our dependence on unreliable allies – the paid officers. We do this with their help when we can, but we do it whether they help or not.

When the CWC issued this statement during the First World War, 'act independently' often meant taking unofficial strike action, but it should be interpreted more broadly. Building the capacity of workers to act independently in smaller ways is central to a rank-and-file approach. If we can't hold a meeting, take a collective decision, produce a leaflet or deal with the employer without approval from paid officers then we aren't likely to be ready to walk out! The more capacity workers have to do things for ourselves, the less vulnerable we are to paid officers pulling the plug on a campaign or diverting resources elsewhere. Ironically, the less we need paid officers' support, the more likely we are to get it, because a campaign that succeeds when they withhold backing is somewhat embarrassing.

If you want to do some organising but are blocked through the official structures, look for ways round. Teachers in Chicago, faced with a dismal union branch, set up a separate group (Caucus Of Rank and file Educators, CORE) which campaigned against school closures and discrimination. One of their activists explained that they 'did what the union should have been doing', rather than burning energy in unproductive conflict with the bureaucracy. Campaigning built profile, networks and power. Eventually CORE was able to win elections to replace the branch leadership and then lead an inspiring and successful strike. There are also examples of activists faced with an obstructive branch using a neglected part of the structure, such as a women's committee, to organise and campaign.

The union bureaucracy isn't monolithic – there are many divisions within it along sectoral and political lines as well around personal loyalties. Radical members and paid officers in unions often organise 'broad left' groups to press for better policies and rules, and to try to elect supporters to various positions. Such groups can play a useful role, but they tend to focus on internal left–right divisions and faction fighting rather than building workers' power. The most important division is between workers and employers. The division between paid officers and rank-and-file members is secondary, and the differences between left and right within the union are the least important, though they still matter – particularly when workers' resistance to employers is low. Even the best of the paid officers tend to side with the rest of the bureaucracy when the stakes get high, while workers' political views can change rapidly in struggle. We shouldn't aim our fire at paid officers – keep it aimed at employers and the government. But when paid officers get in the way, we shouldn't hold our fire to prevent them being caught in the crossfire.

What I've described in this chapter are pressures and tendencies. The behaviour of individuals varies considerably. You may find your efforts being obstructed by lay activists but have a paid officer who is willing to help break down the barriers. For example, it's not uncommon for branch officers or senior lay reps to be committed to a partnership approach, while an officer can see that it isn't working and supports a more robust approach. Don't make the mistake of assuming officers are never willing or able to help you – work with them when you can.

A rank-and-file approach includes trying to replace bad paid officers with better ones and democratising the union to tip the power balance within it in workers' favour. Those who pursue a rank-and-file strategy often try to build rank-and-file organisations. The CWC was a particularly fine one, but there have been many in different industries over the years. These aren't rival unions but organise activists within and across the unions in an industry or area. In periods when few workers are taking high-impact collective action, there's a limit to how far rank-and-file organisation can be built, but we should do what we can. Building direct links with activists in other workplaces reduces dependence on official structures. Similarly, grassroots fundraising for strikes reduces dependence on paid officers and the strike funds they control.

STANDING UP TO THE UNION BUREAUCRACY

While you shouldn't waste energy banging your head against a bureaucratic brick wall, don't accept obstructive behaviour. The union bureaucracy is made up of people and they aren't all the same. It is often worth arguing with individuals. Be very clear what you want them to do – not only does this make them more likely to help, but it educates members if they don't. Involve members in pushing for what you need, rather than doing it as an individual. For example, it's harder for paid officers to block a course of action that members have voted for. This can also make it harder for paid officers to cultivate divisions between reps to prevent you pushing for what you need. Getting lots of members to contact a paid officer directly about a problem may convince them that working with you to address it is preferable. The bureaucracy is neither completely under the control of the members, nor does it have a completely free hand – its room for manoeuvre depends on the circumstances.

Complex structures and rules empower those who know them best at the expense of most workers. While it's not most people's idea of fun, you do need to familiarise yourself with the structures and rules so that it's harder for people to block and bamboozle you. Sadly, some people with positions in unions even make up entirely bogus rules to fob you off, so don't take what you're told as gospel. It helps to build your network beyond your own workplace (see Chapters 2 and 9) so you know plenty of people who can help you navigate your way through the union apparatus. This isn't just about advice.

Someone supportive and influential having a word can often get things moving. It shouldn't be down to who you know, but often it is.

Another tool in the kit of the obstructive bureaucrat is control of information. How can you organise effectively if you don't know what's going on in your own union and can't find out who does what or how to do things? If you get elected to any union committees then report back as widely as possible. When I was on the national executive and other committees of the Amicus and Unite unions, I ran a blog[1] via which I reported on meetings and conferences, as well as posting other information such as appeals for solidarity. This wasn't always popular with those at the top, but many activists said it was their main way of keeping informed.

The latest weapon in the bureaucrat's armoury is GDPR (General Data Protection Regulation), the rules on data protection. Unions must comply with data protection principles[2], which include only holding personal data they need to and restricting access to those who need it for legitimate purposes. But GDPR is widely used as an excuse to deny people the information they need to perform their role in the union, even if they have been elected to that role. Don't be afraid to call bullshit on GDPR excuses or to ask what needs to be put in place to enable you to perform your role.

I'll end this chapter with an example of the rank-and-file strategy in practice. In 2011, seven big construction employers tried to impose a new deal – the Building Engineering Services National Agreement (BESNA) – which included 35 per cent pay cuts and deskilling for electricians. Workers got together at meetings and via social media and organised protests at sites around the country. Initially, the official union response was hostile, opposing any action before the change had been implemented. One senior paid officer described the rank-and-file group organising the protests as a cancer in the union. Workers pressed on with increasingly militant protests, including blockades and rushing site entrances to occupy and hold meetings inside sites. Gradually, supporters (mainly from the left) won arguments in Unite committees to support the workers. Once there was official backing from parts of the union, it was easier to build support for the protests and momentum grew to the point where a large part of the union executive, including the chair, took part in shutting down a site at Blackfriars station. In this context, Unite finally agreed a strike ballot of workers at Balfour Beatty, the main company behind BESNA. Once that came through, BESNA collapsed. It's an example that illustrates workers organising independently of the paid officers, focusing on the employer instead of internal arguments, but not ignoring official structures and working with paid officers where possible.

Key points

- Get to know your union structure and the people in it, and make use of them.
- Dealing with employers and politicians puts people under pressure to accommodate to them.
- Paid officers are neither workers nor bosses but mediate between the two. They are unreliable allies.
- The division between economics and politics disarms workers.
- Use a rank-and-file approach to build the capacity of workers to act with the paid officers when possible, independently when not. Democratising the union helps workers control it. Focus on building power to resist the employer: that will give workers more control over their union too.

Discussion questions

1. What do you need to find out about your union structure and who does what?
2. How can you widen your networks within your union?
3. What are your experiences of any differences or conflicts between members, reps and paid officers?

12

Overcoming difficulties and limitations

In this chapter, I'll discuss some of the common pitfalls to check for if you aren't making the progress you expect. If you hit problems, don't just talk to other activists directly involved – use your networks to get fresh ideas. Just explaining the situation to someone new can clarify matters in your own head. Even bad suggestions can prompt you to look at things differently.

In *Rethinking Industrial Relations*, John Kelly (1998) describes a number of key links in the chain between an employer action that generates a sense of injustice or illegitimacy and workers taking action. Considering how strong each link is in your campaign can help identify the problem:

> Employees must also acquire a sense of common identity which differentiates them from the employer; they must attribute the perceived injustice to the employer; and they must be willing to engage in some form of collective organization and activity. This whole process of collectivization is heavily dependent on the actions of small numbers of leaders or activists.

I'll look at pitfalls under two broad categories – problems with the campaign and problems with the campaigners. I'll then discuss the issue of activist burnout, and end by returning to some of the limitations of organising in unions and how they might be overcome.

CAMPAIGN PITFALLS

If your campaign isn't going well, it's time to revisit some of the key points covered earlier in the book. Chapter 5 covered choosing and communicating about issues. If you've picked the wrong issue then your campaign will struggle. Consider testing your issue again to make sure it really is suitable for organising around. If you've got a good issue for your campaign, you may not have framed it well. Poor framing can draw the dividing line in the wrong place, undermine a united sense of 'us' and prevent the attribution of blame to 'them'. It makes it harder to fan workers' feelings of injustice.

If you've been carrying out structure tests, your mapping and charting (see Chapter 6) will show whether the problems are with the whole campaign or in certain areas. If support is weak in certain teams then it's likely you haven't correctly identified the most influential workers or you haven't really got them on board.

Chapter 8 included making a plan to win. It's hard to motivate people to take action if your plan isn't credible, you haven't communicated it clearly or what you are asking people to do doesn't connect well to the overall plan. You can't get high participation if people can't see the point of an activity.

PROBLEMS WITH THE CAMPAIGNERS

Most of this book has been about the process of organising, but people – with all our strengths, weaknesses and interactions – are central to its success or failure. The dynamics and organisational culture of the group trying to organise can cause major problems – preventing people learning or developing, deterring participation and causing people to drop out. These can be harder to rectify than problems with the campaign itself because they involve the behaviour and feelings of individuals as well as the habits of a group.

Sometimes the problems can be obvious. If discriminatory behaviour (whether deliberate or not), bullying or harassment are tolerated, they will exclude, drive out and put off many people. Sometimes problematic behaviour can be harder to pin down though. Someone can be so unpleasant that people just don't want to work with them, even if they don't cross obvious lines. Your starting point in tackling those cases should be the person's commitment to the cause. If they weren't supportive, they wouldn't be there to cause problems. You can try explaining to the person what they are doing, how it is impacting on the campaign and how you would like them to behave. Is there a way of de-escalating or resolving conflict informally? Could someone act as a mediator? Try to find out if there are reasons why they are behaving destructively, in case that suggests ways to help. Ultimately, if they can't change, ask them to change role or leave. This feels harsh, especially if someone is committed and hardworking, but you can't allow being polite or feeling squeamish to undermine the campaign. Becky Bond and Zack Exley (2016) have good advice on this in a chapter titled 'Fight the Tyranny of the Annoying'.

Other problems can be more collective, about organisational culture. A core issue is how you deal with setbacks. While organising, you will try lots of things and many of them won't work, or at least not how you hoped. If, as the saying goes, you learn from your mistakes, then any organiser should be learning a lot. And we shouldn't expect to win every battle either. As rail union leader Bob Crow said, 'if you fight you might not win, but if you don't fight you always lose'. Sadly, there's a culture in many unions of not admitting mistakes or defeats in the belief this would 'undermine confidence'. It's true that being honest about mistakes and defeats undermines confidence in invincibility or infallibility – but such confidence would be misplaced. To boost confidence, do more to celebrate genuine successes – something the movement is not always great at. Being honest about problems builds trust and enables learning. We are relying on workers' own activity, so we need workers to be educated about our movement and its struggles, not kept in the dark. Restricting knowledge about setbacks to an inner circle is an elitist 'not in front of the children' approach. As the 1199 union's advice to rookie organisers puts it 'workers are made of clay, not glass' (McAlevey, 2016). Only by discussing and thinking about our setbacks can we draw the right lessons from them. If you don't discuss them, people draw lessons anyway, but often the wrong ones.

When people don't understand why things went badly, they are more likely to blame each other. Frustration can lead to activists blaming workers for not participating, not sharing their views, and so on. Stamp this out. If the causes lie in other people, they are outside your control, so this mindset offers no way forward and creates a cynical atmosphere. Heather Wood describes[1] how when things got very stressful for women organising in Easington, County Durham, during the 1984–85 miners' strike, they included in their meetings a section for each person to air how they were feeling so that conflicts could be discussed and the group could move on united.

Activists' deep commitment to their cause can feed a 'macho culture' where we are all expected to be indestructible super-activists who never have a bad day, a life outside activism, exhaustion or a wobble in our resolve, and who never need a break. Such cultures are deeply damaging. They set the bar at an unrealistic height, making most people feel they can't contribute, feeding feelings of inadequacy and imposter syndrome. They discourage people from raising and resolving difficulties and from supporting each other. A macho culture will reduce participation, hinder learning and increase the risk of activists burning out – to which I'll turn shortly.

One pressure on activists to conform to the superhero model is that if workers are looking to you and they see you having a wobble, that can spread. It does matter that you hold your nerve when things get tough. Discuss concerns with relevant people and get support as a matter of routine. Bottling them up risks blurting them out in circumstances you wouldn't have chosen or losing your temper. You can't help others without looking after yourself.

BURNOUT AND ORGANISATIONAL CULTURE

The World Health Organisation (WHO) defines burnout[2] as a product of chronic stress resulting specifically from work, but the term is widely used in activist circles and the WHO definition is all too recognisable:

- feelings of energy depletion or exhaustion
- increased mental distance from one's job, or feelings of negativism or cynicism related to one's job
- reduced professional efficacy.

It should be no surprise then, that the six factors which the Health and Safety Executive identify as the organisational causes of work stress[3] are also relevant for activists:

- *Demands*: this includes issues such as workload, work patterns and the work environment.
- *Control*: how much say the person has in the way they do their work.
- *Support*: this includes the encouragement, sponsorship and resources provided by the organisation, line management and colleagues.
- *Relationships*: this includes promoting positive working to avoid conflict and dealing with unacceptable behaviour.
- *Role*: whether people understand their role within the organisation and whether the organisation ensures that they do not have conflicting roles.
- *Change*: how organisational change (large or small) is managed and communicated in the organisation.

Many activists think burnout is caused by doing too much, but busy periods are often amongst the most satisfying, as long as we don't sustain intensity too long without respite. These are some factors I've seen contribute to activist burnout:

- defeats and setbacks we don't learn from
- inadequate attention to political education causing unrealistic expectations or preventing understanding of difficulties
- awareness of the gap between what's needed and our forces
- feeling responsible for more than we can control
- overcommitting, then guilt
- putting too many eggs in one activism basket (when that goes badly)
- unproductive political conflict
- others pushing our organisations in directions we don't like
- uncomradely behaviour – knocking down rather than building up, rudeness, non-constructive criticism, not listening or engaging in good faith
- bullying, harassment and discrimination
- lack of reflection on successes or affirmation of our efforts
- macho culture

- lack of spaces to discuss what we want, particularly things we are struggling with
- lack of a network of trusted and supportive people
- poor internal communication
- resenting or blaming others who contribute less.

We should try to build organisational cultures that help prevent people suffering burnout. Such cultures would encourage:

- understanding the situation, difficulties and setbacks
- ability to discuss when we're struggling or things go badly
- realistic goals, plans and expectations
- excitement – new ideas, new people, new experiences
- celebrating successes
- clarity about what we're trying to do, why, and how people can contribute
- remembering why we're doing this and how our activism connects to our big goals
- not trying to do everything, spreading yourself too thin or being a 'grasshopper' between campaigns without building anything lasting
- prioritising longer-term areas of interest so you can build relationships, organisation and learn, alongside some variety
- democracy and avoiding cliques
- collectivising responsibilities to reduce the extent that some people, usually women, are playing leading roles in the campaign, in childcare and housework, and neglecting themselves and their relationships or feeling guilty about excessive expectations
- supportive, friendly culture including open disagreement
- giving feedback routinely – positive or constructive criticism
- checking in on other activists if you think they may be struggling
- encouraging others, but if they don't do what you hope, avoiding getting frustrated, disappointed or feeling you have to take on their tasks
- taking responsibility collectively as well as individually
- a culture in which it's better to say you can't do or haven't done something than to hide
- spotting the signs of burnout before it is overwhelming
- feeling able to take short breaks or ease off for a while.

Organising is a marathon and any sprints in it should be short – we need to balance our sense of urgency with patience and care for ourselves and each other. As activists, we have a responsibility to try to look after ourselves and to seek and accept support when appropriate, so that our stresses don't cause problems for others in the movement. Employers often talk about self-care and wellbeing, but they cause the problems that wreck our mental health. Tackling those problems is a collective project. Workers don't need superheroes doing everything for them.

ARE UNIONS ENOUGH?

This chapter has so far looked at problems you might encounter in specific campaigns, or in particular groups of people, and the building of an organisational culture to sustain high participation. For the final section, I want to turn to some of the more structural limitations of organising unions, building on the discussion in Chapter 11 about unions as institutions and a rank-and-file strategy.

I have argued throughout this book that we should focus on organising workers rather than on recruiting into unions, which is just one part of that process. I have argued that unions are inherently contradictory organisations, divided between a bureaucracy and the rank and file, and enabling both resistance to capital and accommodation to it. And I have argued that organising at work should not be counterposed to organising in other spheres of life – we are strongest when struggles at work and in the community support and reinforce each other. Given the sorry state of affairs in Britain today, building strong unions would help greatly, but the limitations and contradictions of unions mean we need to aim beyond them.

Union organisation gives us more power to influence the market for our ability to work (our labour power). But it takes for granted our exploitation – the fact that we as workers are sellers of our labour power and that a minority are capitalists who can buy it to make profit. That's why every union victory is temporary – and, thankfully, so is every defeat! The technology and process of work keeps evolving and the labour market changes too. Employers keep coming back with new demands and changes, and we have to defend past gains. Polish/German socialist Rosa Luxemburg (1999a [1900]) had good reasons to describe trade unionism as a 'labour of Sisyphus', after the mythological king of Corinth who was condemned to eternally roll a huge stone to the top of a hill, after which it rolled down again. A better world, one not founded on the grotesque inequality of wage labour and the pursuit of profit, means replacing capitalist society with a socialist one, rather than just reducing the degree of our exploitation.

The word 'socialist' has been used as a label for so many different political projects that it's worth specifying what I mean by it – a society where democracy is meaningful and extends into economic life, enabling an end to exploitation, oppression and the pursuit of profit. People debate whether it's possible to avert the worst of the developing climate catastrophe under capitalism. We can be sure that we won't do so without resisting the short-term pressures of capitalist competition between companies and states. These same pressures drive states towards war. We will only see an end to working-class men and women being sent to murder and maim each other when democratic control replaces the competitive drive for profit.

Even when workers don't make socialism their explicit aim, the question can force itself on the working-class movement. In Chapter 11, I gave the example of radical union leaders, in a dispute over pay and hours, backing down when the prime minister said the government was at the unions' mercy and that they would have to take over the functions of the state or withdraw. Unions aren't equipped for such a role and the 'leaders' chose defeat over too big a victory.

I discussed the importance of maximising workers' capacity to act independently of paid officers, and building rank-and-file networks to support that. The most successful union organisations include almost all the workers in the parts of the labour market they cover, giving the workers enormous potential power. I say 'almost' because unions shouldn't include organised fascists since fascist movements crush all democratic organisations, including unions. The strongest unions protect members by excluding fascists from the workforce, not just membership. Unions also need to ensure women (and occasionally men) aren't prevented from participating because we have failed to deal with perpetrators of gendered violence in our ranks. After #MeToo, nobody should still imagine that attempting to brush such issues under the carpet is good for an organisation.

Workers don't all agree – there's always a significant minority who vote Tory, or worse – and workers have a wide range of opinions on many practical questions that arise as you organise. Unions, and even rank-and-file organisations, are therefore sites of struggle themselves, between individuals and formal or informal factions promoting different approaches. As Colin Barker puts it in *Revolutionary Rehearsals in the Neoliberal Age* (Barker, Dale and Davidson, 2021):

> [I]n just about any social and political crisis there will be voices inside movements urging that we should negotiate with the powers that be, that we should 'moderate' our aspirations and demonstrate our 'realism,' that we should recognize that many people are put off by aggressive militancy but might be won over if we only slowed the pace and narrowed the scope of our demands. Those voices may be 'honest brokers' or may be hoping to make their own political fortunes; they may be disillusioned former revolutionaries. Whatever their motivations, their presence and influence can't be wished away.

This implies that workers don't just need unions that organise all workers and rank-and-file organisation to facilitate action independently of paid officers. We also need socialists within both to be organised independently to fight our corner. The importance of this is clearest when the movement is strongest. I will give two more examples.

During the First World War, strikes were illegal in Britain but workers saw their bargaining power increasing because labour was in great demand. New technologies and working practices disrupted the 'deal' at work and employers profiteered. Workers, particularly in engineering, responded with strikes and the growth of a rank-and-file movement of shop stewards, which included workplace delegates forming Workers' Committees in industrial areas. Given that strikes disrupted the war effort, it is unsurprising that anti-war socialists were at the fore, even though the movement was politically diverse and took no position on the war. The Workers' Committees created a national structure, but it was primarily administrative. One of the stewards' leaders, John Thomas Murphy, recognised in his book *Preparing for Power* (1972 [1934]) that the theories the national committee held, which meant referring all matters back to the rank and file, prevented it giving the leadership the movement needed.

One of the big issues facing workers was conscription to the bloodbath at the front, which 'skilled' engineers had resisted. By 1918, the Bolshevik Revolution in Russia had forced that country's withdrawal from the war, while the British army was demanding yet more conscripts. Cliff and Gluckstein (2014 [1986]) explain that the stewards' national leadership gave the UK government an ultimatum to scrap new conscription laws and consider Bolshevik peace proposals. But their newspaper, *Solidarity*, cast doubt on whether German workers would take similar action, and there was no effective action behind the ultimatum. Cliff and Gluckstein describe the tragedy: 'at the very moment Solidarity voiced its fear of German workers, 400,000 German engineers struck against the war, only to find themselves isolated internationally'. The dispute had focused on the protection of 'skilled' engineers from conscription. Dodging the political issue of opposition to the war made it easier for them to be split off from other workers.

The weaknesses of the rank-and-file movement were twofold. Firstly, in reaction to the experience of bureaucracy, many activists rejected 'leadership' in favour of an entirely bottom-up approach. This ignored the reality that various people *were* leading the movement and made their role and views less explicit and open for debate. Secondly, a politically diverse rank-and-file movement cannot provide political leadership within itself. To win workers to strike against the war, political organisation of anti-war socialists was required, independent from those afraid of undermining the war effort. Tragically, such organisations were inadequate.

Another great example is from the Solidarność (Solidarity) union which erupted in Poland in 1980–81, triggered by the sacking of Gdansk shipyard worker and activist Anna Walentynowicz. Strikes and occupations spread across Poland and the union rapidly grew to ten million members, 80 per cent of the Polish workforce.[4] Workers' committees sprang up to coordinate action between workplaces. There were plenty of people who preached moderation, including Solidarność's intellectual advisers and the church's Cardinal Wyszynski, but those who wanted workers to take power had no significant organisation. When hundreds of police beat up union members and one of Solidarność's leaders in the city of Bydgoszcz, strikes erupted and plans were laid for a general strike. The cardinal had a private meeting with strike leader Lech Wałęsa, after which Wałęsa called off the strike, throwing the movement into retreat and paving the way for more repression and then the imposition of martial law and the banning of Solidarność. There wasn't socialist organisation capable of arguing against the retreat within the movement and preventing it. It wasn't until 1986 that Solidarność was legalised. In the 1990s, Solidarność was in government but a disaster for workers, who were now marginalised because the organisation accommodated to global capital and its former enemies within Poland.

In addition to unions and rank-and-file organisation, the working-class movement needs socialists who are committed to completely replacing capitalism, in order to be collectively organised independently of the compromisers. Such organisation can help make connections between different parts of our movement, in work and communities, overcoming sectionalism and localism. It can encourage convergence between workers resisting their oppression and exploitation and other groups confronting capitalism, such as those resisting other forms of oppression or environmental breakdown. It can campaign against those inside and outside our movement who preach the moderation and unnecessary compromise that so often cause defeat. Its members can pool their ideas and experiences to collectively hammer out what needs to be done and put those arguments across a country and internationally. Such an organisation will be absolutely indispensable when struggles reach a higher level, but would also make a difference every day now. In a country like Britain, it would need hundreds of thousands of members, rooted in every workplace and community.

The current state of the left is a million miles from what we need. In Britain, the working-class movement has been on the back foot since the mid-1970s. This book doesn't aim to cover how we build revolutionary socialist organisation, but given the scale of the crises we face, organising at work needs that wider context. Organising at work can improve our lives in myriad ways today. Without organising at work, we lack the power to effectively tackle inequality, poverty, discrimination, housing, health and care, education, repression, war or environmental catastrophe. In every one of those struggles we don't just face bad individuals. The very structure of capitalism is based on competition between companies and states, and on the pursuit of profit at any cost. We fight more effectively today, even for the smallest reforms, if we aren't held back by a commitment to the system that causes our problems. Being in a socialist organisation today, despite all such organisations' inadequacies, can connect you with a wealth of ideas and experience and make you a more effective activist, as well as being a tiny step towards the organisation we need.

Union activism may be an unending Labour of Sisyphus with no permanent victories, but Bob Crow was right that if you never fight you always lose. We're better off with temporary victories than no victories at all. And rolling that giant rock up the hill makes our movement stronger. One day, we will use that strength to smash that rock and liberate humanity.

Key points

- If things aren't going well, use your networks to get fresh ideas.
- Check the chain between an unjust employer action and workers' action to identify the weak links.
- Common problems with campaigns include choosing the wrong organising issue, framing it badly, not communicating a credible plan to win, and not confirming through structure tests that you have correctly identified and won over the influential workers in every area.
- Stamp out behaviour from people in your campaign that deters participation.
- Build a supportive culture where people can talk about concerns and problems.
- Even strong unions with a powerful rank-and-file movement have limitations because of their relationship to capitalist society, which is inherently exploitative, oppressive and environmentally destructive.
- Socialist organisation is required to oppose the compromisers in our movement. Such organisation also helps us be more effective organisers now.

Discussion questions

1. If you have previously been part of a campaign, whether in work or elsewhere, what was its organisational culture like?
2. How do you see the relationship between unions, rank-and-file groups and political organisations?

Postscript

I hope you found the book useful and are trying out some of the ideas. What you do can make a difference. Remember that nobody has all the answers about how best to organise. You will need to try lots of things, see what works, adapt some and scrap others. One of the weaknesses of the working-class movement is how bad we are at sharing our successes and what we learn from failures. This is partly because of the fear of employer reprisals, partly because we underestimate the value of our experiences and partly because recent decades with few strikes have left activists disconnected from each other.

Little in this book is entirely original – I have spent a lifetime picking the brains of other activists, attending meetings and training sessions, reading books and trying things out. I'm grateful to all those who helped me learn what I know and hope the book is in some small way 'paying it forward'. I was working as an organiser for the socialist group rs21.org.uk when writing the book. Their support was invaluable practically and in clarifying my ideas.

You can help continue the collective learning process by building and using your networks for advice, support and solidarity. The website I've set up for this book (workers-can-win.info) is intended to help, so please send in your ideas, experiences and constructive criticisms, so that the site can provide updates and additions that others can read alongside this book.

Go get organised!

Notes

CHAPTER 1

1. P&O Ferries intentionally broke the law: workers-can-win.info/ch1-1

CHAPTER 2

1. Trade unionists in many countries face violence: workers-can-win.info/ch2-1
2. Social reproduction: workers-can-win.info/fr-16
3. Statistics on employment in the UK, October 2021: workers-can-win.info/ch2-3

CHAPTER 3

1. TULR(C)A 1992 s146–151: workers-can-win.info/ch3-1a; TULR(C)A 1992 s152–167: workers-can-win.info/ch3-1b; ERA 1996 s44: workers-can-win.info/ch3-1c; ERA 1996 s103: workers-can-win.info/ch3-1d
2. Ruling that industrial action can be union activity: workers-can-win.info/ch3-2
3. www.google.co.uk/alerts
4. Information from Companies House: workers-can-win.info/ch3-4
5. Gender pay gaps: workers-can-win.info/ch3-5
6. How to make a Freedom of Information request: workers-can-win.info/ch3-6
7. www.bailii.org
8. lrd.org.uk
9. Unite's Work Voice Pay resources: workers-can-win.info/ch3-9
10. Research skills for trade unionists: workers-can-win.info/ch3-10
11. TUC union finder: workers-can-win.info/ch3-11
12. TUC reps' training: workers-can-win.info/ch3-12
13. gftu.org.uk
14. *Acas Code of Practice on Facility Time:* workers-can-win.info/ch3-14
15. Thompsons' solicitors' newsletters: workers-can-win.info/ch3-15
16. TUC email subscriptions: workers-can-win.info/ch3-16
17. Trades councils: workers-can-win.info/ch3-17

CHAPTER 4

1. ERA 1999 s10: workers-can-win.info/ch4-1
2. *Acas Code of Practice on Disciplinary and Grievance Procedures*: workers-can-win.info/ch4-2
3. Understanding legislation: workers-can-win.info/ch4-3

4. EU legislation and the UK: workers-can-win.info/ch4-4
5. NMW rates: workers-can-win.info/ch4-5
6. National Minimum Wage Act 1998: workers-can-win.info/ch4-6
7. Acas early conciliation: workers-can-win.info/ch4-7
8. Employment Tribunals: workers-can-win.info/ch4-8
9. Survivor-centred approaches: workers-can-win.info/ch4-9
10. UCU advice on migrant workers taking industrial action: workers-can-win.info/ch4-10

CHAPTER 5

1. The original leaflet included a great cartoon by Bob Simpson and Estelle Carol under the pen-name Carol Simpson: workers-can-win.info/ch5-1
2. Buzzword bingo workers-can-win.info/ch5-2

CHAPTER 6

1. This first successful unionisation of an Amazon warehouse in the USA illustrates the importance of influential workers: workers-can-win.info/ch6-1
2. Influential workers and organising in a pub chain: workers-can-win.info/ch6-2
3. Unite did get fined for a GDPR breach, but that was for unsolicited marketing to members, not organising: workers-can-win.info/ch6-3
4. workers-can-win.info/ch6-4

CHAPTER 7

1. Umbrella companies: workers-can-win.info/ch7-1
2. Judgement where Uber drivers won 'worker' status: workers-can-win.info/ch7-2
3. Right to a written statement of employment particulars: workers-can-win.info/ch7-3
4. TUC guide to health and safety rights: workers-can-win.info/ch7-4
5. Health and Safety at Work Act 1974: workers-can-win.info/ch7-5
6. Safety Regulations: workers-can-win.info/ch7-6
7. Allocation of safety enforcement responsibilities: workers-can-win.info/ch7-7
8. 'Suitable and sufficient' risk assessments: workers-can-win.info/ch7-8
9. Competent persons: workers-can-win.info/ch7-9
10. Young people: workers-can-win.info/ch7-10
11. HSE management standards for stress: workers-can-win.info/ch7-11
12. Safety consultation regulations: workers-can-win.info/ch7-12
13. Equality Act 2010: workers-can-win.info/ch7-13
14. Terms used in the Equality Act: workers-can-win.info/ch7-14
15. Judgement about what counts as a PCP: workers-can-win.info/ch7-15
16. The social model of disability: workers-can-win.info/ch7-16
17. Identifying discrimination in selection: workers-can-win.info/ch7-17
18. PSED in the Equality Act 2010: workers-can-win.info/ch7-18

19. The TUC guide to PSED: workers-can-win.info/ch7-19
20. TULR(C)A 1992 s188 covers redundancy consultation: workers-can-win.info/ch7-20
21. A ruling on objecting to a TUPE transfer: workers-can-win.info/ch7-21
22. Whistleblowing in the ERA 1996: workers-can-win.info/ch7-22
23. TULR(C)A 1992 covers union duties, learning reps and activities: workers-can-win.info/ch7-23a. The *Acas Code of Practice* covers facility time for reps and learning reps: workers-can-win.info/ch3-14. The brown book covers safety reps: workers-can-win.info/ch7-23c. Information for collective bargaining is covered on WorkSmart: workers-can-win.info/ch7-23d and TULR(C)A 1992: workers-can-win.info/ch7-23e
24. How to apply to the CAC: workers-can-win.info/ch7-24a; Legislation on statutory union recognition: workers-can-win.info/ch7-24b
25. The CAC: workers-can-win.info/ch7-25
26. Legislation on the bargaining unit for statutory recognition: workers-can-win.info/ch7-26
27. *Code of Practice on Unfair Practices During Recognition Ballots*: workers-can-win.info/ch7-27
28. *ACAS Code of Practice on Facility Time*: workers-can-win.info/ch3-14
29. Information and Consultation of Employees Regulations 2004: workers-can-win.info/ch7-29
30. *Using Information and Consultation Rights: A Union Rep's Guide*, November 2016
31. CAC documents about ICE: workers-can-win.info/ch7-31
32. EU Directive on EWCs: workers-can-win.info/ch7-32
33. The 1999 EWC Regulations: workers-can-win.info/ch7-33a were amended by the 2010 ones: workers-can-win.info/ch7-33b

CHAPTER 8

1. Examples of the debates prompted by the Amazon Bessemer recognition bid: workers-can-win.info/ch8-1a, workers-can-win.info/ch8-1b, workers-can-win.info/ch8-1c and workers-can-win.info/ch8-1d
2. Interviews with Go North West bus strikers: workers-can-win.info/ch8-2
3. Examples of criticism of Alinsky can be found in Jane McAlevey's *No Shortcuts* (2016) and Aaron Petcoff's article in *Jacobin*: workers-can-win.info/ch8-3
4. For example, in Scotland you might use the Fair Work Convention: www.fairworkconvention.scot
5. During the Go North West bus strike, community protesters took to wearing body-cams because a thug opposed to the strike snatched phones to avoid being filmed while threatening and assaulting people.

CHAPTER 9

1. A list of nonviolent action methods: workers-can-win.info/ch9-1
2. Strikes may be unlawful but aren't illegal: workers-can-win.info/ch9-2

3. Section 100 of ERA 1996 provides the equivalent for dismissal.
4. *Code of Practice on Industrial Action Ballots*: workers-can-win.info/ch9-4
5. TULR(C)A 1992 on ballots: workers-can-win.info/ch9-5
6. Community blockades: workers-can-win.info/ch9-6
7. Unite's policy on direct action was set by Composite 33, which included Motion 165. See page 52 of workers-can-win.info/ch9-7
8. Pickets aren't necessarily to stop workers going in: workers-can-win.info/ch9-8
9. 'Slow walking' tactic copied from anti-fracking protesters: workers-can-win.info/ch9-9
10. 80-year-old arrested under terrorism legislation for wearing a t-shirt: workers-can-win.info/ch9-10
11. Anti-terror legislation used against sacked electrician: workers-can-win.info/ch9-11
12. The Pentonville Five dockers: workers-can-win.info/ch9-12
13. Opening a bank account for a strike fund: workers-can-win.info/ch9-13
14. *Code of Practice on Picketing*: workers-can-win.info/ch9-14
15. Women in the 1984–85 miners' strike: workers-can-win.info/ch9-15
16. Interviews with Go North West bus strikers: workers-can-win.info/ch8-2
17. UCU branch delegate meetings: workers-can-win.info/ch9-17
18. Delegation work: workers-can-win.info/ch9-18
19. Who owns the media: workers-can-win.info/ch9-19
20. The *Guardian*'s guide to writing a press release: workers-can-win.info/ch9-20
21. Media tips from the Electronic Frontier Foundation: workers-can-win.info/ch9-21

CHAPTER 10

1. Video of Professor Phil Taylor speaking on performance management, Lean and stress: workers-can-win.info/ch10-1

CHAPTER 11

1. www.iansunitesite.org.uk
2. ICO guide to data protection principles: workers-can-win.info/ch11-2

CHAPTER 12

1. Women in the 1984–85 miners' strike: workers-can-win.info/ch9-15
2. WHO definition of burnout: workers-can-win.info/ch12-2
3. HSE management standards for stress: workers-can-win.info/ch7-11
4. The rise of Solidarność: workers-can-win.info/ch12-4

Bibliography of sources and further reading

Below, I list the books, articles and resources referenced in this book, along with a few extras. I include a short comment about some of the most interesting ones. Most web links which appear in notes have not been duplicated here. All web links were accessed 27 December 2021. A full list of references and links is available at workers-can-win.info/further-reading and it will also be updated if links become broken over time.

Alinsky, Saul, 1972. *Rules for Radicals: A Practical Primer for Realistic Radicals*. New York: Vintage Books.

Allinson, Ian, n.d. *Guide to Striking for Climate and the Law.* [online] Available at: workers-can-win.info/climate-strike

Allinson, Ian, n.d. *Organising Conversations Crib Sheet.* [online] Available at: workers-can-win.info/conversations

Angry Workers, 2020. *Class Power on Zero Hours*. London: Angry Workers.

Armstrong, Peter, Goodman, Jeffrey and Hyman, Jerahn, 1981. *Ideology and Shop-floor Industrial Relations*. London: Croom Helm.

Barker, Colin, Dale, Gareth and Davidson, Neil (eds), 2021. *Revolutionary Rehearsals in the Neoliberal Age: 1989–2019*. Chicago: Haymarket Books.

Batstone, Eric, Boraston, Ian and Frenkel, Stephen, 1978. *The Social Organization of Strikes*. Oxford: Blackwell.

Bergfeld, Mark, 2020. *Research Skills for Trade Unionists Who Want to Build Power.* [online] Available at: workers-can-win.info/ch3-10

Bevan, Aneurin, 1952. *In Place of Fear*. London: William Heinemann Ltd.

Bishop, I., 2021. *Trade Union Membership, UK 1995–2020: Statistical Bulletin*. Available at: workers-can-win.info/fr-1

Bond, Becky and Exley, Zak, 2016. *Rules for Revolutionaries: How Big Organizing Can Change Everything*. White River Junction, Vermont: Chelsea Green Publishing.

Bradbury, Alexandra, Brenner, Mark and Slaughter, Jane, 2016. *Secrets of a Successful Organizer*. Detroit: Labor Notes.

Labor Notes, based in the USA, produces lots of good books on aspects organising. Their website includes some downloadable handouts for group exercises: labornotes.org/secrets

Brook, Paul, 2013. Emotional Labour and the Living Personality at Work: Labour Power, Materialist Subjectivity and the Dialogical Self. *Culture and Organization*, 19(4), pp. 332–52.

Brown, William, 2010. Negotiation and Collective Bargaining. In: Trevor Colling and Mike Terry (eds), *Industrial Relations: Theory and Practice*, 3rd ed. Chichester: Wiley. pp. 255–74.

Butcher, Matthew and Edwards, Polly, 2019. *Press Officer Handbook: A Guide to Progressive Media Work.* [online] NEON. Available at: workers-can-win.info/fr-2

Cliff, Tony and Gluckstein, Donny, 2014 [1986]. *Marxism and Trade Union Struggle: The General Strike of 1926.* [online] Marxists Internet Archive. Available at: workers-can-win.info/fr-3

The Cliff and Gluckstein book is far more useful and relevant than its title suggests. It is a great survey of the ways rank-and-file workers attempt to make their unions work for them and the limitations of trade unionism in periods of great conflict.

Equality and Human Rights Commission, 2021. *What Are Human Rights?* [online] Available at: workers-can-win.info/ch2-2

Ferguson, Susan, n.d. *Social Reproduction: What's the Big Idea?* [online] Pluto Press. Available at: workers-can-win.info/fr-5

Fox, Alan, 1966. Industrial Sociology and Industrial Relations. In: *Donovan Commission Research Paper No. 3*. London: HMSO. pp. 2–14.

Fox-Hodess, Katy and Santibáñez Rebolledo, Camilo, 2020. The Social Foundations of Structural Power: Strategic Position, Worker Unity and External Alliances in the Making of the Chilean Dockworker Movement. *Global Labour Journal*, [online] 11(3). Available at: workers-can-win.info/fr-6

Freeman, Jo, n.d [1970]. *The Tyranny of Structurelessness.* [online] Available at: workers-can-win.info/fr-7

Gahan, Peter and Pekarek, Andreas, 2013. Social Movement Theory, Collective Action Frames and Union Theory: A Critique and Extension. *British Journal of Industrial Relations*, 51(4), pp. 754–76.

Gallacher, Will, 1915. *Clyde Workers' Committee: To All Clyde Workers.* [online] Marxists Internet Archive. Available at: workers-can-win.info/fr-8

Garneau, Marianne, 2021. *The Problem with Leaders.* [online] Available at: workers-can-win.info/fr-9

Graf, Arnie, 2020. *Lessons Learned: Stories from a Lifetime of Organizing.* Chicago: ACTA Publications.

Hardy, Jane, 2021. *Nothing to Lose but Our Chains: Work and Resistance in Twenty-First Century Britain.* London: Pluto Press.

Hardy debunks many of the myths about the world of work, past and present, and includes accounts of inspiring struggles from workers who are often low-paid, outsourced women or migrants.

Henaway, Mostafa, 2022. *First We Take Staten Island: Lessons from the Unionization of Amazon's JFK8.* [online] Available at: workers-can-win.info/ch6-4

Hinton, James, 1973. *The First Shop Stewards' Movement.* London: G. Allen & Unwin.

Hinton's book is an inspiring history of the explosion of rank-and-file organisation around the First World War.

Holgate, Jane, 2021. *Arise: Power, Strategy and Union Resurgence.* London: Pluto Press.

Hyman, Richard, 1975. *Industrial Relations: A Marxist Introduction*. London: Macmillan Press.

Hyman, Richard, 1989. *Strikes*. 4th ed. Basingstoke: Palgrave Macmillan.

The two Hyman books above are excellent introductions to many of the key issues in industrial relations, despite being written when the times were very different.

IWW, 2009. *Organizing 101 Trainer's Manual*, version 2.2.

Joyce, Simon, 2015. Why are there so few strikes? *International Socialism*, [online] (145). Available at: workers-can-win.info/fr-10

Kelly, John., 1998. *Rethinking Industrial Relations: Mobilization, Collectivism and Long Waves*. London: Routledge.

King, Martin Luther, Jr., 2010 [1968]. *Where Do We Go from Here: Chaos or Community?* Boston: Beacon Press.

Lees, M.K., 2019. *Pushing: On the U in AEIOU*. [online] Organizing work. Available at: workers-can-win.info/fr-11

Levitt, Martin Jay and Conrow, Terry, 1993. *Confessions of a Union Buster*. 1st ed. New York: Crown Publishers.

Lorde, Audre, 2007, *Sister Outsider*. Berkeley: Crossing Press.

Luxemburg, Rosa, 1999a [1900]. *Reform or Revolution*. [online] Marxists Internet Archive. Available at: workers-can-win.info/fr-12

Luxemburg, Rosa, 1999b [1906]. *The Mass Strike, the Political Party and the Trade Unions*. [online] Marxists Internet Archive. Available at: workers-can-win.info/fr-13

Marx, Karl, 2015 [1867]. Part II, Chapter 6: The Buying and Selling of Labour-Power. In: *Capital: A Critique of Political Economy, Vol. 1*. [online] Marxists Internet Archive. Available at: workers-can-win.info/fr-14

McAlevey, Jane, 2014. *Raising Expectations (and Raising Hell): My Decade Fighting for the Labor Movement*. London: Verso.

McAlevey, Jane, 2016. *No Shortcuts: Organizing for Power in the New Gilded Age*. New York: Oxford University Press.

Both McAlevey's books above are very readable accounts of some impressive organising efforts. The article below is a great explanation of big and open bargaining.

McAlevey, Jane and Lawlor, Abby, 2021. *Turning the Tables: Participation and Power in Negotiations*. [online] UC Berkley Labor Center. Available at: workers-can-win.info/fr-15

Moody, Kim, 2015. *Precarious Work, 'Compression' and Class Struggle 'Leaps'*. [online] rs21. Available at: workers-can-win.info/fr-16

Monbiot, George, 2001. *An Activist's Guide to Exploiting the Media*. London: Bookmarks.

Murphy, John Thomas, 1972 [1934]. *Preparing for Power: A Critical Study of the History of the British Working-Class Movement*. 2nd ed. London: Pluto Press.

ONS, 2020. *Enterprise Employees by Employee Size Band 2008 to 2020*. Available at: workers-can-win.info/fr-17

ONS, 2021. *Tribunal Statistics Quarterly: January to March 2021*. Available at: workers-can-win.info/fr-18

Popovic, Srdja and Miller, Matthew, 2015. *Blueprint for Revolution: How to Use Rice Pudding, Lego Men, and Other Nonviolent Techniques to Galvanize Communities, Overthrow Dictators, or Simply Change the World.* New York: Spiegel & Grau.

Pudd'nhead, Mike, 2020. *A-E-I-O-U: Agitate, Educate, Inoculate, Organize, Union / pUsh (from 'Wages So Low You'll Freak' by Mike Pudd'nhead).* [online] libcom.org. Available at: workers-can-win.info/fr-19

Silver, Beverly, 2003. *Forces of Labor: Workers' Movements and Globalization since 1870.* Cambridge: Cambridge University Press.

Taylor, Phil, 2013. *Performance Management and the New Workplace Tyranny.* [online] Available at: workers-can-win.info/ch10-1

Tressell, Robert, 2003 [1914]. *The Ragged Trousered Philanthropists.* [online] Project Gutenberg. Available at: workers-can-win.info/fr-20

Tressell's classic novel tells the tale of a socialist painter and his efforts to win over his workmates. It has sold over a million copies and is often called the builders' bible.

Walton, Richard and McKersie, Robert, 1965. *A Behavioural Theory of Labor Negotiations.* London: McGraw Hill.

Wood, Heather, 2018. *Women in the Miners' Strike.* [online] Working class history. Available at: workers-can-win.info/ch9-15

Workplace Organising, 2016. *Set Up a Bank Account Well Before You Go on Strike.* [online] Available at: workers-can-win.info/ch9-13

Wright Mills, Charles, 1948. *The New Men of Power.* New York: Harcourt Brace.

x362014, 2021. *My Thoughts After Attending the 'Workers Rising Everywhere' Training.* [online] Organizing work. Available at: workers-can-win.info/fr-21

About the authors

Ian Allinson started organising while working in a largely un-unionised multinational outsourcing company. He led strikes which won union recognition, saved jobs, defended pensions and improved pay, sick pay and holidays. In 2009, he led the first national strike in the notoriously difficult to organise British IT industry, which won a national agreement despite the employer not recognising the union nationally.

Ian has been involved beyond his workplace too, serving on the national executive committee and standing in 2017 as a grassroots socialist candidate for Unite general secretary. He is involved with the Manchester trades union council, served as its president, and coordinates its solidarity for disputes and its campaigning on climate issues.

As well as direct experience, Ian's journey to writing this book involved learning from countless activists, from training and education, from books and discussions. After dismissal from his IT job in 2018, Ian spent a couple of years working as an organiser for rs21, the socialist group he's involved with, and rs21 supported him writing this book. He has written extensively on workers' movement issues for rs21 (rs21.org.uk/author/ian_allinson/) and elsewhere. Ian has supported workplace activists across many industries.

Colin Revolting's cartoons have been published by New Musical Express, rs21.org.uk and the Ramblers Association. They can be found at Artivists at Work (Instagram @artivistsatwork). Colin has twice been dismissed for organising at work – once in a large public institution and later in a small charity. He is still trying to organise at work, hence the ridiculous pseudonym.

Index

Thanks to our Patreon subscribers:

Andrew Perry
Ciaran Kane

Who have shown generosity and comradeship in support of our publishing.

Check out the other perks you get by subscribing to our Patreon – visit patreon.com/plutopress.

Subscriptions start from £3 a month.

PGIL2021USA